"We are at an inflection point in our nation. We can either continue with the racial status quo or earnestly engage in the long-overdue process of repair. Kwon and Thompson marshal deep research, theological acumen, and pastoral tenderness to make a timely call for reparations and the dignity of all people."

—**Jemar Tisby**, CEO of The Witness Inc.; author of the bestselling book *The Color of Compromise*

"*Reparations* is challenging in the best way: it challenges Christians to look squarely at our history, to take responsibility for our complicity in evil, and, most importantly, to take our mission as the church seriously. This book is a clarion call to understand the context of our mission and how that context must shape our work and community."

—**Tish Harrison Warren**, Anglican priest; author of *Liturgy of the Ordinary* and *Prayer in the Night*

"How do we make things whole? That is the question *Reparations* helps us answer. Kwon and Thompson walk us through our complicated racial past and give us a glimpse of a future that is reconciled, just, and ultimately more like Christ. This book should be essential reading for every single believer who cares about justice and equality. The history is sound, the facts are compelling, and the ultimate case must not be ignored."

—**Joshua DuBois**, CEO, media commentator, and former director, White House Office of Faith-based and Neighborhood Partnerships

"Kwon and Thompson have listened to their African American brothers and sisters. They tell us the sad truth about the significant role the church has played in the problem of racism. They demonstrate that reparations is a thoroughly biblical concept and a work of the gospel. And most importantly, with empathy and hope, they show us how we can start repairing our racial brokenness through local and community-based efforts that every one of us can be part of."

—**Latasha Morrison**, founder of Be the Bridge and *New York Times* bestselling author of *Be the Bridge: Pursuing God's Heart for Racial Reconciliation*

"Kwon and Thompson do a compelling job of laying out the historic legitimacy, the moral necessity, and the biblical urgency for reparations from slavery. With a kind of whiplash effect, they frequently let centuries-old voices speak into this very moment with shocking immediacy. May Christ's loving reign over new hearts, minds, and systems reorder the powers of this world that all may freely and justly live."

—**Mark Labberton**, president, Fuller Theological Seminary

"Arguments for reparations have often veered into emotional and moral appeals without careful theological, biblical, and historical reasoning. This book ends the era of poor pro-reparations arguments and silences the criticisms of those who suspect reparations as a kind of 'reverse injustice.' Kwon and Thompson have given us the careful yet daring, gracious yet trenchant, historical yet relevant, principled yet persuasive teaching the church and the world has desperately needed."

—**Thabiti M. Anyabwile**, pastor, Anacostia River Church

"Writing in the prophetic tradition, Kwon and Thompson are unrelenting in indicting the American church for its complicity and collusion in keeping its relative silence regarding the ongoing cries of the African American communities in the Civil War, during the civil rights movement, and in contemporary contexts. However, along with stinging words of indictment come words of invitation. Kwon and Thompson invite the readers to reimagine the shape of human flourishing in the church *if* we were to seek ways to repent for past sins, repair the breaches of the present, *and* rejuvenate communities for a more beautiful future. By engaging with their pastoral counsel and prophetic courage, we will have a better understanding of what it means to see the image of God in every human person."

—**Paul Chang-Ha Lim**, award-winning historian and
professor, Vanderbilt University

"In a Nazi concentration camp, Dietrich Bonhoeffer pondered the future of the German church as it lay in the ruins of its fatal allegiance to Hitler. 'What is bothering me incessantly is the question what Christianity really is, or indeed who Christ really is, for us today.' Has the church so cheapened its witness to the gospel that it now seems incapable of speaking a redemptive word to humanity and the world? Kwon and Thompson give us a profound and urgent answer in the context of the American church crisis. Their book illuminates the costs and joys of discipleship in a nation marked by White privilege and its theological disfigurations—to which I can imagine Bonhoeffer replying, 'Yes and amen.'"

—**Charles Marsh**, University of Virginia; author of
Strange Glory: A Life of Dietrich Bonhoeffer

"Admittedly, I am still working through what my own response will be to this convicting, sometimes disorienting book written by two pastors whom I respect greatly. Wherever you end up landing in relation to their message and conclusions, I pray that this book will stir you up as it has me."

—**Scott Sauls**, senior pastor of Christ Presbyterian Church; author of
Jesus Outside the Lines and *A Gentle Answer*

REPARATIONS

REPARATIONS

A CHRISTIAN CALL FOR REPENTANCE AND REPAIR

DUKE L. KWON *and*
GREGORY THOMPSON

BrazosPress

a division of Baker Publishing Group
Grand Rapids, Michigan

Published by Brazos Press
a division of Baker Publishing Group
PO Box 6287, Grand Rapids, MI 49516-6287
www.brazospress.com

Printed in the United States of America

Library of Congress Cataloging-in-Publication Data
Names: Kwon, Duke L., 1976– author. | Thompson, Gregory, 1971– author.
Title: Reparations : a Christian call for repentance and repair / Duke L. Kwon and Gregory
    Thompson.
Description: Grand Rapids, Michigan : Brazos Press, a division of Baker Publishing Group,
    [2021] | Includes bibliographical references and index.
Identifiers: LCCN 2020042366 | ISBN 9781587434501 (cloth)
Subjects: LCSH: Race relations—Religious aspects—Christianity. | Reconciliation—Religious
    aspects—Christianity. | Restitution—United States. | African Americans—Reparations.
Classification: LCC BT734.2 .K96 2021 | DDC 277.30089—dc23
LC record available at https://lccn.loc.gov/2020042366

Scripture quotations are from The Holy Bible, English Standard Version® (ESV®), copyright © 2001 by Crossway, a publishing ministry of Good News Publishers. Used by permission. All rights reserved. ESV Text Edition: 2016

21 22 23 24 25 26 27   7 6 5 4 3 2 1

The real cost lies ahead.

—Martin Luther King Jr.

To deepen your reading and reflection on the issues raised in *Reparations*, a study and discussion guide for individual or group use may be found at www.reparationsproject.com.

CONTENTS

INTRODUCTION

Generations without Recompense

An Overdue Response

On August 7, 1865, former slave Jourdon Anderson sat at a table in his Dayton, Ohio, home and dictated a letter to his former owner, Colonel Patrick Anderson. Jourdon was purchased as a boy by the colonel's father, General Paulding Anderson, to be a personal slave and playmate for the general's young son Patrick. It was a good investment: Years later, as the Civil War approached, Patrick owned not only Jourdon but also his wife Amanda and their children. But like many slaves, Jourdon Anderson saw himself and his family not as resources to be exploited but as human beings to be honored. And so, in 1864, with the help of Union soldiers, and after some thirty years of bondage, Jourdon Anderson and his family escaped to freedom.

One year later, shortly after the end of the Civil War, learning of his former slave's whereabouts, Colonel Anderson wrote to Jourdon and requested his return. Lamenting that his thousand-acre estate was faltering and confessing his desperate need for Jourdon's help with the coming harvest, Colonel Anderson promised that if Jourdon returned, he would treat him kindly. The request of the former master was audacious. The reply by the former slave was masterful.

Dayton, Ohio
August 7, 1865
To My Old Master, Colonel P. H. Anderson, Big Spring, Tennessee

Sir: I got your letter, and was glad to find that you had not forgotten Jourdon, and that you wanted me to come back and live with you again, promising to do better for me than anybody else can. I have often felt uneasy about you. I thought the Yankees would have hung you long before this, for harboring Rebs they found at your house. I suppose they never heard about your going to Colonel Martin's to kill the Union soldier that was left by his company in their stable. Although you shot at me twice before I left you, I did not want to hear of your being hurt, and am glad you are still living. It would do me good to go back to the dear old home again, and see Miss Mary and Miss Martha and Allen, Esther, Green, and Lee. Give my love to them all, and tell them I hope we will meet in the better world, if not in this. I would have gone back to see you all when I was working in the Nashville Hospital, but one of the neighbors told me that Henry intended to shoot me if he ever got a chance.

I want to know particularly what the good chance is you propose to give me. I am doing tolerably well here. I get twenty-five dollars a month, with victuals and clothing; have a comfortable home for Mandy,—the folks call her Mrs. Anderson,—and the children— Milly, Jane, and Grundy—go to school and are learning well. The teacher says Grundy has a head for a preacher. They go to Sunday school, and Mandy and me attend church regularly. We are kindly treated. Sometimes we overhear others saying, "Them colored people were slaves" down in Tennessee. The children feel hurt when they hear such remarks; but I tell them it was no disgrace in Tennessee to belong to Colonel Anderson. Many darkeys would have been proud, as I used to be, to call you master. Now if you will write and say what wages you will give me, I will be better able to decide whether it would be to my advantage to move back again.

As to my freedom, which you say I can have, there is nothing to be gained on that score, as I got my free papers in 1864 from the Provost-Marshal-General of the Department of Nashville. Mandy says she would be afraid to go back without some proof that you were disposed to treat us justly and kindly; and we have concluded to test your sincerity by asking you to send us our wages for the time we served you. This will make us forget and forgive old scores, and rely on your justice and friendship in the future. I served you faithfully for thirty-two years, and Mandy twenty years. At twenty-five dollars a month for me, and two dollars a week for Mandy, our earnings would amount to eleven thousand six hundred and eighty dollars. Add to this the interest for the time our wages have been kept back, and de-duct what you paid for our clothing, and three doctor's visits to me, and pulling a tooth for Mandy, and the balance will show what we are in justice entitled to. Please send the money by Adams's Express, in care of V. Winters, Esq., Dayton, Ohio. If you fail to pay us for faithful labors in the past, we can have little faith in your promises in the future. We trust the good Maker has opened your eyes to the wrongs which you and your fathers have done to me and my fathers, in making us toil for you for generations without recompense. Here I draw my wages every Saturday night; but in Tennessee there was never any pay-day for the negroes any more than for the horses and cows. Surely there will be a day of reckoning for those who defraud the laborer of his hire.

In answering this letter, please state if there would be any safety for my Milly and Jane, who are now grown up, and both good-looking girls. You know how it was with poor Matilda and Catherine. I would rather stay here and starve—and die, if it come to that—than have my girls brought to shame by the violence and wickedness of their young masters. You will also please state if there has been any schools opened for the colored children in your neighborhood. The great desire of my life now is to give my children an education, and have them form virtuous habits.

Say howdy to George Carter, and thank him for taking the pistol from you when you were shooting at me.

From your old servant,
Jourdon Anderson[1]

Thanks to the efforts of abolitionist Valentine Winters, Jourdon Anderson's letter was reprinted in the *Cincinnati Commercial*, the *New York Daily Tribune*, and Lydia Maria Child's *The Freedmen's Book*, and became something of a national sensation. Rightly so. It is at once satirical and serious, compassionate and candid, vulnerable and shrewd, personal and prophetic. Indeed, it is difficult to read this letter without being led, in the span of but a few sentences, to both laughter and tears. But perhaps the most important aspect of this letter is the light it sheds on what is, at heart, its essential theme: *reparations*. Jourdon Anderson's letter was, fundamentally, a call for his former master, one who had long benefited from Anderson's unrequited labor, to begin the work of repair. This book is a long overdue response to Jourdon Anderson's letter, a response that seeks to engage seriously with his essential theme.

Convictions

Our response is framed by seven core convictions that we believe are foundational to a constructive engagement with the work of reparations. The first regards the nature of racism itself (the subject of chapter 1).[2] Before proceeding, we should briefly state that *racism*, as used in this book, has three elements to it. First, classifying human beings into distinct "races" due to presumably fixed and hereditary physical characteristics. Second, assigning notions of inferior mental or moral capacities correlated to those physical characteristics. Third, pushing people who are seen to have those physical, mental, and moral qualities to the margins of a given social order. Over the course of preparing this work, we have come to see that when people look at racism, they often see very different things and, further, that these various ways of seeing racism elicit varying responses to it. Some, for example, view racism personally, as a form of personal prejudice whose remedy is personal repentance. Others view it socially, as a form of relational estrangement that requires racial reconciliation. Still others view it institutionally, in terms of discrete institutional injustice whose redress lies in institutional reform. Each of these accounts holds important truths about the nature of racism and what it means to respond faithfully to it. Even so, we believe that none of these capture the whole truth, that still another view of racism is required.

Our conviction is that racism is best understood *culturally*, as a force that shapes the entire ecosystem of meanings, values, ideas, institutions, and practices of American culture. Seeing racism in this way—as embedded in an entire cultural order—is important not only because it reminds us that each of us, simply by virtue of living in this culture, is implicated in and affected by the reality of American racism but also because it reminds us just how expansive the work of repairing racism ultimately will be.

Our second conviction, addressed in chapter 2, is that the best way to understand the cultural order of racism is through the lens of White supremacy. White supremacy has been present since the founding of America, pervasive across all of its institutions and enduring throughout its history. Because we understand the difficulty of this claim for many of our readers, a difficulty we ourselves feel, we want to take a moment to elaborate on just what we mean.

There is a certain revulsion in hearing this word *supremacy*, and even more so the phrase *White supremacy*. It is a difficult phrase, and this is important to acknowledge. But it is also important to ask why it is so difficult for many of us to speak of White supremacy. Part of the difficulty lies in how we understand its meaning. For many, White supremacy is understood in fairly narrow terms: as hooded riders in the forest, torch-bearing marchers in the streets, or trolls on the dark web, promoting open, active animus against people who are not White. This is understandable. Since the early twentieth century, these images of White supremacy have been deeply and deliberately etched into the popular American imagination. And they are real. When understood in these terms, it is reductive at best and cynical at worst to describe America in this way. But this is, in our view, an overly narrow account, one that obscures more than it illumines by mistaking the periphery of White supremacy for its essence. As we will see, the truth is that White supremacy is much broader than these occasional spasms of violence, much more ordinary and mundane than these moments of dark spectacle suggest.

Another difficulty some might have with the language of *White supremacy* regards not necessarily what it means but how it *feels*. Even if one grasps this more comprehensive meaning of White supremacy, and even if one sees something of the fullness of its historical reality, it is nonetheless possible to object to this language simply on the grounds that it is offensive. Indeed, we have met more than a few sympathetic people who have suggested that we use different language precisely on these grounds: "I agree with what you're trying to say. But can't you just find a different way to say it?" In considering these suggestions, two things have become clear to us. First, to cease to use the language of *White supremacy*, even though it is historically accurate and broadly used in minority communities, simply because it offends the sensibilities of White people is, in our view, to perpetuate the logic of White supremacy itself. We see no way around this. Second, if, as we will demonstrate, the American social order disproportionately (and deliberately) benefits those deemed to be White, even as those who are not deemed White are enslaved, degraded, and marginalized, what other term does honesty permit us to use?

But perhaps the most important obstacle to the language of *White supremacy* comes from those who, often in good faith, doubt its *reality*, who ask whether it really is the case that American society is one in which Whites have been at the top of the social hierarchy and have had virtually exclusive access to its benefits. This seems to us to be a fair and important question. The work of chapter 2 is to show that the unequivocal answer is yes.

The third conviction, developed in chapter 3, is that White supremacy's most enduring effect, indeed its very essence, is *theft*. We believe White supremacy to be a multigenerational campaign of cultural theft, in which the identities, agency, and prosperity of African Americans are systematically stolen and given to others. As we will show, we believe that while this theft took many forms, its most significant and enduring forms are the theft of truth, the theft of power, and the theft of wealth.

Our fourth conviction is that the Christian church in America, a church that emerged and has endured in the context of White supremacy, has a fundamental responsibility to respond to this theft, for several reasons. The first reason derives from the church's complex history, at times embracing and justifying White supremacy and at times resisting it. The church in America is not and never has been an innocent bystander to White supremacy. It has, to the contrary, been present—as both friend and foe—every step of the way. This reality entails the obligation to own this history and to take public responsibility for addressing it. This responsibility also comes from the church's inner life. One of the glories of the Christian church is that, even in the midst of its deep brokenness, it takes the work of love seriously. Indeed, it is a community constituted by an act of love and committed to the work of love in the midst of the world. This love expresses itself as the burden, in the words of Jesus, to "proclaim good news to the poor" and "liberty to the captives" (Luke 4:18). The church is a community that, by its very nature, exists to address harms like those done by White supremacy. Last, the church's responsibility derives from its need for missional integrity. It is easy to forget that the Christian church in America carries out its mission in one of the longest-standing White supremacist social orders in the history of the world. For this mission to have integrity, the church has to take this context seriously. If the church in America carries out its work of engaging culture, transforming cities, bringing the kingdom of God, and making all things new, without deliberately engaging the reality of White supremacy, both the integrity and the efficacy of its mission are diminished. This is the subject of chapter 4.

Our fifth conviction is that one of the most important contributions of the church to the work of reparations is its historic ethic of culpability and restitution. As we will show, there is a long scriptural and deep theological tradition in the Christian church that teaches, very simply, that when you take something that does not belong to you, love requires you to return it. This ethic of culpability and restitution, embodied most clearly in the story of Zacchaeus, is a crucial element of any Christian vision of reparations. Related, our sixth conviction is that, in addition to restitution, the Christian tradition also teaches another response to theft: restoration. Even when not culpable for a theft, the Christian still has the obligation to restore what was lost. This ethic of restoration, seen clearly in the story of the good Samaritan, is a crucial element of the Christian vision of reparations. These two ethical responses to theft—restitution where we are culpable and restoration even where we are not—provide a broad foundation for a Christian account of reparations. In this account—and this is critical for our argument—*reparations is best understood as the deliberate repair of White supremacy's cultural theft through restitution (returning what one wrongfully took) and restoration (restoring the wronged to wholeness).* We discuss these two elements in chapters 5 and 6, respectively.

Our final conviction (developed in chapter 7) is that as the church undertakes this work of reparations it must mirror the threefold theft wrought by White supremacy: not only the theft of wealth (as is generally understood) but the theft of truth and the theft of power as well.

Approach

In writing this book, we are painfully aware not only of the many approaches to these convictions but also of the frustrating limitations inherent in adopting a single approach. However, the nature of such a book requires embracing these limitations. As a way of setting expectations for our readers, we want to foreground our approach to clarify what we are, and are not, trying to do in this book.

As the subtitle of this book suggests, our book is *Christian*. We orient our discussion of reparations both from and to the Christian church, broadly conceived. In saying this, we do not intend to suggest that other communities cannot benefit from these reflections. Indeed, we very much hope that they will. Likewise, we do not intend to suggest that the church alone is responsible for (or indeed capable of) the work of reparations. When the work of reparations comes to fruition in America, it will be a collaborative effort, just as White supremacy was. Nor do we intend to suggest that all expressions of the church are identical in their need for a work such as this. To the contrary, some Christian communities—especially African American churches—have long labored toward the work of reparations, even as other churches have labored against it. We simply want to acknowledge candidly that our reflections on this issue are deeply informed by our own formation in the Christian tradition and that our specific exhortations are oriented primarily toward those who embrace this tradition as their own.

Our book is also *focused*. Reparations is an extraordinarily complex subject, one that by its very nature addresses issues of human identity, social history, political economy, and moral obligation. In order to provide focus, both for ourselves and for our readers, this book explores reparations in the fairly specific context of anti-Black racism in the United States. We realize that this decision leaves other historically marginalized communities—both nationally and internationally—beyond the scope of our consideration. The most obvious of these, of course, are the various communities of Native peoples within the borders of the United States. As with African Americans, the history of the United States with respect to these communities is one of virtually unbroken theft. The only hope for any type of healing from these enduring harms is reparations.[3] Our hope is that others will take what we have done here and, insofar as it is useful, apply it to reparations in those contexts as well.

Even with this relatively narrow focus, however, a comprehensive treatment of reparations to African Americans is also beyond the capacity of a single volume. Because of this, we intend for this book to be *introductory*. Many of our readers will not only have little familiarity with the topic of reparations but also have significant questions about its basic historical and theological foundations. Because of this, our modest ambition is simply to introduce a broad audience to the historical and cultural context, moral logic, and potential trajectory of the work of reparations, providing the reader with the necessary foundation for further exploration.

Finally, our approach to this work is *synthetic*. While it addresses matters of history, theology, economics, and politics, it is not strictly speaking a work of history, theology, economics, or politics. Rather, it is an attempt to synthesize some important insights from each of these into a coherent whole. In doing this, we run the risk of producing a book that is at once too much and too little. Indeed, at times we ourselves have felt it to be each of these. Insofar as our readers share this sentiment, we can only offer you the consolation that in this respect you are not alone.

Contributions

Though we intend for this book to be introductory, we also hope that it will make substantive contributions to larger conversations regarding reparations both inside and outside of communities of faith. Even as we introduce some of our readers to the topic of reparations, we also hope to engage with scholars, theorists, and practitioners of reparations in a constructive manner. Some of our readers may be surprised to learn that a robust conversation around reparations exists at all, and even more surprised to learn that it exists outside and inside the Christian church, both today and throughout history. Part of the purpose of this book is to orient our readers to that conversation. It is also our purpose to shape that conversation and to contribute to its maturation. Though the extent of our contribution will only be seen in time, we believe that our work contributes to this conversation in several important ways.

The first of these is that we set our treatment of reparations not simply against the backdrop of slavery but against the much larger backdrop of White supremacy. As will be abundantly clear, in doing this we do not intend to diminish the significance of slavery. To the contrary, we seek to embed it in a much larger and more enduring context that illumines both its essential meaning and its enduring effect. Nor do we intend to critique organizations or movements such as the American Descendants of Slavery (ADOS) who, as their name indicates, largely center the descendants of those enslaved in America in their account of reparations.[4] Even so, we deliberately join others in taking a broader approach.[5] Doing so provides a more accurate historical picture of both the character and the duration of White supremacy's cultural theft, a theft that preceded American chattel slavery and endures beyond it. In our view, it is only as we set reparations in the context of the entire history of American White supremacy, a history that includes but is not confined to slavery, that the full picture of reparations can come into view.

Our second contribution lies in our characterization of White supremacy as theft. While this is central to our argument, we also confess that it is a point in which our argument is vulnerable. After all, White supremacy expressed itself as a symphony of vices: not least idolatry, covetousness, lying, adultery, and murder. Even so, the simple fact is that American White supremacy originated in the theft of Black bodies, sustained itself through the theft of Black wealth, and justifies itself through the theft, the erasure, of truths that expose its lies. Theft is, therefore, not simply an expression of White supremacy; it is, rather, both its most elemental impulse and its most enduring effect. We believe that characterizing it in this way helps not only to clarify its essential logic but also to chart a clearer path toward reparations.

We also contend that this theft is best understood not merely in terms of wealth but in the more comprehensive terms of truth and power. This is an important feature of this work that distinguishes it from most of the literature on reparations. A great deal of the literature frames reparations in largely economic terms, as a form of redress for the incalculable wealth lost to African Americans caused both by slavery and by subsequent decades of continued inequality. As we will show in chapters 3 and 7, we are in deep sympathy with this view and fundamentally agree that there is a critical monetary horizon of reparations. Even so, we resist reducing reparations to this horizon. To view White supremacy as a theft of not only wealth but also truth and power provides important insights regarding White supremacy's inner logic. It is also a more accurate account of White supremacy's devastating cultural reach. To frame the harm done by American White supremacy in exclusively economic terms is actually to obscure the nature and magnitude of that harm. In our view, this broadened perspective opens up new horizons for reparations by reminding us that the true imperative of reparations is not simply for a debt to be repaid but for an entire world to be repaired.

Another contribution of this work is its focus on the church. We hope that this book will introduce Christian readers to the reparations conversation, to the role of Christian thought in those conversations, and to the incredible potential of the church to bring those conversations to the forefront of the national imagination and to enact them in their local contexts. In doing this, however, we have subtly shifted the institutional backdrop of this conversation. Most treatments situate reparations against the institutional backdrop of the federal government. Even as these treatments differ from one another in their accounts of history and their elaboration of debt, most believe that reparations is, finally, the work of the government. We, too, believe that the United States government is morally responsible for the work of reparations—both for the ways that it sheltered White supremacy and the ways in which it benefited from that sheltering. Indeed, throughout its history the government has paid reparations to Native peoples, to Japanese Americans interned during World War II, and most relevantly, to *slave owners* following emancipation. The United States government has already demonstrated its capacity to enact reparations when it finds the moral and political will to do so.[6] And, pragmatically speaking, we believe that the scale of reparations is such that the resources of the United States government, combined with the governments of other nations, are necessary. That said, given the history of our government's indifference to reparations to Black Americans, and given the profound divisiveness of our political moment, we are not sanguine that the United States government will take up the work of reparations with any real intentionality or efficacy in the foreseeable future. And yet the need for reparations remains.

Because of this, we believe that churches can and should play an important role in catalyzing and demonstrating the power of reparations in our communities. Indeed, the church's complicated history, moral tradition, committed membership, considerable resources, local knowledge, collaborative potential, and divine power render it the perfect context for the work of reparations. As with all civil organizations, the church's efforts will, structurally speaking, be smaller in scale than those made possible through governmental resources. But they will be a beginning, which with labor and time may yet amount to the whole.

Our final intended contribution is our insistence that reparations requires what the Christian community refers to as repentance. Which is to say, the work of reparations requires us to become different kinds of people. The sad, though understandable, truth is that conversations over social change, especially those surrounding racial redress, are fraught with self-righteousness and venomous recrimination. Rarely are these conversations characterized by the presumption that perhaps we are wrong, that we are the problem, and that our social goals require our personal repentance. Indeed, there is a discernible vanity in both religious conservative "patriots" and secular liberal elites that presumes that social change can somehow bypass personal repentance, that the world can change while we remain the same. This false presumption obstructs the work of reparations because it inevitably focuses our attention on defending our rightness rather than on repairing the wrong before us. This tendency is evident everywhere around us, but perhaps its greatest expression lies in the almost total unwillingness of many Americans and of our collective government to stand before our African American citizens and before the world and say, "We did this, it was wrong, and we want to repair what we have done." But if we are to heal the wounds of White supremacy, this is precisely what we must do.

Though reparations will not be accomplished simply by changing who we are, they cannot be accomplished without it.

Concerns

One reality of writing a book on reparations is that, with a consistency that borders on the comic, people's first response upon hearing about the book is *concern*. Some of these concerns are personal and typically sound something like this: "Why are you doing this to yourself?" "Delete your Twitter account." "Don't expect to be invited to any Christmas parties." Though offered tongue-in-cheek, they indicate what most of us already know: the topic of reparations bears on some of the most vulnerable, painful, and heavily fortified elements of our common life. Talking about it is just not going to be easy for anyone.

Much more important than these personal concerns, however, are concerns about the substance of the work itself. Over the course of writing this book, we have benefited greatly from people around the country who have taken the time to raise these concerns. In what follows, we want to foreground some of the most consistent and important concerns that we heard. In doing this, we do not intend to suggest that we have either comprehensively seen or fully resolved these concerns. We simply want to be transparent about them and to invite the reader into them with us.

The first and, perhaps, most obvious of these is, very simply, *why us?* Why is a book on reparations being written by two men, one White and the other Korean American? This important question, understandably, seeks to safeguard African Americans from yet again having the voices of others—rather than their own voices—tell their story and shape their experience. In many conversations, both before beginning this project and throughout its production, we engaged with one another and with African American friends and colleagues about this concern. In so doing, we have come to believe that the conversation around reparations is, by its very nature, a conversation between two parties: those who owe reparations and those to whom reparations are owed. In our view, each of these parties have important things to say—and not to say. We are writing from the vantage of those who owe reparations and who have benefited from the thefts of White supremacy. We believe that our role is to tell the truth about this theft, to own the complex ways in which we are implicated in it, and to struggle toward the work of repair. Further, we have the responsibility to exhort others who are similarly implicated to do the same. We believe, in other words, that we *have* to say these things, that reparations itself requires it.

That said, there are also things that we believe we should not say. We should not, for example, speak as authoritative interpreters of African American experience. These experiences are most faithfully articulated by African Americans themselves. Because of this, we have been careful to anchor our account and interpretation of American history in those given by African American theorists and writers. In like manner, we should not decide the ultimate shape that reparations should take. This shape should be determined—and overseen—by African Americans. Chapter 7, which illustrates potential trajectories for reparations, is based not exclusively on our own ideas but on both the work and the advice of African Americans around the country. We have tried to say what we believe we ought to say, and, having done that, to let others speak.

The second concern is that of *paternalism* and its correlate, *victimization*. This important concern raises questions about power and power's diminishment. The concern with paternalism is that this work—in both its motivation and its substance—is yet another manifestation of the broadly held presumption that people other than African Americans are more equipped to solve the problems affecting African Americans than are African Americans themselves. Likewise, the concern with victimization is that this work simply reinforces tropes of African American helplessness and, thereby, rather than empowering African Americans, actually serves the forces of their disempowerment. In response to this concern, we would like to say two things. First, it is a point of historical fact that African Americans have been wronged—profoundly, devastatingly, and perpetually—by the culture of White supremacy. Reparations is predicated upon our collective acknowledgment and ownership of this fact. In this sense, and this sense alone, we may objectively speak of African Americans as victims. This is not to say, as some suggest, that African Americans are the psychologically defeated and passive pawns of historical forces. To the contrary, history itself bears witness to the undeniability of African

American power and exposes this caricatured account of victimization to be little more than an ignorant trope of White supremacist self-justification. Second, we wish simply to say that we have labored to write this book not from the perspective of the paternalist or from a spirit of messianic presumption. It is, rather, written from the perspective of the perpetrator and the penitent.

Another frequently heard concern regards *entitlements*, and whether reparations might contribute to a culture of entitlement among African Americans. We will limit ourselves to two responses. First, this concern fundamentally mischaracterizes the issue at hand. The implication is that reparations are primarily to be evaluated in terms of their potential effects. But this is mistaken: reparations are not primarily given in light of a hoped-for future; they are given in light of an actual past. Consider an analogy. Imagine that someone steals your car and, one year later, the thief is caught and a judge orders your car returned. Now, imagine that the thief protests this return on the grounds that walking seems to have done you good and, further, that you might get into an accident if you begin to drive again. You would, of course, realize that the thief's concerns about the potential consequences of returning the stolen car are completely beside the point. The point is that the car is not his, that it never was his, and that his role is simply to return what he stole and let you get on with your life. The terms of the return, in other words, are not his to dictate. The concern regarding entitlement often falls into the thief's error, and in this respect gets the matter exactly backward.

Second, this concern often entails the barely concealed assumption that entitlement is the particular affliction of the African American community and that the desire for outside economic support entails a form of civic vice. The truth, however, is that the history of American economic policy is a history of government subsidization of White Americans. As we will show in chapter 3, from the very beginning of the republic, the economic well-being of White Americans has been the fruit not simply of their personal initiative but also of critical entitlement instruments such as land grants, homestead acts, wage standardization, mortgage subsidies, education grants, and tax deductions—almost all of which, for the majority of American history, have excluded African Americans from their benefits.

The simple truth, historically speaking, is that the White middle class was created by entitlements. The fact that those who have themselves most benefited from entitlement tools are also those who most frequently raise concerns about the bestowal of those tools upon African Americans is a fact that warrants serious moral reflection.

A fourth concern is whether, by talking about White supremacy and employing the racialized language of "White" and "Black," we are *perpetuating racial divisions* in our communities and obstructing the type of healing to which we aspire. This concern seems largely born of weariness, of a desire to simply move past the trauma of race in America and on to other things. We understand this desire, and we are empathetic with this weariness, but this concern misunderstands the nature of our collective racial trauma. The trauma of racism, as we see it, comes not from the continued deployment of racial categories but from the continued existence of the destructive social realities from which those categories emerged and to which they refer. The way to heal from American racism is not to change our words but to change the social order that put those words in our mouths in the first place. Until we do this, no matter what language we use, our racial divisions will remain.

Finally, there is a more academic concern regarding our conception of human identity and history. The Christian tradition understands human identity not fundamentally in terms of race but in terms of the image of God. This unspeakable glory, bestowed on all human beings, is the ultimate anchor of human identity. Likewise, the Christian tradition understands history not primarily as the unfolding of ideological or material forces in the world, but as the unfolding of God's mysterious and redemptive love, made known in Jesus and expressed by the Spirit in the world. We ourselves view the nature of identity and the meaning of history in just this way.

That said, like many writers on race in America, we also speak of human identity in racial terms, and of history, especially American history, as subject to and shaped by the forces of White supremacy. This might lead some to ask whether, in so doing, we have bestowed upon each of these an essential quality and have thereby embraced notions of identity and history that are divergent from the Christian tradition. We recognize in this concern a desire to take theological categories seriously and to ensure that they are deployed faithfully, and we honor this desire. This is all the more the case given that some prominent writers on race and White supremacy explicitly repudiate Christian accounts of both identity and history. However, we believe that with respect to our work this concern is doubly misplaced. First, we believe it to be perfectly reasonable to speak of the power of historical realities like race and White supremacy without thereby ascribing to those realities some sort of metaphysical essence or eschatological force. We are not, in other words, confused about the difference between the historically contingent and the theologically normative. Second, we sense in this concern a lurking tendency toward ecclesial self-interest, a subtle shift of focus away from a concern for historical injustice and toward a concern for theological self-preservation. We wish to resist this tendency at all costs. It gives the impression that the *real* issue before us, the *real* battle to be fought, is the battle to preserve the integrity of the church and its theological formulations. But this issue, while important, is not ours. Our concern is not to defend the Christian church from its alleged ideological victimization but to defend our neighbors from their actual victimization by repairing the harm done by White supremacy in our communities. Indeed, we believe that this work, rather than being a threat to our theology, is, to the contrary, its proper fruit.

Hopes

This leads us to our hopes for this work. We honestly don't know what the impact of this project might be. At times, the harm done by White supremacy, the work required to repair it, and the comparative smallness of our own labors seem overwhelming. But, if we may be vulnerable, here is what we hope.

Our hope for ourselves is that the call to reparations will continue to change us, to shape our imaginations, our loves, and our labors. We hope to become people whose lives are inexorably bound to the vocation of repair. Our hope for our children is that each of you will renounce the beguiling myths that tempt us and instead see the truth about the world. And not only that you will see the truth, but that in seeing it you will give yourselves, in your own ways, to the work of repairing the world. We know this means that your lives will often be marked by grief, anger, and struggle. We grieve this for you. But this also means that your lives will be marked by the truth and by the faith, hope, and love that true lives require. As you labor to live the truth, remember that you are crowned with light.

Our hope for the church is that the work of reparations, the work to repair our communities from the ravages of White supremacy, will become central to its mission. Our hope is that the language of *White supremacy* and *reparations*, now so unfamiliar and awkward, will one day become as fixed in the church's imagination and fundamental to its vocation as the language of repentance and reconciliation is today. This is the only way that the church can fully live with integrity, and the only path to beholding the joy of redemptive love made flesh in the streets of this world. Our hope for our nation is that we will renounce our willful blindness to our history, confess, and give ourselves collectively and collaboratively to the work of repairing what we have done. Until we do this, we will never embody the meaning of our creeds, never escape the secret shame and uneasy conscience that shadows our national identity, never know peace in our cities.

Most of all, however, our hopes are for our African American friends and neighbors. Our hope is that the singular harm wrought by White supremacy, the theft it has visited upon you and those you love, will broadly be seen for what it is. Our hope is that when it is seen, it will be confessed. Our hope is that when it is confessed, it will be renounced. Our hope is that when it is renounced, the world that it made will pass away, and its weight will fall from your shoulders. Our hope is reparation. We labor toward this hope. This work is for you.

I

The Call to See

I am invisible, understand, simply because people refuse to see me.

—Ralph Ellison, *Invisible Man*

The Call to See

On the rainy afternoon of February 1, 1968, two young African American men stepped out from the back of a city garbage truck and onto the suburban Memphis street. Hearing the truck pull up in front of her home, a White woman watched absentmindedly from her kitchen window as they loaded the trash inside the giant compactor. Suddenly she was startled to attention by the sound of screams and banging from outside, and she watched in horror as the two men—first one, and then the other—were pulled into the compactor and crushed to death in front of her eyes. In an interview with authorities later that night, she said, "It looked like the big thing just swallowed him."[1]

The two men, Robert Walker, 29, and Echol Cole, 35, were part of an unseen generation of African American men who, fleeing the perpetual poverty and foreclosed opportunity of the farms of the Deep South, had come to Memphis in search of work. Their hope was that Memphis, the swinging city built on the bluffs of the Mississippi River, would provide the opportunity for a different sort of life than that offered by the endless expanse of the surrounding Delta. When they arrived in Memphis, however, most of these men found their conditions little changed. As in the Delta, the jobs typically available to African American men were the most physically difficult—storm and drainage work, street and asphalt repair, and trash pickup. And these jobs provided the least economic security. Almost all of these African American men were contract employees who started at $1.27 per hour, unpaid on days when weather prevented their work, and without any form of protection from the caprice of the supervisors who oversaw them. In spite of their hopes and labor, the poverty and diminished opportunity of the farms they fled were waiting for them in the city.

This was the lot of Robert Walker and Echol Cole, and also of the nearly 1,500 other men who worked alongside them in the city's sanitation department. On an average morning, in heat and in cold, these men would wake before dawn and walk or catch a ride to the lot where the city's garbage trucks were parked. As White supervisors slid behind the wheel of the truck, the African American men held on to the sides or, in the event of rain or snow, sat in the back with the trash. Stopping in front of homes, the African Americans would climb out and begin to pick up the bins of trash. These bins, typically lidless cans sitting open in the rain or sun, were filled with rotting, liquefying trash. Shouldering the bins, water and filth would spill over the sides or out of holes in the bottom and drip into their hair and down their backs as the men dumped the trash into the truck. At day's end, because the sanitation department provided neither uniforms nor showers, the men left for home in the same filthy clothing in which they had worked all day. Because of this, they were unable to ride in cars or to take public transportation. They walked, in heat and in cold, to their homes where they would wait on their porches while family members hosed them down and picked maggots from their hair.[2]

No one knows exactly how Robert Walker and Echol Cole were pulled into the trash compactor that day. The most likely account is that after dumping the trash into the back of the truck, they sought shelter from the rain and climbed in as well. Somehow the internal wires short-circuited, starting the compactor with the men inside. But these are speculations. So much about that day was, as the witness said, simply swallowed.

What is clear, however, is that at the news of their deaths the anger of the sanitation workers—long simmering over their poor working conditions, poverty wages, and lack of negotiating power—began to boil over. In a matter of days, 1,300 sanitation workers went on strike. Every day for nearly two months they gathered at Clayborn Temple, the historic African Methodist Episcopal church in downtown Memphis. There they listened to the Reverend James Lawson, one of the architects of nonviolent resistance in the civil rights movement, remind them of their ineradicable dignity, the rightness of demanding civic recognition of that dignity, the necessity of nonviolence, and the transformative power of love. Then they rose from the pews, stepped through Clayborn Temple's arched doorways, lined up, and made their way up Beale Street and down Main Street to city hall, just over a mile away.[3]

As in many cities marked by protest, the leaders of Memphis sought to obscure the nature of this cause. Some characterized the protest as simply a ploy launched by Martin Luther King Jr. and other civil rights leaders to stir up trouble and gain attention. Others characterized it as a movement of violence launched by Black nationalists aiming to seize control of the city. Still others characterized it as a strategy of northern union leaders to extend their reach and enrich their organizations by establishing new labor unions in the South. But for the protestors themselves, the meaning of the cause was very simple: the truth of their own humanity. They came together, in defiance of American racism, and demanded to be seen and treated as human beings. Proof could be found in the signs that the protestors printed in the basement of Clayborn Temple and carried with them as they marched: a plain white background with four simple words in black:

I <u>AM</u> A MAN

These signs immediately became icons of the long African American struggle against racism[4] in America, and remain so to this day.[5] These signs were both a confrontation and a calling. With devastating simplicity, they confronted American racism, its multigenerational refusal to recognize the full humanity of enslaved Africans and their descendants, and the ways in which this racist refusal takes social and economic form.[6] And yet in another respect, these signs called to America; they called America to renounce its racist blindness and to view African Americans in terms of their full humanity. They were, in other words, a call to *see*.

Ways of Seeing Racism

We have encountered many people struggling to answer this call, laboring daily to see the truth about American racism and the way it shapes both our individual and common lives. This is not true of everyone, of course. In every community, some are deeply resistant to seeing the truth about American racism and resistant to the vulnerability that this seeing entails. Even so, all across the United States—in churches in Memphis, college campuses in Georgia, auditoriums in Pennsylvania, dinner tables in Washington, DC, and cocktail bars in Charlottesville—we have encountered people who want both to see the truth about American racism and to respond redemptively.

Over time, however, we have noticed that while many people are concerned with racism in America and are committed to engaging it, few have thought deeply about the role of reparations. While many Americans see the reality of racism, they see it in ways that—while substantively true and ethically important—are not yet robust enough to lead to the work of reparations. Many of us need a different way of seeing race in America, one that makes reparations not only plausible but inevitable. The task of what follows is twofold: First, we explore three dominant ways of seeing American racism and the responses to which each of them inclines. Second, we gesture toward a different way of seeing American racism—to be more fully developed in chapters 2 and 3—that serves as the foundation of this work.

Racism as Personal Prejudice

In 2016, African American social commentator Heather McGhee was a guest on C-SPAN's *Washington Journal*. McGhee, then president of Demos, a "think-and-do" tank that focuses on equitable democratic reform, was invited to discuss the role of progressive politics in the 2016 presidential election, then underway. During the call-in portion of the show, a White man from North Carolina spoke to McGhee with unusual candor about his own racism. Introducing himself, he simply said, "I'm a White male and I am prejudiced." Given our cultural moment, upon hearing these words one might have expected either for this man to launch a fleet of justifications for his racism or for McGhee to shame him for it. However, neither did so. For his part, the man began simply to talk about his fears. For her part, rather than rolling her eyes or turning away, McGhee looked directly into the camera and gave this man her full attention. As she did so, he said something almost wholly unexpected: "What can I do to change, you know, to be a better American?" Upon hearing these words, she closed her eyes, gathered herself in kindness, and spoke directly to the camera:

> Thank you, so much, for being honest, and for opening up this conversation because it's simply one of the most important ones we have to have in this country. You know, we are not a country that is united because we are all one racial group that descended from one tribe and one community. That is actually, I think, what makes this country beautiful, but it is our challenge. We are the most multi-racial, multi-ethnic, wealthy democracy in the world. And so, asking the question you asked, "How do I get over my fears and my prejudices?" is the question that all of us—and I will say people of all races and ethnicities and backgrounds hold these fears and prejudices. Most of them are actually unconscious, right? You'll say to yourself, "I'm not prejudiced" but of course we all have them. And so your ability to just say, "This is what I have, I have these fears and prejudices and I want to get over them" is one of the most powerful things that we can do right now at this moment in our history. So thank you.[7]

In the following days a video of the exchange began to show up on Facebook pages, Twitter feeds, and other media outlets. Some viewers responded with contempt for the man, the ignorant southern racist who had the gall to ask an African American woman to help him with his racism. Others responded with criticism of McGhee, accusing her of coddling a fragile White man who should have been confronted instead. But many responded with something like gratitude—thanking both of them for showing us something that we rarely see: the willingness to have a painful conversation with both honesty and mutual care.

Embedded in this man's question is a particular way of seeing American racism. Specifically, seeing racism as a form of personal prejudice, as a disposition of the heart and mind. In this view, racism is largely understood as a set of individual perspectives, attitudes, and biases that shape how we value—or devalue—human beings. As McGhee noted, one of the common humiliations of our inheritance is that each of us bears prejudicial judgments against other people because of the color of their skin and the cultural heritage that this color suggests.[8]

But if racism is a heart issue, then what must we do to address it? Throughout American history, the answer to this question has been relatively straightforward: change the heart. Throughout the eighteenth and nineteenth centuries, anti-racist activists and abolitionists developed strategies aimed at just this sort of change. Through tracts, multiracial speaking tours, and other literature, they sought to reshape the racist heart of Americans.[9] During the early twentieth century, the writers and artists of the Harlem Renaissance continued this work by creating works designed to confront the racist blindness of White America and to help America, in the words of Langston Hughes, "see how beautiful I am and be ashamed."[10]

In our own time, this work of dispositional change continues in families, churches, and schools. In each of these initiatives, across the centuries, the goal has in many respects been the same: to weaken the malignant power of American racism by transforming the dispositions of the heart and mind.

In the Christian tradition, the language for this deep internal change is *personal repentance*, a sacred dimension of the Christian vision of the moral life. We have seen many Christians—including ourselves—take up this work of repentance with respect to racism. And rightly so. In the Christian tradition, personal prejudice is a form of violence that harms the other by denying their God-given dignity. Seeing these prejudicial dispositions in the heart, the Christian begins the long, renunciative work of uprooting them from the heart and rebuilding new dispositions in their place. This is essential work, and we ourselves are deeply committed to it. Even so, this particular way of seeing racism as a personal prejudice that chiefly requires the work of personal repentance is not the complete picture.

Racism as Relational Division

In 1994, Spencer Perkins and Chris Rice published a book that became something of a sensation in the American church. The book, *More*

Than Equals: Racial Healing for the Sake of the Gospel, was an extended treatment of both the necessity and practicality of living in cross-racial relationships as a way of bearing witness to the reconciling power of God. Perkins, the son of legendary African American civil rights activist John Perkins, and Rice, a northern White Mennonite who lived in an intentional interracial community in Jackson, Mississippi, stood side by side on the cover, and the book was heralded as "living proof that white and black Christians can live together."[11] At the heart of their argument was the claim that the Christian church in America desperately needed to transcend a debilitating contradiction in its life: being a community of reconciliation that contributes to a culture of social estrangement.

Writing in the early 1990s, they recognized a phenomenon that is easily recognizable in our own day. Though America has legally renounced segregation, we nonetheless remain profoundly segregated along racial lines. And the church itself—the community created to bear witness to the reconciling power of God—remains deeply segregated. For Rice and Perkins, the work of developing cross-racial or multiethnic friendships—what they call "racial reconciliation"—is at the heart of the work of the Christian church in America. This book had a considerable impact on the Christian church. Membership grew tremendously in the Christian Community Development Association, a Christian ministry founded by John Perkins and devoted to the work of racial reconciliation. Duke Divinity School created a Center for Reconciliation, led by Perkins and Rice, to train pastors and congregants in the work of reconciliation. In communities across America, deliberately multiethnic churches began to emerge to embody and bear witness to the reconciling power of God. And in our own time this work of raising up multiracial Christian communities continues to grow.

Embedded in *More Than Equals*, and the various endeavors to which it gave rise, is a particular way of seeing American racism. They describe American racism not primarily in terms of personal prejudice but in terms of *relational division*. And rightly so—this is surely part of our racial inheritance. It could hardly be otherwise. From the very beginning, American culture was both rooted in and dependent on an inviolable form of racial distance between White Europeans and the Africans they enslaved. Over time, as Americans chose to become more dependent on slave labor, this division was formalized into highly choreographed rituals of intimacy and distance that characterized the system of slavery that persisted in America from the early seventeenth to the mid-nineteenth century.

For a brief moment in the mid-nineteenth century, emancipation and the process of Reconstruction offered the promise of a different sort of America, but it was not to be. Even the most sweeping legislative changes were ultimately powerless to overcome America's racial division. This division was so deeply entrenched that many Americans—both Black and White—believed that the only possibility for Black freedom lay in colonization: send African Americans back to Africa.

In the face of the abandonment of Reconstruction and the failure of various colonization movements, Americans—especially, though not exclusively, in the South—inaugurated a new era of racial division by means of the Black Codes and, in time, the Jim Crow system of segregation. This comprehensive system of racial apartheid enshrined the principle of racial division in virtually every area of American life: families, schools, businesses, hospitals, political institutions, and even the church itself. And the effects of this system are broadly visible among us today.

What is to be done in the face of this relational division? With surprising consistency, an answer to this question has emerged again and again across American history: the healing of American racism requires the deliberate cultivation of integrated communities. Indeed, from Revolutionary-era movements for abolition, to nineteenth-century radical movements, to twentieth-century civil rights campaigns, to the twenty-first-century movement to birth multiethnic churches, the impulse has been the same: we can overcome racism by closing the relational divisions between White and Black Americans.

The Christian tradition calls this type of relational work *reconciliation*. However, reconciliation is not simply the cessation of hostilities or the willingness to coexist. It is, rather, about the cultivation of friendship and the creation of a community that bears witness to the reality of life beyond estrangement. In the Christian tradition, this relational estrangement is a broken form of human existence. It obscures the truth of the Triune unity of Father, Son, and Holy Spirit, the power of Christ to reconcile all things to himself, and the credibility of the church as an expression of a renewed humanity. From the earliest days of the Christian church, the law of love has required Christians not simply to repent of their personal prejudices but also to labor toward relational reconciliation—to live lives not of exclusion but of embrace.[12] In the past several years, we have seen this work of embrace taking shape in Christian communities around the country, and we continue to labor toward it—however falteringly—in our own lives. And yet we are conscious that this way of seeing American racism, as a relational division that demands the work of racial reconciliation, is incomplete.[13]

Racism as Institutional Injustice

In March 2012 an African American defense attorney named Bryan Stevenson gave a TED Talk called "We Need to Talk about an Injustice." While not yet the household name he has become today, within the legal defense world Stevenson was a deeply admired figure for his work—especially with inmates on death row—through his organization the Equal Justice Initiative (EJI). Wearing a blue blazer and a white, open-collared shirt, and carrying himself with a warmth that both reflected a native kindness and masked a native strength, he stepped onto the stage and began to speak. In the following days multiple friends forwarded us a link to the talk with subject lines such as "Must see" or "Please take time to watch this." In watching, we—like so many others—began to learn of the profound racial injustice at the heart of our criminal justice system.

The statistics Stevenson presents are startling: In 1972, America had roughly 300,000 people in prison, but we now have over 2.3 million—the highest incarceration rate in the world. One-third of African American men in this country between the ages of 18 and 30 are either in jail, on probation, in prison, or on parole (and the rate is 50 to 60 percent in some major cities in America). African American defendants are eleven times more likely than White defendants to receive the death penalty, and twenty-two times more likely if the victim of the crime is White. In many states, these criminal convictions have led to permanent disenfranchisement—the loss of the right to vote. In Alabama, for instance, 34 percent of African Americans have lost this right to vote. By the year 2022, the percentage of disenfranchised African Americans without the right to vote will be higher than before the passage of the Voting Rights Act of 1965. Stevenson paints a picture of a profound racial injustice in our midst. Appealing explicitly to hope, Stevenson reminds us that each of us is more than the worst thing we've ever done, and that we as a people will be judged not by our capacity for technological innovation but by our capacity to care for the poor, the marginalized, and the incarcerated. He invites us to join him in this work of telling the truth about the shadow side of our national history, acknowledging the injustice of it, and laboring toward a criminal justice system that is, well, *just*.[14]

As he concluded his remarks and began to walk off stage, the crowd stood and gave Stevenson an ovation that lasted nearly two minutes. It was a sign of things to come. Over the next few years, this man and this message emerged with greater force in the American imagination. In 2014, Stevenson released his book, *Just Mercy*, a moving personal account of his work to defend the rights of men, women, and children trapped in our national correctional system. In 2016, Ava DuVernay released her award-winning documentary *13th*—a reflection on race, mass incarceration, and the Thirteenth Amendment—and featured Stevenson prominently in its story. In 2018, Stevenson's EJI opened the National Memorial for Peace and Justice in Montgomery, Alabama, which memorializes and honors the victims of lynching in America. It is estimated that nearly ten thousand people attended the opening ceremonies of the memorial, and the *New York Times* named it as a top tourism destination in 2018. In 2019, *Just Mercy*, a feature film starring Michael B. Jordan and Jamie Foxx and based on Stevenson's book, became a national sensation. Stevenson's rise was astonishing. Wherever we went—churches, colleges, conferences, family reunions—we heard people talking not only about Bryan Stevenson but also about the racial injustice at the heart of our legal system and how it could change. And not only talking but *doing*. Both of us have friends who enrolled in law school or who changed the course of their existing legal careers in order to respond to Stevenson's call.

This response indicates a powerful awareness that racism in America expresses itself not merely as personal prejudice or as relational division but as *institutional injustice*. The same prejudices and estrangement that mark our individual and relational lives are encoded—often invisibly—in the institutions that shape our common life. As we will explore in the following chapters, racism in America has never been merely personal or even relational—it has always had an institutional shape. Look no further than slavery itself. This system was never just about the prejudices in the heart of the masters or their broken relationships with the slaves (though both were real). It was, rather, a system that aspired to comprehensive control of the person—bodily, economically, educationally, and politically.

Even after emancipation, the racist impulses of slavery were encoded in virtually every American institution. American culture not only maintained but intensified the racist patterns of American slavery in institutions related to law, education, health care, banking, housing, labor, and criminal justice. And—as Stevenson points out—in our own time, some 160 years after emancipation and 70 years after the legal end of Jim Crow, many of these patterns remain.

Across the centuries Americans have responded to these various forms of institutional injustice with extraordinary consistency, courage, and creativity. At the heart of these responses has been the work of not simply repentance or reconciliation but *reform*—seeking to right specific institutional wrongs. This work of reform has addressed itself to a range of institutional injustices: to abolish slavery, to secure African Americans the right to vote, to provide equal educational opportunities, to abolish prejudicial lending and housing practices, and to reform the practices of criminal justice—to name only a few. This history of reform has inspired our own work to address injustices in each of the discrete institutions in which we ourselves have served. And yet we remain aware of the fact that this, too, is the product of a particular way of seeing racism in America—as a form of institutional injustice that calls forth the work of reform.

Each of these ways of seeing and responding to race in America is probably familiar to the reader. Each of them is, in its own way, a crucial part of truly understanding the dynamics of race in America. We *do* carry personal prejudices that call for the work of repentance. We *do* have broken relationships that call for the work of reconciliation. And we *do* have institutional injustices that call for the work of reform. Even so, as important as these perspectives are, both individually and in aggregate, they fail to offer the full picture of race in America.[15] More importantly, they fail to act in the way that a fuller picture would demand. Because of this, we wish—here and in the chapters to follow—to suggest a fourth way of seeing race in America that, though including the others, overcomes their limitations, leading us not simply to repentance, reconciliation, and reform but beyond them to repair.

Racism as Cultural (Dis)Order

In 2015, journalist Ta-Nehisi Coates published a book entitled *Between the World and Me*.[16] This book, framed as a letter to his son about the experience of being Black in America, was part autobiography, part social history, part fatherly exhortation, and part lament. But it was all fire. At the time, Coates was already well known because of his memoir *The Beautiful Struggle* and the articles he published in *The Atlantic*—most notably, "The Case for Reparations."[17] But *Between the World and Me* amplified his voice to an international audience. His book renders a poet's eye, a theorist's mind, and a father's heart in language that is, at times, equal in beauty and power to any in American letters. But in the years since its publication, something else—something more fundamental to the work than even these things—has captured the imaginations of his readers. In private interviews and in public town halls across the world, it seems that his audiences want to hear him talk almost exclusively about one thing: his view of racism.

For many of us, the notion that we would need to write a letter to our children to guide them through the perils of American racism seems remote, perhaps even unimaginable. But for Coates it is essential. For him and for his son, this is the work of survival. He offers his child not a philosophical but what might best be described as a visceral account of American racism. He struggles to take the chaotic and bewildering phenomena of his body, of his streets, of his life—and of his son's life—and make them visible, intelligible, and actionable. He does so in hopes that his son might, in the fullest sense, live. His account of American racism is, in other words, not the academic musing of the social theorist but the guidance of a desperate, loving father.

To understand this account, it is important to understand three important ideas embedded within it. The first of these is that American society inextricably creates and promotes White people through violence against

Black and brown people. America as we know it is impossible apart from this violence. As Coates puts it, America "was not achieved through wine tastings and ice-cream socials, but rather through the pillaging of life, liberty, labor, and land, through the flaying of backs, the chaining of limbs; the strangling of dissidents; the destruction of families; the rape of mothers; the sale of children."[18] The cultural miracle of a free and prosperous White America—a foundational element of the American dream—depended on the creation of an enduring cultural nightmare of bondage and poverty for African Americans.

The second of his core ideas is that even as America kidnaps, enslaves, tortures, and exploits, it needs to see itself as innocent—to believe, in the very face of this bondage, that it is the land of the free. Again Coates:

> America believes itself exceptional, the greatest and noblest nation ever to exist, a lone champion standing between the white city of democracy and the terrorists, despots, barbarians, and other enemies of civilization. . . . There exists, all around us, an apparatus urging us to accept American innocence at face value and not to inquire too much.[19]

Much like the sanitation workers in Memphis, Coates accuses White America of a form of willful blindness, a sustained commitment to shelter its own brutality under the cloak of myth—what Coates refers to as "the Dream."

His third core claim is that the only way to live with integrity is to wake from this dream, to resist its manifold forms of temptation, and to take our place in the midst of the struggle for our own humanity against the forces of this history. As he tells his son,

> I did not want to raise you in fear or false memory. I did not want you forced to mask your joys and blind your eyes. What I wanted for you was to grow into consciousness. . . . If my life ended today, I would tell you it was a happy life—that I drew great joy from the study, from the struggle toward which I now urge you. . . . The changes have awarded me a rapture that comes only when you can no longer be lied to, when you have rejected the Dream.[20]

This, for Coates, is the only path to a life of freedom—to strip away the vanities embedded in our mythological cultural identities and to struggle as free people against the terror of our inheritance.

Taken together, these claims indicate a belief that American racism is not simply a personal prejudice, a relational division, or a specific institutional injustice, but something much more profound. Specifically, *racism is an entire culture—a comprehensive way of being and doing that is embedded in our structures of meaning, morality, language, and memory and expressed in our patterns of individual, social, and institutional behavior.*

At this point it seems important for us to say two things: First, in saying that racism is fundamental to American culture, we do not intend to say that racism is the *only* thing fundamental to American culture, reducing American culture to racism. Second, we *do* intend to say that racism is not incidental but elemental to American culture—that it goes all the way down. In other words, though one can conceptually distinguish racism from other energies in American culture, it is also the case that, historically speaking, these things have been *functionally* indivisible. Racism is best understood when seen not simply in individual, relational, or discrete institutional terms but in comprehensive *cultural* terms (a perspective developed more fully in chapters 2 and 3).

Since the publication of Coates's book, people have criticized his account of racism as fundamental to American culture as an overly reductive and profoundly cynical account of American cultural history. His view has also been called a basic failure of political hope. It might even be that some of our readers will be concerned about our decision to appeal to Coates, concerned that we have fully aligned ourselves with his intellectual project and that we are, therefore, subject to these same criticisms. Well, yes and no.

First, the no. Coates is straightforward about his hopelessness regarding the healing of America's profound racial wounds. When he looks at American culture, he simply does not see the grounds for such hope. We, on the other hand, have deep hope. We believe that what has been made can be unmade. We believe that what has been hidden can be unveiled. We believe that what has been broken can be made whole. This very book is an expression of that hope. But, crucially, our hope comes not from wistful optimism about the institutions of this nation, nor from a blind faith in the inevitable triumph of democracy. Our hope, rather, comes from our belief in the Father, the Son, and the Holy Spirit. We have hope because we believe that there is a God and that this God loves the world, hates injustice, and promises the healing of all things. God has demonstrated this in the life, death, resurrection, and ascension of Jesus. This is the source of our deep political hope. In this, we differ significantly, though respectfully, from Coates.[21]

Now the yes. We agree with Coates's claim that racism is not anomalous but essential to American culture. While this claim may be disconcerting to many of us, the truth is that this perspective is not unique to him or us. Since the beginning of the American republic, this view—that America is a racist cultural order—has been echoed time and again, becoming an enduring theme in American social and political history. It was echoed by Gouverneur Morris who, at the constitutional convention, argued that the adoption of slavery made America a "cursed" nation.[22] It was echoed by David Walker, a free African American from North Carolina turned Boston abolitionist who in his remarkable 1829 appeal said that American racism tempted the just judgment of God and invited its own destruction.[23] It was echoed by William Lloyd Garrison, a prominent abolitionist who described the American slaveholding nation as "the empire of Satan."[24] It was echoed by Frederick Douglass, who in 1847 said, "I have no love for America, as such. I have no patriotism. I have no country. The institutions of this country do not know me, do not recognize me as a man, except as a piece of property."[25] It was echoed by Ida B. Wells, nineteenth-century journalist, suffragist, and anti-lynching activist, who said that the power of White America had come by means of "fraud, violence, intimidation, and murder."[26] It was echoed by Malcolm X, who in 1964 described racism as "the cancer that is destroying America."[27] And it was echoed by Martin Luther King Jr. who, in a Memphis speech given the night before his death, told his audience that "the nation is sick."[28]

Each of these, and many others like them, while seeing racism in America as personal prejudice, relational estrangement, and institutional injustice, also—indeed primarily—saw racism as more than this. They saw racism as a culture, as a disorder at the heart of the American nation.[29] In this respect, Coates's work, though singularly powerful, echoes the voices throughout American history that have called us to see racism in this way—voices that we ourselves echo in this book.

This different way of seeing racism serves as the foundation of this work: racism is not *simply* a matter of personal prejudice, relational division, or institutional injustice but rather a fundamental cultural (dis)order that is both the source and sum of all these. Because of this, personal repentance, relational reconciliation, and institutional reform—though important—are not enough, indeed can never be enough, to overcome its power. Because racism is a comprehensively broken culture, what is needed—if we are to truly heal—is comprehensive cultural repair.[30]

The Struggle to See

In our own lives, and in the lives of many of our friends, the work of seeing racism in this way has been an ongoing struggle. In truth, seeing clearly almost always is a struggle. In reflecting upon this, we have come to believe that it is important to surface both the reality and the nature of this struggle. Only in doing so can we overcome these incomplete ways of seeing racism.

The Social Struggle

In his 1903 book, *The Souls of Black Folk*, W. E. B. Du Bois writes that "the problem of the Twentieth Century is the problem of the color line."[31] This line of racial division emerged from the headwaters of American culture, scoured every aspect of its development, and utterly shaped its ideas, policies, and practices. It is a line that runs through the very structure of our daily lives.

One of the functions of this line is to keep people on either side of it from really seeing one another. The color line is actually a wall designed to facilitate racial blindness. Consider American plantation life. The very structure of this system—with its hidden staircases, separate dwellings, and overseer system—was designed to render African Americans largely invisible to those who held them in bondage. Similarly, the Jim Crow system of total segregation—in schools, businesses, churches, neighborhoods, and bathrooms—rendered the truth about African American life almost entirely invisible to White Americans. Even in our own time, nearly seventy years after the legal end of segregation in this country, the legacy of this system continues. In many places, White and Black Americans continue to live almost wholly separate lives.

This is not in any way to provide justification for White blindness. Throughout history, we have seen that it is possible for both Whites and African Americans to see the truth and labor to help others see. Even so, for people who have been born into a system of almost total isolation, a certain form of social blindness is inevitable. For many White Americans the issue is not simply that they cannot see across the color line. The issue is that they do not even see that it is there. The segregated structures of American life function as a sort of cataract to true sight.

But this social structure is not simply a cataract. It is also coercive. It not only blinds us from seeing; it also pressures us *not* to see. Many Americans who have tried to see the racial truth about America have been met with a powerful and often deadly force of resistance. In the colonial era they were tarred and feathered. In the early Jim Crow era they were publicly lynched by angry mobs or forced to migrate to other communities. In the civil rights era they were met by jeers and shouts at their schools, by burning crosses in their yards, and by bombs in their churches. And in every era—even into our own—those who have struggled to see and speak the truth have been labeled as "un-American." Which, from the perspective of the racist history of America, is exactly what they were. This coercive force with which the American order meets those who dissent from it is a powerful obstacle to sight. Indeed, it is an incentive to turn away from sight to the relative safety of blindness.

These social obstacles to seeing the truth about American racial history are critical to understand. Not so that White Americans can excuse themselves from the work of seeing, but because overcoming these social obstacles is the first step toward an honest vision of ourselves.

The Personal Struggle

As powerful as these social obstacles are, they are not the heart of the struggle to see. The most powerful obstacles to sight lie instead within ourselves. Indeed, it is fully possible to know the truth about American history, to see the enduring legacy of its violence, and to nonetheless find ourselves indifferent—even hostile—to the repair for which it calls. Many of us resist seeing the truth of American racism not simply for social but for personal reasons as well.

The first of these reasons is that American racial history *threatens our personal identity*. For many of us, especially if you happen to be White and male, to be an American is to lay claim to a heritage of freedom, equality, and opportunity. This heritage bestows a certain form of civic pride, an awareness that no matter how difficult our individual circumstance, we are part of something larger that is both strong and good. This inheritance and civic pride are an important source of identity for many Americans, a crucial part of who we understand ourselves to be. But if the account of cultural racism is true—that America is about not only liberty but bondage, not only justice but oppression, not only the pursuit of happiness but the pursuit of men, women, and children through the swamps and forests of this land—then this identity takes on a different character. No longer may we see ourselves as the benedicted inheritors of a city on a hill. We must also see ourselves as inhabitants of a city that was built on the graves of broken children, and as beneficiaries of that breaking. We must see ourselves not simply as inheritors of history's nobility but also as ones who are implicated in history's nightmares.

Another reason that we refuse to see the truth about race in America is because it *complicates our personal histories*. The history of American racism complicates our relationship with ourselves and with the people, places, and institutions that frame the story of our lives. Consider an example: Many of us have photographs of people from past generations in frames on our walls and shelves. Some of them are admired historical figures; others are simply grandparents and great-grandparents. When we look at those pictures, we see people who lived, loved, and labored, and through those efforts made our lives possible. We see people who gave us our ideals, our eyes, our names, and our dining room tables. We see them with gratitude. As we should. What we see is real. But what if the history of American racism requires us also to see something else? What if it requires us also to see these people—*our* people—as members of one of the longest standing racist social orders in the history of the world? And not only members but contributors and beneficiaries of that order? As people who lived in the midst of some of the most terrible racial violence the world has ever seen? When we look at their faces in light of these things, what do we see?

Or another example: Many of us have places to which we like to escape for vacation—a campground, a mountain cabin, a cottage on the beach. These places—their smells, sounds, architectural details, their very landscapes—infuse us with longing. The beauty that they give to us is real. But what happens when we realize that the coastal vista that we cherish or the dunes on which our children play were once the homes of newly emancipated African Americans? When we realize that—despite promises made in the wake of emancipation—this land was stolen from them and given back to the families of those who formerly enslaved them? That it was later sold to White developers for enormous profits to those families? That African Americans were prohibited from buying homes in those areas? That it is no accident that the people walking around us on the shore are all White? That this place of our rest is the site of another's loss?[32]

One last example: Like many Americans, those of us who are White deeply love the institutions that have shaped our lives. Consider, for example, our colleges, universities, and seminaries. Many of us return to these institutions year after year. We walk the flowered paths, admire the stately buildings, and gather with friends under the ancient trees. We wear hats and sweaters that bear witness to the fact that this place is a fundamental part of our history, one of the treasured institutions of our lives. And we should. The gifts that we received from these institutions are of incalculable value. But if our account of American racism is true, then we must also see that many of these places—especially if they are historically significant or culturally prominent—also have very painful racial histories. What if the bricks of the buildings we love were built by the hands of the tortured? What if the gates that open for us onto shaded groves close behind us in the faces of others? What if the place that built our minds was also a place in which others' bodies were broken? What then?[33]

Finally, we believe there is a third reason that many of us resist seeing the truth about American racism: it *questions our personal aspirations*. To be White in America is to be the recipient of a powerful cultural inheritance of liberty, equality, and opportunity. Embedded within this inheritance from the past is also a set of aspirations for the future. This inheritance asks us to receive these things *and* to make the most of them—to benefit from them in our own lives and to bestow them on the lives of our children. Indeed, many of us are taught to avail ourselves of liberty, equality, and opportunity in the pursuit of happiness. We take these things and from them create lives of incredible education, wealth, experience, and security. Further, we do so with the consoling knowledge that our pursuit of happiness goes with the very grain of the American dream. But what if this is not true? What if the cultural inheritance we have received is not universal but selective and exclusive? What if for every Jacob who revels in the inheritance of his father, there are five Esaus who scrape empty pots? What if, out of no evident fault of our own, our pursuit of happiness entails the sorrow of others? What happens to our aspirations? What happens to the lives we have imagined for ourselves?

It is difficult to overstate the trauma of these discoveries for White Americans. Embracing these truths requires a profound transformation of one's identity, history, and aspirations. With this transformation comes an inescapable sense of disorientation and an enduring form of grief. It could not, and ought not, be otherwise. In the face of this, it is extraordinarily tempting for White Americans—in our anger and shame—either to distance ourselves from this history by denying its reality and our role in it or to simply craft lives of oblivion that allow us to entirely ignore these historical realities and the obligations that they entail. Indeed, non-White Americans are susceptible to a similar temptation. We have seen it in men and women around the country. And we have seen it in our own lives—indeed we see it daily.

But we also see these temptations for what they are: temptations to flee from reality. Temptations to blind ourselves to the truth about who we are as a people and a society, and what will finally be required of us if we are to heal. To succumb to this temptation is to undergo a kind of death—the death of ourselves and of our neighbors and the communities we share. To resist these temptations is to embrace freedom: freedom from blind complicity with evil and freedom to rejoice in the possibilities of a world made new. And so, we continue to struggle to answer the call to see.

2

Seeing the Reality of
White Supremacy

The conundrum of color is the inheritance of every American, be he/she legally or actually Black or White. It is a fearful inheritance, for which untold multitudes, long ago, sold their birthright.

—James Baldwin, *Notes of a Native Son*

The Immeasurable Distance

In the summer of 1852, Frederick Douglass felt lost. Just five years earlier, he had basked in the glow of a meteoric rise to international fame. During his year-long speaking tour of the United Kingdom, crowds gathered in churches in Scotland, pubs in Ireland, and lecture halls in London, straining against one another just for the opportunity to see him. They wept when he left the British Isles, pledging their personal loyalties and financial resources to his abolitionist cause. When he returned to America, a cheering crowd welcomed him home. He had accomplished what few men—and virtually no African American men—had accomplished: he had become an intellectual leader, a moral force, and a personal celebrity on both sides of the Atlantic. And he had done all this before his thirtieth birthday.

What a difference five years had made. As he looked at his life now, he found himself engulfed in attacks on his reputation, conflicts in his marriage, precarity in his finances, dispute with other abolitionists, and a national political crisis that would, he sensed, lead to civil war. In light of these things it was a relief to be asked by the Ladies' Anti-Slavery Society of Rochester to be their honored speaker for their Fourth of July address. Not only would it help to support him financially and promote his fledgling paper, it would also, in a sense, feel like old times.

But these were new times too. No longer was he the novice speaker on the abolitionist circuit, an emerging leader testing out his ideas and gauging his audience. He had matured into a singular force, and he knew it. He gratefully accepted their offer to speak, but he did so on his own terms. Though the event was originally scheduled as part of the community's July 4 celebration, Douglass insisted on giving his address the following day, July 5. In doing so, he identified not with White but with Black Americans who, in response to the tradition of holding slave auctions on July 4, refused to celebrate that day.[1] It was a sign of things to come.

The talk was held in Rochester's newly opened Corinthian Hall. Graced with soaring ceilings and abundant light, it was the most prestigious venue in town for public events. As the hour drew near, nearly six hundred people—the majority of them White—began to claim their seats. Though Douglass had fallen on hard times of late, he maintained his reputation as one of the finest orators in America and one of the most powerful spokesmen for abolition anywhere in the world. Even so, no one was quite prepared for what they heard.[2]

As he often did, Douglass began his speech by humbling himself before his hearers. He told them, among other things, that he approached them "with little experience and less learning . . . trusting to [their] patient and generous indulgence."[3] At face value, Douglass's words were transparently false. He was a once-in-a-generation talent, a man of enormous charisma, learning, and experience. In these respects, not one person seated before him was his equal. But to take them at face value, to hear them merely as self-abnegating flattery offered in hopes of uniting his hearers to himself, is to miss the point. Douglass's words were, rather, an attempt to *divide* himself from his hearers. He sought to remind them of the profound distance between him and them, of the fact that—his enormous gifts notwithstanding—he was still a Black man in America. As he puts it, "The distance between this platform and the slave plantation, from which I escaped, is considerable—and the difficulties to be overcome in getting from the latter to the former are by no means slight."[4] This distance, rather than a mere deferential formality, was to become the speech's central theme.

But not yet. Moving on from his introduction, Douglass seemed to settle firmly into his audiences' expectations—the glories of the Fourth of July. He spoke of the day as the "birthday of your National Independence, and of your political freedom." He described it as their "Passover," a day that "carries your minds back to the day, and to the act of your great deliverance." And not only this, he reminded them—in terms verging on the rhapsodic—that their deliverance was no mere act of providence but the fruit of the bold work of their ancestors, who out of a strong conviction of freedom and justice, "lay deep the cornerstone of the national superstructure, which has risen and still rises in glory around you."[5] This was the Douglass they had come to hear. The Douglass who saw the goodness of their cause, honored the courage of their fathers, and embodied the promises of their nation. One can almost imagine the delighted rapture of the audience as they heard these words, from this man, in this place, on this day.

And yet the perceptive listener could hear something else as well. Even as Douglass honored the founding of America, he distanced himself from it. *Your* independence. *Your* freedom. *Your* deliverance. *Your* fathers. *Your* nation. A hidden repudiation lurked beneath the surface of his words. And then it came:

> Fellow-Citizens, pardon me, allow me to ask, why am I called upon to speak here today? What have I, or those I represent, to do with your national independence? Are the great principles of political freedom and of natural justice, embodied in the Declaration of Independence, extended to us? . . . I am not included within the pale of this glorious anniversary! Your high independence only reveals the immeasurable distance between us. The blessings in which you, this day, rejoice, are not enjoyed in common. The rich inheritance of justice, liberty, prosperity, and independence, bequeathed by your fathers, is shared by you, not by me. The sunlight that brought life and

healing to you, has brought stripes and death to me. This Fourth of July is yours, not mine. You may rejoice, I must mourn.[6]

Douglass laid bare what he had kept hidden in mind from the moment he received the invitation, what he had hinted at through his insistence on July 5, his exaggerated words of deference, his uncomfortable use of the word "your" when speaking to his audience of American history: The America being celebrated on that day was *their* America, not his. It was an America enjoyed exclusively by White people at the expense of Douglass and the African Americans on whose behalf he spoke. Though they were abolitionists themselves, Douglass's audience, arrayed in their patriotic finest, sat chastened before him. Douglass had called into question some of their most cherished beliefs. And he did not relent. In page after page he declared their vision of a universally free America to be a soothing fiction, a fantasy refuted by its continued approval of slavery. From his perspective, both the American nation and the church that solemnly blessed it showed themselves to be the enemy of the Constitution and Scripture, rather than embodying their vision.[7] He summed up his view of the July holiday and the nation that it honored in these famous words:

> What to the American slave is your 4th of July? I answer: a day that reveals to him, more than all other days in the year, the gross injustice and cruelty to which he is a constant victim. To him, your celebration is a sham; your boasted liberty and unholy license; your national greatness, swelling vanity; your sounds of rejoicing are empty and heartless; your denunciations of tyrants, brass fronted impudence; your shouts of liberty and equality, hollow mockery; your prayers and hymns, your sermons and thanksgivings, with all your religious parade and solemnity are, to him, mere bombast, fraud, deception, impiety, and hypocrisy—a thin veil to cover up the crimes which would disgrace a nation of savages. There is not a nation on earth guilty of practices more shocking and bloody, than are the people of these United States at this very hour.[8]

At the conclusion of his speech, the crowd—chastened, awed, thrilled, and inspired—rose in unison and celebrated Douglass's words with "a universal burst of applause."[9] Though they had not yet closed the "immeasurable distance" between themselves and Douglass, between Whites and African Americans, they could, perhaps for the first time, truly see it.

Seeing America

Douglass's speech was a literary lightning bolt, one of those rare events that illuminates the landscape for a moment and strikes with a power that transforms all it touches. Within days his speech had been reprinted in newspapers and read in congregations all around the country. To this day it serves as a touchstone for understanding the nature and effects of racism in America. The power of this speech derives not only from its social courage or from its extraordinary language (although both are true) but from the perspective on America that it proclaimed. That perspective? White Americans are *right* to say that America is founded on the unalienable rights of life, liberty, and the pursuit of happiness. White Americans are *right* to boast that America is devoted to the creation of a social order that enables each of these. White Americans are *right* to celebrate each of these and the blessings that have come as a result. *As long as they know that these things are true only for them.* America, in spite of its democratic ideals, has chosen to bestow its blessings exclusively on those whom it deems to be White. These blessings have come not simply from the providence of God but from violence against human beings deemed not White. In America it is not liberty or equality but *Whiteness* that reigns supreme.

Douglass was the most powerful articulator of this perspective, but he was not alone in it. This view has been shared by many Americans—across races—throughout history. Indeed, it is a view shared by millions of Americans today. Yet, for many of our readers, the notion that America is deeply devoted to the supremacy of Whiteness will be unfamiliar, uncomfortable, and even unacceptable. We ourselves have consistently heard these concerns as we have worked on this project. Even so, with Douglass, we must insist on the truth. While we believe that the ideals and institutions of this nation are a source of singular benefit, we also believe that these benefits have been primarily—and at times exclusively—for White Americans. *This is what we mean when we say that racism is a cultural disorder.* In order to truly see the way that racism is a fundamental part of the American cultural order, we have to see the ways in which America has sheltered the supremacy of Whiteness. Until we do so, we will never respond adequately. Our goal in what follows is to help our readers see what Douglass, King, Coates, and we ourselves have seen: the reality of

White supremacy and the ways in which it has shaped—and continues to shape—American cultural life.

Seeing Whiteness, Seeing Supremacy

In April 2020, the government of the United States began a comprehensive census of the people within its borders. The census, mandated by the Constitution, takes place every ten years and provides important insights into the nation's transforming demographic landscape, insights that determine our political and economic decision-making and that reveal our national identity.

The census also subtly determines the ways in which we conceive of the nation. Not surprisingly, it does so in decidedly racial terms. These racial categories are basic to how we understand ourselves as people, both individually and collectively. What is fascinating, however, is that the census teaches us to understand the *meaning* of these categories. Consider, for example, the way it teaches us to understand the category of "Whiteness." On the page devoted to racial designation, beside the box labeled "White," the survey says this: "Select one or more boxes and enter origins: White (German, Irish, English, Italian, Lebanese, Egyptian, etc.)."[10]

Of course, these different cultural "origins," spread across three continents and consisting of multiple people groups and languages, are profoundly different from one another. Some of these groups have warred against one another, each seeing the other as, well, *other*. Yet in spite of these differences, each of them—German and Lebanese, Irish and Egyptian—are all, in the mysterious alchemy of American racial categories, magically rendered "White." And by virtue of this Whiteness, these people occupy a certain space in the American civic imagination.[11]

It is possible to read too much into the census survey, to see its racial designations as a deliberate reestablishment of social conventions intended to maintain a social hierarchy. We do not see it this way. In our minds, it is simply a descriptive tool that employs existing social categories in a way that reflects their common usage in American life. But it is also possible to see too little in it, to miss what it reveals to us about the history and meaning of racial thinking in America. Embedded in its racial designations is the history of a culture and of a culture's thinking about human beings. This history provides two important insights about the meaning of race in America: First, that race is a *modern invention*, and second, that race has a *social function*. In what follows, we wish to apply these two insights toward developing a clearer understanding of the meaning of Whiteness and the reality of its functional supremacy in American culture.

Whiteness: A Modern Invention

Once upon a time there were no White people. This was, in fact, not very long ago. Yes, there were German people, Irish people, British people, French people, even people with light skin. But not *White* people. Not even one.[12] As W. E. B. Du Bois puts it, "The discovery of personal whiteness among the world's peoples is a very modern thing—a nineteenth and twentieth century matter indeed."[13] For those raised in a context in which racial categories such as "White" and "Black" are axiomatic to—indeed necessary for—navigating cultural life, it can be difficult to imagine a world in which such a statement could be true. However, the historical reality is that "Whiteness," which seems to be a universal fact, is rather an American cultural creation. The story of how people of such diverse cultural origins came to be understood—and to understand themselves—as "White" is complicated, and its full telling is beyond our scope. Even so, it is important to understand something of this story. Only by doing so will we be able to truly see the distinctive—and destructive—meaning of American racism.

The Creation of Blackness

To understand Whiteness we must begin with Blackness. In the emergence of Blackness, Whiteness finds its origin and its meaning. Though the African story traces back to the deepest reaches of history, the uniquely African American story begins in the fifteenth century. Driven together by the early Enlightenment currents of religion, economics, politics, and science, Portuguese explorers and African tribal leaders first beheld one another on the shores of West Africa. In spite of the years of interaction between European traders and the various kingdoms of the African coasts, these Portuguese sailors understood little of the people on whose shores they stood. Europeans knew almost nothing of the distinct cultures, diverse languages, complex political structures, and ancient frameworks of spiritual meaning that framed the lives of the various peoples of the African continent. Because of this, they characterized Africans in terms of the feature that most immediately distinguished them from Europeans: black skin.[14]

It's not quite true that this emphasis on physical Blackness was an early expression of modern racism. Certainly Europeans believed themselves to be superior to Africans. Even so, their sense of superiority was based on religious grounds, that the people before them were pagan worshipers of false gods, and on cultural grounds, that the people before them were uncivilized and devoid of true culture. The prejudice was there, but the racism was still to come.

In the decades following this encounter, European colonial powers struggled to keep up with the insatiable colonial appetite for slave labor. The practical problem was where to get the slaves. There were two obvious markets: the Slavic peoples of Eastern Europe (from which the word *slave* is derived), who for five hundred years had been the favored source of slave labor in Europe, and the Native peoples of the so-called New World.[15] But the constant war that resulted from attempting to enslave people who lived nearby and the ravages of disease made these markets impractical. The slaves would have to be found elsewhere: Africa. Unlike the Slavic and Native peoples, Africans lived a world away, reducing the need for endless border wars. And unlike the Native peoples, Africans proved more resilient to the scourge of European disease. These insights gave rise to a virtually exclusive focus on the trade of Africans. This trade, funded by newly formed European companies and enabled by partnerships with African traders, provided the apparently boundless supply of enslaved labor necessary for extending the religious and cultural ambition of European imperialism into the New World.

Because distinctions between the diverse linguistic, religious, and political backgrounds of the various African tribal peoples were invisible to the European traders, the human beings swept up in the horrors of the transatlantic slave trade were simply designated as "Black." Over time, slavery and a distinctly African form of Blackness became inexorably linked, constituting a significant shift in the meaning of slavery. Whereas, for hundreds of years, slavery was justified largely on religious and cultural grounds, now an additional ground entered the picture: Blackness. Thus, in the emerging cultural logic of enslavement in the New World, and for the first time in history, enslavement and Blackness were indivisibly bound together.[16]

As with all social processes, this emergence took time. Initially, Africans were enslaved not for their Blackness but primarily because Europeans viewed them as culturally unenlightened and religiously pagan. But in time a problem emerged. If, as the European powers claimed, the goal of imperial expansion was to bring culture to the unenlightened and religion to the unconverted, what happens when the project succeeds? What happens when the slaves adopt the master's culture? What happens when the unconverted convert? On what basis do they remain enslaved? This was precisely the question facing slave owners in the American colonies at the end of the seventeenth century. One option, of course, was to free the slaves, to consider the imperial goals accomplished and to enfold the formerly enslaved into the empire. But that would be an economic disaster. Without slavery, the entire imperial project would fail. From the imperial perspective, slavery *had to* continue. This continuation required a new justification for slavery: Blackness alone.[17]

Sustaining this justification required an extension of the meaning of Blackness. The mere color of the skin was not sufficient justification for the enslavement of thousands—and in time millions—of people. Coloration needed to signify something more significant, needed to entail certain qualities that were themselves the basis of enslavement. Blackness, in other words, needed to refer to something that was more than skin deep.[18] Over the course of the eighteenth and nineteenth centuries a new meaning for Blackness emerged. Rather than simply a physical description, it became an account of personal capacity. To be Black was to possess lesser mental, emotional, spiritual, and relational capacity; it was to be *inferior*. It also came to signify moral deficiency, an innate tendency toward laziness, theft, duplicity, and lust. To be Black was to be *dangerous*. As a result of these notions of personal inferiority and moral danger, Blackness also came to take on a new meaning: social marginalization. Blackness became not simply a personal but also a social designation. Over time, Blackness came to indicate not merely dark skin but also dimmed personal capacities, a shadowed moral orientation, and a place at the hidden margins of the social order. By the middle of the nineteenth century, this new meaning had been intellectualized by science, baptized by churches, and, as we will see below, institutionalized across the structures of American life.[19]

The Mirror of Blackness

Understanding this history is crucial because *it is in the context of these emerging notions of Blackness that modern racial notions of Whiteness emerged*. Initially, as notions of Blackness began to emerge as justification for enslavement, slaveholders continued to be understood largely in *cultural* terms—such as Portuguese, Spanish, and British. While the slaves were Black, the masters were not yet White. But by the end of the seventeenth century, a new notion of Whiteness began to emerge.[20] As enslavement was identified with Blackness, slaveholding was increasingly identified with those who were "not Black." Across the various colonial powers, even amid hotly contested disputes over territorial boundaries, these powers were in agreement about one thing: slaves were Black, and they were not. This early emergence of a nascent Pan-European identity in response to slavery reveals the original meaning of Whiteness: to be White meant simply to be not Black.

But over time Whiteness came to mean more than this. The mere fact of not having dark skin was not enough to justify the act of holding another in bondage. Whiteness, too, needed to go beneath the skin. The process of this expanded meaning of Whiteness mirrored the expanding of Blackness; as Blackness took on new meaning, Whiteness took on its opposite. Where Blackness signified inferior personal capacity, Whiteness signified superior personal capacity. Where Blackness signified moral deficiency, Whiteness signified moral virtue. Where Blackness signified the margins of society, Whiteness signified a rightful claim to the center. To be White came to mean not only having lighter skin but also possessing elevated personal capacity, inherent moral virtue, and an assumed place at the center of the social order. And, as with Blackness, by the middle of the nineteenth century, the presence of this newly invented notion of Whiteness was clearly visible in American cultural life. But the fullness of its social implications was yet to be seen.[21]

Supremacy: Its Social Function

The creation of hierarchical racial categories for human beings was an anthropological revolution of the Enlightenment era. It created "a new epistemology of human difference,"[22] a model of knowing that brought into existence new ways of being human. But, not surprisingly, the real impact of this development, the true expression of its power, lies in its social and political expression. Modern racial categories were framed in the context of enormous social transformations: the renaissance of the sciences, the rise of colonial powers, the expansion of global markets, the flowering of humanistic ideals. Emerging in this context, racial categories were never merely a form of anthropological classification; they always entailed, and were in service to, social and political functions. The social function of Whiteness was to secure for Whites the dominant role in the hierarchy of the emerging world and an *exclusive* claim to its incalculable benefits. The social function of Whiteness was, in a word, *supremacy*.[23] Understanding the social and political supremacy of Whiteness in America is critical not only for understanding the nature of American racism but also for beginning the work of meaningfully engaging it. To that end, in what follows we seek to show that the social supremacy of Whiteness was *original* to the founding of America, *pervasive* across its institutions, and *enduring* throughout its history.

White Supremacy as Original

As in all nations, the origin story of America is, culturally speaking, sacred. It serves as the basis of national identity, the justification for national behavior, and the touchstone for national aspirations. Americans teach this story in schools, celebrate it in parades, summon it in speeches, exhibit it in museums, pin it on lapels, and pledge allegiance to it, hand over heart. To suggest that White supremacy is original to that story is, at best, complicated.

This challenge is all the more exaggerated in our cultural moment in which competing accounts of American origins are deployed as weapons in a profoundly divisive cultural and political contest. There are those whose account of American origins is almost exclusively a tale of throwing off the bonds of royal oppression and founding a new nation of liberty and justice for all. In this rendering, America is understood in heroic terms, a lone defender of freedom in a world of widespread political bondage. Anything that might shadow that heroism is wholly obscured from view. There are others whose account of American origins is exclusively a tale of White supremacy and bondage, an economic and political tragedy in which the unfathomable suffering of some enabled the unimaginable enrichment of others. In this rendering, America is understood wholly in terms of villainy, as a singular example of the racialized horrors of bondage, extraction, and violence. Anything that might complicate this account is often viewed with dismissive suspicion. For a great many Americans, the conflict between these two zero-sum accounts is a source of personal stress and political agitation. Each side frames its claims not simply in historical but in moral terms, each views the other exclusively as the enemy, and each accepts nothing less than absolute allegiance. It is not our intention or desire to participate in this conflict or to have our view of American origins weaponized in the service of American culture wars. We are not seeking to offer a comprehensive theory of America or to imbue the complex origins of America with a single meaning. Our claim about American origins is much more modest. Simply put, it is this: *The social supremacy of people characterized as White—in other words, White supremacy—was present and powerful in the founding of America.*

The most obvious expression of this fact is the decision to maintain and protect the institution of slavery. This institution existed as part of the old colonial world for nearly three centuries before the formal founding of America. But crucially, even the American founders—who were casting off much of that old world, casting off institutions that were as ancient and powerful as monarchy itself—*chose* to bring slavery into the New World with them. This language of choice is critical. The enslavement of human beings in the United States of America did not just happen. It was embraced and sustained through a series of choices made by other human beings, the founding fathers of the new nation.

It is true that this choice was contested at the time, even by those who made it. It was broadly understood that the American choice to perpetuate the enslavement of human beings directly contradicted America's legitimating ideals. This was obviously the opinion among Black Americans, who before, during, and after the American Revolution struggled for freedom from White supremacy. In South Carolina, for example, White crowds marched through the streets protesting the 1765 Stamp Act with cries of "Liberty," and their African American slaves took up the chant in their own right, creating panic among the slaveholding community there.[24] Likewise, northern African Americans, such as Philadelphians Richard Allen and James Forten, seeing the emancipatory logic of America's revolutionary ideals, worked to establish those ideals in hopes of making their people free. Other African Americans joined the British army, seeing the defeat of the American revolution as their only hope for freedom. To make the point, many of these marched into war with a patch on the shoulder of their uniform that read "Liberty to Slaves."[25] Still others, despairing of any freedom under the rule of either the Americans or the British, sought to take their liberty into their own hands through a series of largely ill-fated insurrections.[26]

This criticism of White supremacy and its embodiment, slavery, was not limited to Black Americans. Criticism came also from White Americans, even those at the very center of the founding of America.[27] In the years of tension that preceded the revolution, as democratic ideals began to coalesce more broadly in the popular mind, the colonies saw the emergence of an unprecedented number of antislavery writings. And in the wake of the publication of the Declaration of Independence and the inauguration of the war for independence, a number of American slaveholders—Virginian James Madison among them—began the process of voluntary (if limited) manumission.[28] In the minds of not a few Americans, the logic was fairly straightforward: the conviction that God had endowed human beings with unalienable rights to life, liberty, and the pursuit of happiness was fundamentally at odds with the dehumanization, misery, bondage, and death intrinsic to the slave system.[29] A letter written by Abigail Adams to her husband and future president John Adams is illustrative of this sentiment: "It always seemed a most iniquitous scheme to me to fight ourselves for what we are daily robbing and plundering from those who have as good a right to freedom as we have."[30]

Even so, such sentiments, though powerful in the imagination, were not to prevail in the actual institutions of the new nation. America enslaved human beings even as choruses of liberty were sung in its streets. And not only was slavery to continue in the new republic, it was to be politically privileged. At the Constitutional Convention of 1787, the Three-Fifths Compromise, which determined state population (and thus political representation) by counting not only free citizens but also three-fifths of a slave, guaranteed the political dominance of the slaveholding South for generations to come. America was left to bear the contradiction between its animating ideal of liberty and justice for all and its actual practice of liberty and justice for a few, with bondage and injustice for many. Emblematic of this contradiction is Thomas Jefferson himself. Jefferson, the poet laureate of revolutionary republicanism, was also Jefferson the trafficker of human beings. Neither he nor the nation he founded was ever able to escape this contradiction.[31]

The inescapable implication is that from the moment of its founding, the United States of America was a willing participant in the legal kidnapping, torture, sale, bondage, and murder of thousands, and in time millions, of human beings. It willingly justified these things on the contrived racial grounds of "Blackness." And the fruit of this decision has indelibly marked our fields and our cities, our churches and our banks, our bodies and our shame. Any version of American origins that conceals this reality behind the thrill of revolutionary ideals or the elegance of colonial gardens is a lie. In light of these things, it is essential that when we tell the story of American origins we tell the truth about the presence and power of White supremacy within it. This means to embrace not merely the fact of its existence but also that this existence was not marginal but central, not an inevitability but a choice, and that this choice unalterably marked what America was and what America would become.

White Supremacy as Pervasive

In the years following the war for independence, the men who were once colonists and then insurrectionists took on a new mantle: founding father. In so doing they began the momentous task of transforming America from a possibility into a polity, from a set of ideas into a system of institutions.

That was the point all along, of course: not simply to write pamphlets about liberty and equality but to build a social order conducive to their flowering. In a true marvel of political entrepreneurship, they created the new institutions of the nation, each giving particular expression to the meaning of American ideals.

As with the Revolution, it is tempting to tell the story of this institutional unfolding in a way that fails to disclose the role of White supremacy. Sadly, this omission is an American pastime. The truth, however, is that White supremacy, rather than being an unfortunate and aberrant weed in the garden of democracy, was in fact a native species that grew into and flowered out of every institution that the American founders created, in every region of the nation. *In other words, White supremacy was pervasive.* It is impossible to tell the story of the scope of White supremacy in a few pages. There are entire shelves of literature devoted to exploring the presence of White supremacy in a host of discrete regional and institutional domains. The best we can do is to gesture toward this comprehensiveness and to persuade the reader that while there is more that could be said about the scope of White supremacy in America, there is, alas, certainly not less.

The years following the Revolution seemed to offer the possibility of a change in African American fortunes. The endurance of prerevolutionary abolitionist sentiment, the desire to build strong relationships with skeptical European allies, and the early stages of a new religious awakening led to a surprising (if small) trend toward manumission and open conversations about the role of free African Americans in the new republic. True equality was never on the table, but it was at least plausible to imagine a short-term future in which America would resolve its inherent tension between liberty and bondage.

It was not to be. The liberation of African Americans, while formally consistent with the founders' revolutionary ideals, created problems for their actual institutions. Most pressing was the concern about the role of the growing number of free Blacks in a system of representative government. Given White beliefs about the limited personal and moral capacity of Black Americans, and given White fears of the possibility of Black political influence, any notion of Black citizenship was out of the question. But if they were not slaves and not citizens, then what were they? How were they to be governed? And, perhaps most important of all, how were they to relate to Whites? Rather than resolving these difficult questions by enfolding African Americans into the American republic, the founding fathers established two approaches to African American life, approaches that transformed the nature of American institutional life. The first of these was segregation. Already firmly established in American plantation life, segregation extended through increased restrictions on social relations between White and Black Americans and through the creation of separate social and religious institutions. But by the turn of the century, a more dramatic solution had begun to take root: colonization. If Black Americans deserved freedom but could not live as free people in America, perhaps they should be sent back to Africa. This was strongly opposed by both northern Blacks who believed that they should be citizens and by southern Whites who believed that they should be slaves. Even so, it was embraced by a number of America's political leaders as the only viable solution to America's internal contradictions. By 1817, the American Colonization Society was formed and experiments in returning free Blacks to Africa had begun.[32] This anxiety about Black political and social power and the emergence of both segregation and colonization in response demonstrate in the clearest possible terms the power of White supremacy in the early American imagination. In its institutional practice, America was a country for Whites. And while being Black in America no longer guaranteed enslavement, it also did not yet mean freedom.[33] This early institutional structure was contested, of course. Abolitionist communities, both Black and White, struggled to turn public sentiment against enslavement in particular and White supremacy in general. But these movements, though powerful, were no match for the political and economic power of the American South. The early American institutionalization of White supremacy, with its perpetuation of slavery, its insistence on segregation, and its pressure toward colonization, remained intact for nearly a century.

In the intervening years, the central question of American political life was what would happen to those institutions as the nation expanded into new territories. Would the agricultural slave economies of the American South dominate these territories (and thus the nation) or would the more urban and abolitionist energies of the North expand their power? It was a question that would only be answered by war.

As with the Revolution, the years following the Civil War opened a new window for African American freedom. The seeds of this freedom were sown in the enlistment of Black soldiers and, in time, emancipation of Black slaves. As the war ended, these seeds of freedom flowered in rapid succession. Congress passed the Civil Rights Act of 1866, establishing citizenship for everyone born in the United States without respect to race, color, or previous condition of servitude and requiring the free exercise of the privileges of this citizenship.[34] Several months later, the Fourteenth Amendment, which permanently established these rights in the Constitution and—for the first time—gave Congress the power to enforce this law, was passed and sent to the states for ratification. And in 1870, the Fifteenth Amendment, prohibiting the denial of the right to vote to any male citizen—including African Americans—was ratified as well. In an almost miraculous turn, Black Americans' long insistence on their own equality had transformed from an unanswered personal plea into an established constitutional right.

In truth, however, it was a fragile transformation. In spite of the events in Washington and the ecstasies of the abolitionists, much of the nation remained deeply opposed to African American equality. And in 1877, when the federal government ended its commitment to Reconstruction and withdrew military forces from the South, this opposition consolidated power with astonishing speed. Almost overnight, communities across the United States, especially (though not exclusively) in the South,[35] reestablished a hierarchical racial order as the basis of social and political life. And they perfected and policed it with an unprecedented level of violence. Thus was born Jim Crow—a comprehensive institutional expression of American White supremacy. Over time, as this system solidified, virtually every aspect of American institutional life—voting, education, employment, lending, housing, health care, transportation, policing, and even religion—took the shape of White supremacy. By the twentieth century, in spite of the ideals of the revolution and the promises of emancipation, America's original commitment to White supremacy had taken a dominant and pervasive institutional form that would endure for the next eighty years. As W. E. B. Du Bois puts it, "The slave went free; stood a brief moment in the sun; then moved back again toward slavery."[36]

White Supremacy as Enduring

In 1955 a young activist named Rosa Parks staged a planned protest on a bus in Montgomery, Alabama. Parks, a veteran anti-racist who spent years documenting White violence against Black women in the South, was the perfect choice.[37] She possessed not only an absolute commitment to dismantling White supremacy but also a strong personal character and an impeccable public reputation. She and local NAACP leaders believed that she was the right person to help force the issue of segregation into federal court and to force the southern states to comply with federal law. Thus began the classical era of the civil rights movement, the period in the middle of the twentieth century in which the legitimacy of White supremacy was systematically challenged across the entire landscape of American institutions. In 1954, the landmark case *Brown v. Board of Education* successfully challenged the legitimacy of White supremacy in public schools. In 1955, the Montgomery Improvement Association, led by Martin Luther King Jr., challenged its legitimacy in public transportation. In 1957, the Little Rock Nine challenged the legitimacy of states to obstruct federal integration law. In 1958, the NAACP Youth Council carried out a sit-in protest to challenge the legitimacy of segregated lunch counters in Kansas and Oklahoma. In 1960, student groups carried out sit-in protests in businesses across the United States. In 1961, the Freedom Riders challenged the legitimacy of segregation in interstate travel. In 1962, James Meredith challenged the legitimacy of segregated public universities. In 1963, some 250,000 people gathered in Washington, DC, to protest racial inequality at the March on Washington for Jobs and Freedom. In 1964, college students from across the country joined the Freedom Summer movement in Mississippi to challenge its legitimacy at the polls. That same year, protests in Memphis challenged the legitimacy of segregated churches. In 1965, protestors challenged White supremacy in police departments in Selma, Alabama, and Los Angeles. In 1966, King moved to Chicago to protest the role of White supremacy in housing inequality, and the Black Panther Party emerged in Los Angeles to address it. In 1967, in *Loving v. Virginia* the Supreme Court rejected state bans on interracial marriage. And in 1968, just a few days before his murder, King joined the sanitation workers in Memphis to protest unequal wages and employment practices. This period was, by any measure, the most astonishing assault on institutionalized White supremacy since the era of Reconstruction and one of the most dramatic moments of social transformation since the revolution.

Even so, the triumphs of this movement and the power they exert over our collective imagination can serve to obscure two important realities. The first is the fact that it had to happen at all. Remember, this time period—in which Rosa Parks was arrested, Black students were dragged from White establishments, Black children were blocked from going to White schools by screaming adults, buses were bombed in Alabama, churches were burned in Mississippi, and Martin Luther King Jr. was shot in the face—was nearly *two hundred* years after the Revolutionary War and *one hundred* years after emancipation. Centuries after the American founders chose to institutionalize White supremacy in the new republic, Americans were still at war over that choice. This points to one of the most important features of White supremacy: its *endurance*. Far from being a discrete phenomenon locked away in one or two unfortunate and easily dismissed periods of American history, it is, rather, a constant. Contrary to popular perception, the civil rights movement did not simply emerge out of the context of mid-century southern American racism. It was, rather, a contemporary expression of one of the most abiding struggles in American culture—the struggle against the enduring dominance of White supremacy.[38]

The second important reality is that White supremacy did not come to an end after that particular era of the civil rights movement. One of the most cherished and consoling myths of American culture is that the triumph of the civil rights movement over the powers of mid-century segregation was a triumph over White supremacy itself. The truth is more complicated. True, the work of the civil rights movement secured important victories with respect to the power of White supremacy in American institutions—both public and private. The fruit of these victories is real. And yet so are their limitations. The civil rights movement dealt a powerful blow to White supremacy, but the blow was not fatal.

The endurance of White supremacy was evident in the years following the civil rights movement. In the weeks after King's murder in April 1968, cities across America were engulfed in flames of protest, and not simply because King had been killed but because the movement he symbolized—which had come so far—still had so far to go. Legally speaking, Jim Crow had ended, but its two defining characteristics, separation and inequality, remained defining features of American life. In response to this, the early 1970s saw the birth of several Black coalitions devoted to filling the leadership gap created by the death of King and to closing the social gap created by the endurance of White supremacy. Over the following decade, they focused their work on continuing the integration of schools, consolidating African American political power, securing rights for African American workers, and creating a holiday in celebration of Martin Luther King Jr.'s legacy. In the 1980s these leaders continued to make important gains in the broader application of nondiscrimination laws in voting, housing, and employment. These efforts continued throughout the 1990s, while presciently adding a more deliberate focus on racially motivated police misconduct. This led to a series of attempts to reopen unsolved murders from the civil rights era that resulted in the convictions of Byron De La Beckwith (assassin of Medgar Evers in 1963) in 1994 and Edgar Ray Killen (the ringleader of the Mississippi civil rights murders of 1964) in 2005, as well as the indictment of James Bonard Fowler (the murderer of Jimmie Lee Jackson in 1965) in 2007. In spite of these real victories, however, public attention to violence against Black communities has only grown in recent years, leading to the founding of Black Lives Matter in 2013 and the broader coalition organization Movement for Black Lives in 2014. And all along, even as violence and policing have taken center stage in the public eye, resistance to White supremacy has continued to take place across a range of issues and institutions including voting, hiring, housing, capital investment, and philanthropy.[39]

Though by no means comprehensive, this brief account of recent attempts to oppose White supremacy illustrates the endurance of White supremacy in American culture. It reminds us that White supremacy is not merely a historical accident, an occasional emergence in an otherwise egalitarian history. Rather, White supremacy is original to America and pervasive across its institutions, enduring from the beginning of its history to the present moment.[40]

Seeing Ourselves

Douglass's invitation to his hearers that day, much like the sanitation workers who followed him a century later, was an invitation to see. To see—perhaps for the first time—what America is as a nation and who we are as a people. It was an invitation to see ourselves, to see that both we and the culture we share have been profoundly disordered by the reality of racism. Seeing this requires us to see the reality of White supremacy. It means seeing that America has used modern racial categories as a fundamental way of understanding human beings and ordering relations between them. These racial categories have had an anthropological, as well as a social and political, function. Douglass's invitation means seeing that the social function of being White entails supremacy, holding the dominant role in the social hierarchy and a disproportionate claim to its privileges. It means seeing that this supremacy is not accidental but a result of specific choices we have made as a people. It means seeing that these choices were original in the founding of America, pervasive across American institutions, and enduring throughout American history. For it is only in seeing the reality of White supremacy that we can begin to come to terms with the profound limitations of other ways of seeing racism—as merely personal prejudice, relational estrangement, or institutional injustice, important as these are—and begin to see racism in *cultural* terms. It is only in seeing the reality of White supremacy that we can begin to come to terms with the incalculable darkness of its effects.

3

Seeing the Effect of
White Supremacy

___

What are kingdoms without justice but large bands of robbers?
—Augustine, *City of God*

Even unto Death

On July 4, 1826, just twenty-six years (and one day) before Frederick Douglass gave his speech in New York, Thomas Jefferson died in Virginia. Not surprisingly, Jefferson was prepared for the occasion. He lived through the uncertainty of revolution, watched the institutions of the republic come into being, and saw the young nation grow in size, population, and reputation. Indeed, he presided over each of these. Before his death, he had turned to his legacy, to determining which parts of his past years would define him for generations to come. He had choices: member of the Continental Congress, governor of Virginia, author of the Declaration of Independence, ambassador, secretary of state, vice president, president, architect, inventor, political philosopher, and more. Sifting through these accomplishments, he settled upon three. Sketching a tombstone design in his notebook, he directed that it be inscribed as follows:

Here was buried
Thomas Jefferson
Author of the Declaration of American Independence
Of the Statute of Virginia for Religious Freedom
and Father of the University of Virginia[1]

Though surprising at first glance (who would omit the presidency?), they were a perfect choice. The Declaration of Independence told his republican political story, articulating his vision of free citizens. The Statute of Virginia for Religious Freedom told his Enlightenment philosophical story, articulating his vision of a free mind. But the University of Virginia told perhaps his most important story, his American cultural story, his vision of what a free society could be.

The neoclassical architecture of the buildings rooted the ideals of the republic in the soil of classical culture. The design of the campus, centering on the library (rather than the chapel), instantiated his commitment to the primacy of reason. The curricula, which included natural philosophy, moral philosophy, law, medicine, chemistry, mathematics, and languages (but, notably, not divinity), expressed his vision of the educated citizen. And his choice of the setting expressed his preference for an agrarian (rather than urban) future for the new nation.[2]

But like the republic itself, Jefferson's university was bound to the contradictions of White supremacy. His decision to locate the university in bucolic Virginia was no coincidence. It was, rather, a reflection of his desire to form students not simply in an agrarian setting but in a *southern* setting. "He believed that a southern institution was necessary to protect the sons of the South from abolitionist teachings in the North," which he described to a friend as "against us in position and principle."[3] He embedded this principle of racialized enslavement in every part of the university. As construction began, enslaved human beings cleared the trees, moved the soil, marked the plots, laid the brick, and cut the trim. As the university opened, enslaved human beings cut the firewood, lit the fires, slaughtered the animals, tended the gardens, prepared the food, did the laundry, and ran menial errands on behalf of the students and professors. As they performed these tasks, they were largely—and deliberately—invisible to the students and professors. They worked behind tall brick walls. They lived in small basement rooms. Essential though they were, Jefferson erased them from view.

For most of the university's history, the enslaved at the University of Virginia have remained invisible, neatly excised from its public identity. The dirty yards where the enslaved labored are now quiet, flowering gardens. The small basement rooms where they lived are now storage spaces. If one were to walk around the university today, it would be difficult to know anything at all about its history of White supremacy.[4] Unless, that is, you happen to visit the cemetery. A beautiful place filled with towering trees, stone walls, and fading tombstones, the cemetery is divided into three sections. Through the main entrance is the first section: the Confederate cemetery. At the center of this cemetery stands a large pedestal supporting the towering statue of a soldier and engraved with the words, "Fate denied them victory but crowned them with glorious immortality." Simple gravestones marked with the names, dates, and home states of the dead line the spacious field.

A gate in the stone wall opens to the original section of the cemetery. Built between 1829 and 1830 by an enslaved man named Sebra and expanded over the years, it serves as the resting place for the university's luminaries and their families. Varied gravestones tell their stories: professors, physicians, statesmen, scientists, judges, soldiers, wives, and children. The graves are framed by worn paths and spreading ivy and are sheltered by branching trees.

At the back of the cemetery a gate opens into a third space: a small field enclosed by a simple wooden fence. Apart from a few young trees, the space is unmarked: no stones, no flowers, no paths. Indeed, one would have no reason to suppose it part of the cemetery at all. This is the African American burial ground, the final resting place of many of the human beings held in bondage at the University of Virginia. Discovered by accident in 2012 through an environmental study for a university expansion and corroborated by archival evidence, the plot contains sixty-seven unmarked graves. Varying in size and arranged in rows, the unexcavated shafts suggest the remains are not simply of individuals but of families, of multiple generations, buried unacknowledged beneath the ground.[5]

Though largely invisible, this burial ground bears living witness to the reality of White supremacy in the American republic, to the "immeasurable distance" between White and Black Americans that endured even unto death. But crucially, it also powerfully illustrates what we take to be the central *effect* of White supremacy on the lives of African Americans: theft. *At the heart of our case for reparations lies the claim that White supremacy is best understood as a massive, multigenerational project of cultural theft.* In the name of White supremacy, America stole Black bodies from their homes, stole the labor from those bodies, stole the fruit of that labor, stole the wealth from that fruit, and in the end stole the very memory of those it victimized from the annals of the earth. Not only this, America then used its ill-gotten gain to build monuments to its own genius on top of the very graves of the forgotten. This theft, every bit as much as the Declaration of Independence, is the legacy of both Thomas Jefferson and the republic for which he stands.

The notion that White supremacy is fundamentally an act of theft, a culture in which the bodies, labors, and histories of African Americans were stolen and used for the benefit of White Americans, is foundational to the logic of reparations. Without this insight, the work of reparations will continue to be marginal to the work of racial healing. But if people truly see this theft, the work of reparations will be mandatory, not marginal. Because of this, we seek to elaborate on the meaning of this theft by demonstrating White supremacy's theft of *truth*, *power*, and *wealth*.

White Supremacy and the Theft of Truth

American White supremacy is rooted in and sustained by an account of the world, a cherished collection of myths—about the nature of humanity, the character of society, and the obligations of morality—whose purpose is to normalize the political and cultural supremacy of White Americans. The powerful impact of this account—both on the American historical imagination and the American social order—is evident everywhere around us. And yet this account is, in fundamental respects, a lie. As with all lies, it obscures reality and leads all who believe it into the dark. This is what we mean when we say that White supremacy is the theft of truth. In what follows, we seek to highlight two aspects of this theft: the theft of identity and the theft of history.

The Theft of Identity

Our first claim is that White supremacy stole the truth about the identity of African Americans. In saying this, we are not speaking of identity in the theological sense. In much of the Christian tradition, and certainly in the Scriptures, human identity is grounded in the reality that God loves human beings and crowned them—all of them—with the glory of his image. We are speaking of identity in a different sense, not in the ineradicable theological sense but in the constructed and contingent *social* sense—that is, to the meaning and value assigned to a given person or group of persons by the social order in which they live.[6] Our claim is simply that the social identity assigned by the order of White supremacy was a powerful theft of the truth of African Americans' inherent dignity.[7]

This theft expressed itself generally in the artificial category of race itself. Through the appropriation of the category of "Blackness," Whites viewed African Americans not in terms of their individual personhood, their familial background, or their tribal connections but through the lens of race. Over time, this physical description took on deeper meanings related to personal and moral capacity. By more fully understanding these deeper meanings, we can grasp the degree to which White supremacy stole the truth about African American identity and replaced it with lies.

Black Animalization

The first of these lies is that of Black *animalization*. Though Whites have throughout American history understood Black people to be human, many have also believed that they were not fully so. They saw them as "animalized humans."[8] The origins of this view are complicated, but it seems clear that it emerged in the context of enslavement, with the identification of African Americans as domestic beasts of burden. Like animal laborers, African Americans were considered brutes whose proper use was labor in service of White interests. This perspective was justified not only by the advent of a racialized pseudoscience that emerged in the eighteenth century and remained popular until the middle of the twentieth century,[9] but also by the support of religious leaders who offered divine approval for Black animalization.[10] Justified by this powerful combination of science and religion, Black animalization was popularized through the highly exaggerated portrayals of African American physical features designed to demonstrate their animalistic nature and codified in laws that, for all practical purposes, gave African Americans the social status of a horse.[11] They could be owned, used, abused, freed, and even—after a fashion— loved, but they could never be fully human.[12]

Black Demonization

In response to animalization, African Americans and those who supported their equality worked hard to highlight the achievements of extraordinary African Americans. Though fraught with paternalism and with the pressure to conform to White norms, this strategy was effective. Because of their efforts, the notion of Black animalization became increasingly implausible. The dwindling appeal of Black animalization, however, was also partly caused by White supremacy itself. One of the most horrible features of White supremacy was the degree to which it concealed the rape of African American women. The unforeseen result, however, was the relativization of the physical attributes of "Blackness." As more and more enslaved children were born bearing the physical features of "Whiteness," attempts to justify their enslavement by appealing to their animal features became increasingly fraught.

These two developments led to a new American framework for African American identity: Black *demonization*. In this framework, the inferiority of Blacks is not merely physical but *moral*. This had long been part of the logic of subjugation: Whites broadly characterized Blacks as lazy, deceptive, and duplicitous. But in the years following the Civil War this framework took an even more destructive turn: Blackness was now seen as dangerous. To understand this turn, it is important to remember that the boundaries of segregation were not simply social but moral. By the nineteenth century, policing these boundaries was an American obsession. This obsession was fueled by the convergence of a number of variables: White supremacist mythologies of blood purity,[13] the resurgence of long-held theological justifications for Black inferiority,[14] and Victorian convictions of feminine delicacy and male honor.[15] The social, and in particular *sexual*, anxiety created by this convergence is almost impossible to overstate. The threat of Black-White sexuality became *the* moral offense of the White supremacist order.[16] This view profoundly affected the development of Black identity—especially that of African American males. No longer simply viewed as lazy, they were now considered predatory. White supremacists used these fears of Black predation to reassert the legitimacy of White rule and to reestablish that rule through one of the most terrible eras of racially motivated violence in American history.[17]

Black Infantilization

Despite the power of these frameworks, the need arose for still another form of Black identity—Black *infantilization*. Unlike animalization, which was driven by putative physical characteristics, or demonization, driven by alleged moral corruptions, infantilization was driven by the presumption of impaired capacity. Infantilization was born as a precedent for slavery and arose from the needs of White supremacy. Simply put, White society needed Black labor. And though the tropes of animalization and demonization were useful to White people both psychologically and socially, they were less useful domestically. After all, if Black people were simply animals and predators, who would clean the house, cook the food, and raise the children? Whites needed a framework that allowed them to retain their commitment to Black inferiority and to express that commitment in a form more conducive to social functioning. That strategy was infantilization. The core assumption of infantilization is diminished capacity—the fixed conviction that no matter how reasonable, talented, helpful, loyal, or even beloved an African American may be, there remains within them an unerring quality of helpless dependency.[18]

These three constructions of Black identity (animalization, demonization, infantilization) were created in the service of Whiteness to legitimize its cultural, economic, and political supremacy. But this creation, even as it brought diminished notions of Blackness into the world, also took something away. It stole the truth about Black identity and replaced that truth with lies.

The Theft of History

White supremacy also stole the truth about history. It could hardly be otherwise. White supremacy, after all, was not simply an anthropological account but a cultural order, a world. As a world, it required an account of itself that could render this world believable. Yet the believable history it created was a lie sustained by two powerful forces: *romanticization* and *erasure*.

Romanticization

In the years following the Civil War, the opposing sides began the inevitably fraught process of finding their way back to one another. Each side had lost husbands, fathers, and children at one another's hands, and the South had lost its economy and its way of life. Added to this, Reconstruction kept America's sectional hostilities close to the surface. However, as southern Whites regained political power and the northern appetite for Reconstruction fizzled, the nation began to search for a new story of one *United* States of America.

The story they found was an old one. Long-standing American themes of resistance to tyranny and the struggle for freedom could credibly be appropriated (though with different meanings) by North and South alike. The theme of American resilience, the capacity to improvise and endure, powerfully reemerged in the post-war period. After all, Americans had a democracy to save and a nation to rebuild, with the entire world watching as they struggled to do so. They needed to reconcile in a way that ensured such a war could never happen again.[19] So in the wake of the most profound sort of social crisis—civil war—Americans joined one another in the age-old stories of freedom and resilience.

There were new stories too, new elements of the emerging American myth, that became fundamental to an American account of history.[20] The first of these is *the myth of the honorable war*. As with most wars, the American Civil War began in the context of recrimination, with each side viewing the other as a mortal enemy so dangerous that it must be destroyed. But with the ending of the war and the rebuilding of the nation, these accounts no longer served the national interest. Thus, a new account of the war emerged. This new account asserted that, contrary to what had been proclaimed by each side just years before, both sides fought an honorable war. For the North, it was the honor of preserving the Union. For the South, it was the honor of defending itself against tyranny. By characterizing the war in this way, each side could understand itself as honorably American and understand the other not as an enemy of democracy but as a collaborator in its reconstruction.

The power of this myth notwithstanding, the truth is that in war there are winners and losers. How can a winner and a loser collaborate in the construction of a new life together? This challenge led the nation to embrace a second myth: *the myth of the Lost Cause.* The Lost Cause is a nostalgic and highly edited view of the antebellum South and the war that was fought to preserve it. In this post-war re-narration, the war was not over slavery. In this retelling, slavery was "incidental."[21] It was, rather, a valiant if doomed effort to preserve a way of life characterized by honorable men, socially refined and sexually pristine belles, benevolent masters, happy slaves,[22] fruitful soil, and—above all—political self-determination. It was a nostalgic account, a view of the world imbued with the melancholy of tragedy, a post-Edenic disposition of exile from paradise. And yet this exile was made bearable, even beautiful, by the mere knowledge that the paradise had once existed, that it was of their making, and that their struggle to defend it—even in defeat—had been glorious. This account was crucial for post-war reconciliation because it allowed the North to acknowledge the South's martial defeat, and it allowed the South to render that defeat in terms of moral triumph.

This led to a third myth in the work of national reconciliation: *the myth of the tragedy of Reconstruction.* One of the most consequential realities of American history is that Reconstruction, the decade-long attempt to re-build the post–Civil War nation on terms established by the federal government, was ultimately a failure. From the perspective of many northerners, this failure was the tragic result of the intransigence of southern racism and the power of southern politics. From the vantage of southerners, however, Reconstruction was simply a continuation of northern aggression whose real tragedy was that it existed at all. In order for national reconciliation to proceed, however, the sectional bitterness over Reconstruction needed to be addressed. Each side needed to acknowledge Reconstruction's failure, but in terms that avoided mutual recrimination. This led almost immediately to a national revision of the era of Reconstruction, in which the real tragedy was not the aggression of the North or the intransigence of the South but the disastrous ways in which African Americans expressed their newfound freedom in political vindictiveness and sexual license. Not only was this account of the failure of Reconstruction utter nonsense, it also differed sharply from both northern and southern accounts offered just years before.[23] Like each of these myths, it served the interest of national unification. By displacing the anger of southern and northern political leaders off one another and onto African Americans, this account of Reconstruction removed yet another obstacle to sectional cooperation and set the stage for the nation to come together to face the new world.[24]

This points to the fourth, and perhaps most important, element of the post-war history: *the myth of the problematic Negro*.[25] Though it is true that White Americans viewed Blackness as a problem, it is also true that, with the right amount of willful moral blindness and violent social control, Blackness proved to be both socially and economically beneficial. This was never more true than in the years following Reconstruction. In spite of the conciliatory spirit sweeping America, real sectional differences remained below the surface. After all, the myths of the honorable war, the Lost Cause, and the tragedy of Reconstruction could only go so far in uniting the country. Because of this, America's political and economic leaders found recourse in the one thing that could unite them across these sectional lines: Whiteness. Indeed, the late nineteenth and early twentieth centuries saw an unprecedented rise in the promotion and appropriation of Whiteness as a category. Crucially, however, this decision to sublimate sectional differences under the politically expedient banner of Whiteness led to a renewed emphasis on the problem of Blackness. This emphasis took many forms, but its most basic conviction was that the presence and growing power of Black people in America was a fundamental threat to the American way of life. In order to protect America from this threat, White Americans needed to take direct steps to answer the problem of Blackness and to reestablish the romanticized order of the lost America. The answer was Jim Crow.

Each of these romanticized accounts of history served the (White) national interest of sectional reunion. They allowed both the South and the North to interpret itself with honor, to renounce the politically unpopular program of Reconstruction, and to identify the locus of America's social problems in the presence of African Americans in a White man's country. These accounts of history became pillars of White America's post-war mythology, a mythology from which Black Americans would be systematically erased.

Erasure

The decades following Reconstruction were the heyday of American national storytelling. With the creation of a new mythology as the foundation of a new America, the story needed to be told. From the 1880s to the 1920s, an explosion of articles, books, films, and memorials appeared, all devoted to perpetuating the new American story.[26] Across the nation, the romanticized myths of post-war America could be read in papers, viewed in theaters, and beheld in towering monuments of stone.[27]

As important as what is said, however, is what is *not* said, what books are *not* written, what films are *not* made, what memorials are *not* erected. In post-Reconstruction America, those untold stories were African American. This is not to say that images and accounts of African Americans were not part of the new era of national storytelling. But these images and accounts, when they did appear, were invariably perversions of the truth: crude reiterations of the conventional tropes of Black identity offered in the service of White supremacy. In this new American self-narration, the most important truths about African Americans were simply erased from the story. Erased were the truths of the dignity of their humanity. The crime of their abduction. The violence of their subjugation. The endlessness of their captivity. The rape of their bodies. The significance of their labor. The sale of their children. The desperation of their resistance. The courage of their flight. The resilience of their communities. The shrewdness of their institutions. The brilliance of their art. The power of their religion. The legitimacy of their demands. The triumph of their mere survival. Where are the monographs and monuments to these truths? In the White supremacist mythology of post-war America, the answer is *nowhere*.

This erasure, this "willed forgetting,"[28] reveals something deeply important about the nature of American racism: its aim was not, fundamentally, to hate African Americans; its aim was to *not see* them. Its aim was to render invisible their humanity and its claims upon White Americans. This is why White Americans cloaked Blackness in the guise of inhumanity, why it hid Black labor behind walls, directed them to hidden staircases, banished them to separate restrooms and schools, zoned them in different neighborhoods, excluded them from children's textbooks, and buried them in unmarked fields. America did not want to see. This was the goal of the racist re-narration of post-war America: to erase everything that did not serve the narrative of White supremacy, filling the resulting emptiness with spectacular and beguiling monuments designed to distract White Americans from the depths of their collective self-deceit.[29] The enormous and tragic consequences of this mass theft of history condemned multiple generations of Americans to live in utter ignorance about the truth of their own history, and it robbed them of the opportunity to reckon with this history and to begin to heal its wounds.

White Supremacy and the Theft of Power

White supremacy's theft of truth created the foundation for a second form of theft: the theft of power. Racism was never merely an attempt to re-narrate the truth. It was, rather, an attempt to legitimize the theft of power by bending the truth to that end. In the succinct phrase of Bruce Baum, "Race, in short, is an effect of power."[30]

Personal Power

In its most elemental sense, this theft expressed itself as the theft of *personal* power, of an individual's ability to express agency of body or mind. This theft began with the Black body. Throughout history, the subjugation of Black bodies is White supremacy's most basic requirement. The clearest expression of this requirement is slavery itself. Slavery was possible only by the abduction of bodies, the chaining of bodies, and the forced transportation of bodies in the reeking holds of ships. It was profitable only through the evaluation and commodification of bodies, the forced labor of bodies, and the sexual violation of bodies. And it was sustainable only through the deprivation of bodies, the whipping of bodies, and the hunting of bodies in the night.[31]

However, this subjugation did not end with the end of slavery. Like other elements of White supremacy, the theft of Black bodily power reinvented itself in forms conducive to the needs of the moment. After Reconstruction, this theft expressed itself in the lynching of bodies, the shooting of bodies, the burning of bodies, and, to underscore the point, the photographing of these mutilated bodies surrounded by crowds of smiling White faces.[32] For thousands more, it expressed itself in the brazen abduction and exploitation of bodies in the sulfuric mines of the convict leasing system.[33] As the twentieth century unfolded, these expressions of bodily subjugation continued and were supplemented by new instruments of control: fire hoses, dogs, billy clubs, tear gas, zoning laws, wrongful convictions, and unaccountable police shootings.[34] Though varied in form, each of these bears irrefutable witness to White supremacy's long-standing need to dominate the Black body.[35]

And yet this theft of personal power sought to extend its rule beyond the body to the control of the mind, not merely the physical but the psychological as well.[36] In saying this, we do not intend to suggest that all African Americans are or were psychologically enslaved. American history is filled with the reality of African Americans seeking to overcome their physical and social constraints precisely *because* they were psychologically free. That said, as sociologist Orlando Patterson has shown, slavery by its very nature seeks not just the physical but the *total* domination of the enslaved, including the mind.[37] In American slavery, this domination expressed itself as the attempt to force the enslaved to understand the meaning of their lives—their identity, their thoughts, their feelings, their work, their relationships, their aspirations—exclusively in terms of the will and word of their master. In the years following Reconstruction, this struggle for psychic dominance was reframed in exclusively racial terms. African Americans were taught to think of themselves—both their individual and social existence—in relation to Whiteness, in terms created by White supremacy and reinforced by every dimension of the social order.

As noted above, throughout history many African Americans have resisted this psychological abuse and the sense of inferiority that it sought to instill. Even so, this abuse has not been without effect. This reality was poignantly born out in the doll tests created by Kenneth and Mamie Clark in the 1940s. In these tests, designed to study the psychological effects of segregation, African American children were shown four dolls, each identical except for the color of the doll's skin, and asked to identify the race of the dolls. When asked to say which doll they preferred, a majority of the Black children chose the White doll. The results of these tests were used as evidence in the 1954 case *Brown v. Board of Education* to demonstrate the psychological damage inflicted on African Americans by the White supremacist social structure. This damage—described by Martin Luther King Jr. as "mental slavery"[38]—illustrates the point: White supremacy sought to steal personal power, of body and mind, from generations of African Americans. We write these words with tears.

Political Power

This theft of power was also *political*. Democratic polity, in theory, depends on the political power of the people. In America, this political power expresses itself in many ways: in speech, in assembly, in the press, and perhaps above all in the right to vote. The right to vote—enfranchisement—enables each of these others to exist; it is the essential expression of democratic political power. In the unformed moments of the early American republic, because the meaning of citizenship was not yet clearly defined and the Constitution did not stipulate the terms of enfranchisement, voting practices varied from state to state. By the end of the eighteenth century, however, the right to vote increasingly belonged exclusively to White men. By the middle of the nineteenth century, this exclusivity was virtually a universal American practice.[39] African Americans, though they could live in the United States, even as "free" people, were deprived of the fundamental political tool for shaping the nation.[40]

In the years immediately following the Civil War, African American political fortunes began to change. This change was largely due to the passage of the Fifteenth Amendment, which did two important things: it prohibited states from denying someone the right to vote based on "race, color, or previous condition of servitude," and it gave the federal government the power to intervene should a state refuse to comply. Imperfect though it was, this amendment empowered tens of thousands of African American men to shape their political reality by means of the vote. For example, in 1860, there were no African Americans registered to vote in the state of Georgia. But just over ten years later, there were more than thirty African Americans elected to political office in Georgia alone, including in the United States Congress. It is no wonder that African American leaders of the time referred to Black male enfranchisement as America's "second birth," the completion of the American revolution.[41]

Alas, this revolution was short-lived. With the end of Reconstruction, the federal government effectively set aside its power of enforcement and left the matter of enfranchisement to the states. The states were not idle. In keeping with the post-war White anxieties of Black political power, states began to systematically reverse Black enfranchisement. This reversal took various forms: violence, intimidation, fraud, and the creation of a series of poll taxes and tests administered to African Americans at the discretion of their White registrars. This was catastrophic for African American enfranchisement. By the 1890s, registered African American voters were reduced to a fraction of those who were eligible. And by the early twentieth century, the Reconstruction-era gains in African American enfranchisement and political power were largely lost.[42]

This was still the situation in 1964—nearly one hundred years after the passage of the Fifteenth Amendment—when college students from around the country descended on Mississippi to inaugurate one of the largest voter registration drives in American history.[43] When Freedom Summer began, less than 7 percent of Mississippi's African Americans were registered to vote. To remedy this, civil rights organizations launched a campaign that aimed to increase African American registration and to give their disenfranchisement national attention.[44] While only a small number of the attempted registrants were successful (only 1,200 out of nearly 17,000 applicants), the murder of three civil rights workers in Philadelphia, Mississippi, captured the attention of the nation and influenced the passage of both the Civil Rights Act of 1964 and the Voting Rights Act of 1965.[45] This voting act was a sweeping federal prohibition of voter suppression and of the taxes and tests that served as barriers to African American enfranchisement. Like the Fifteenth Amendment on which it was based, it gave the federal government powers of enforcement. The immediate impact was extraordinary. With respect to voter registration in the South, nearly 250,000 African Americans registered in 1965 alone, and by 1967 a majority were registered in all but a few states. Between 1965 and 1985 the number of Black state representatives increased from three to nearly two hundred.[46] Even so, the Voting Rights Act has faced repeated legal challenges to its constitutionality, and in 2013 (*Shelby County v. Holder*) the Supreme Court voted to weaken some of its provisions. The final effect of this weakening remains to be seen, but it has already had the demonstrable (and utterly predictable) effect of significantly reversing African American enfranchisement, and thereby weakening African American political power.

Taken together, the theft of personal and political power expands our understanding of the harm White supremacy has done to Black Americans. Not only has White supremacy written history in a way that denies African American dignity, it has also structured a society that resists their agency.[47]

White Supremacy and the Theft of Wealth

These two forms of theft, of truth and of power, enabled the third form: the theft of wealth.[48] In turning to wealth, we turn to what is perhaps the most familiar theme in reparations: White supremacy has systematically stolen wealth from African Americans, creating demonstrably racialized economic inequality in American society.[49] Though complicated and varied, this theft has expressed itself in two ways: through the *extraction* of wealth and through the *obstruction* of wealth.

Theft by Extraction

As with all economies, White supremacy's economy is rooted in a prior conception of the world itself and of its value. After all, what one believes something to be (or not to be) shapes one's valuation of it. As theologian Willie James Jennings has shown, White supremacy's approach to wealth is rooted in a fundamentally dominative and extractive view of the world, a distinct "theological vision of creation."[50] In this account, the created world, rather than having its own integrity that lays claim on human beings, enabling and limiting their actions, is instead a shapeless thing to be claimed, controlled, and ultimately used according to the desires of those who presume mastery over it. This view of creation drove European presumptions of "discovery," dominating and extracting the value from what they "discovered." As Jennings puts it, "European vision saw these new lands as a system of potentialities," and that the "reconfiguration of living spaces is the first reflex of modernity in the new world."[51] This point might strike our readers as tangential, but the idea that the practices of economy are rooted in an account of creation is deeply important. It reminds us that, in spite of our exonerative illusions regarding the "natural laws" and "invisible hands" of our economies—illusions that allow us to distance ourselves from the consequences of our choices—our economy was built as a deliberate expression of human convictions about the nature of the world, built by hands that were not only visible but visibly White. It is also important because it reminds us that the economy we have was not inevitable, that with a different account of the world, things might have been otherwise. That they may yet be otherwise.

This view of creation gave rise to an economy that mirrored its pathologies. The clearest expression was, again, slavery. Though the enslavement of human beings had both a social function (reinforcing the cultural supremacy of Whiteness) and a political function (preserving the power of White Americans), its most transparent function was economic. It was, after all, the slave *trade*.

Enslaved human beings *were* wealth: economic assets under the control of their owners. Their bodies were evaluated for strengths and weaknesses, placed in auctions, and purchased by strangers.[52] They were branded to ensure the clarity and the perpetuity of their purchase.[53] They were "bred" so as to further enrich their owners. They were used as collateral to secure credit for their owners. And, when the time came, they were sold away from all they had known for the profit of their owners. This was the fate of nearly twelve million human beings caught in the slave trade between the fifteenth and nineteenth centuries in America: they were living currency, hoarded and traded for the enrichment of others.[54]

Economically speaking, more important than the enslaved person's status as wealth was their role in the *creation* of wealth. They created wealth by growing food, constructing homes, building furniture, tending livestock, and bearing children who were themselves commodified. But none of these, important as they were, come close to the wealth created by

African Americans in the global trade of cotton. Though it is easy to view cotton as little more than a quaint agricultural heirloom in our national memory, the truth is that its production and trade created the world's first truly international economic empire.[55] The beginnings of this empire lay in England. Over time, England became *the* global center for the manufacture and distribution of cotton, a status that greatly contributed to the foundation and enrichment of its modern financial institutions. But the heart of the cotton empire lay not in the factories where it was processed or the harbors from which it was distributed but in the fields where it grew. And those fields were in America.

This development took time. In the early days of the republic, cotton was a meager part of the American economy and almost nonexistent in the global economy. But in the span of a few decades, the United States became the global leader in cotton production.[56] The economic windfall that accompanied this status enabled "the young country to grow from a narrow coastal belt into a vast, powerful nation with the fastest-growing economy in the world."[57] This emerging economy was the result not simply of the sale of raw cotton but of the other forms of economic expansion that it enabled. The liquidity provided by the sale of cotton was foundational to the development of the banking institutions, credit system, and investment practices of the United States economy, each of which expanded that economy by generating even more wealth.[58] In other words, the production of cotton in the United States was the foundation of its once and future economic power.

At the center of this production were enslaved human beings. They marked the fields, cleared the trees, and pulled the stumps from the ground. They furrowed the brown earth and planted the seeds in its heart. They watered those seeds, cleared the weeds from the seedlings, and watched them branch out under the sun. They looped bags over their shoulders, walked paths to the white fields, bent their backs, and used their hands to pull the bolls from the prickly stems. They shouldered those bags from the field, laid them on the scales to be weighed, and emptied them into piles. They fed the cotton into gins, spun the cotton in the gins, and pulled it out of the other side. They bound the cotton into bales, loaded bales onto wagons, and drove wagons to anchored barges. Without their labor, the world's largest economy simply could not have emerged with either the speed or the power that it did. And yet every day, every month, and every year, decade after decade, through the turning of centuries, the wealth created by their labor was taken from their hands.[59]

It is tempting to create a barrier between the historically distant economy of slavery and the economy of our own time, to imagine that the two economies are sealed off from one another. But this distinction, consoling as it might be, is false. The two economies are in fact one economy in history, and the enslavement of human beings is its foundation. In the haunting words of historian Edward Baptist, "the whole history of the United States comes walking over the hill behind a line of people in chains."[60]

Theft by Obstruction

In the years following the Civil War, that line of people coming over the horizon began the process of laying down their chains. As part of laying down their chains, African Americans began the work of acquiring wealth of their own. Given the centuries of enslavement, African Americans were at a profound economic disadvantage, and they knew they needed to close the gap. The struggle to close this gap took two forms, both of which were deliberately obstructed by American White supremacy.

The first of these was the struggle for land. In the largely agricultural world of nineteenth-century America, land was the basis of the American economy. To control land was to control one's economic destiny. That this is so may be seen in the continued westward expansion of the American populace, in which Americans staked, claimed, settled, and cultivated lands from coast to coast. This expansion, enabled by federal government land programs such as the Homestead Act of 1862, allowed a broad cross section of American citizens—through land acquisition—to have real agency in shaping their economic life. This act, however, applied only to White Americans. In the 1860s, as the prospect of African American freedom began to rise, Black land ownership was critical for making that freedom a reality.[61]

The Confiscation Act of 1862, granting the federal government the power to confiscate Confederate lands, opened the door to the possibility of Black land ownership. Under the oversight of the Department of the

Treasury, thousands of acres along the South Carolina coast were redis-
tributed to the African Americans who lived there. This act allowed the
wartime federal government to benefit financially from cotton production,
and it laid the foundation for African American ownership. Thus began the
Port Royal Experiment, in which thousands of formerly enslaved African
Americans began to cultivate their own crops on what, they were assured,
would become their own land. For the majority, however, it was not to
be. Rather than transferring the lands to African Americans outright, the
federal government decided to sell the land at auction. While it is true that
the government made the land available to African Americans at submarket
rates, the formerly enslaved population simply could not compete in an
open auction. They were outbid by northern business leaders seeking to
extend northern control over the economic potential of the soil. And so
this land, held so long by White men from the South, became land held by
White men from the North.[62]

This scenario was repeated in January 1865 in the wake of General
Sherman's famous Special Field Orders, No. 15. This order reestablished
African American claims on coastal lands. Each African American family was to be allotted not more than forty acres of tillable soil and tools.
Further, the order specified that "no white person, whatever," except
for military personnel, "would be permitted to reside there."[63] However,
the land was issued through a series of "possessory titles" that granted
African Americans ownership of the land but only on the grounds that
others did not lay claim to it. In May 1865, those others came. Even as
the war continued to be fought, President Andrew Johnson issued an
amnesty proclamation that not only granted former Confederates complete amnesty from criminal charges but also mandated restoration of all
their former property except the enslaved. Though challenged in court
and resisted in Congress, President Johnson got his way. African Americans lost their land and were faced with a terrible decision: leave the only
home they had ever known or continue to work the fields of their former
enslavement.[64]

African Americans, in their struggle for wealth, also sought to acquire
money. Unable to purchase either land or homes outright, African Americans began to work for the money necessary to make their new lives of

freedom possible. The chief vehicle for this savings was the Freedman's Savings Bank, a bank for African Americans chartered by the federal government in 1865.[65] As northern political leaders contemplated the shape of life after the war, they understood that the poverty of Black Americans was a central issue in Reconstruction. In response, the federal government, using the unpaid salaries of African American soldiers killed in the war—some $200,000—created a bank for African Americans. Congress appointed a board of trustees consisting of prominent—and all White— northern bankers and philanthropists. The bank's board of accomplished financial professionals and its backing by the federal government gave it enormous credibility in the eyes of many African Americans. In a few short years, thousands of African Americans opened accounts and placed their savings—some $3 million—in its care. Sadly, their trust was misplaced. Though initially established as a savings and lending entity, the trustees, without the knowledge of their account holders, transformed it into an investment bank, allowing the trustees to use the bank's assets to invest in the stock market.[66] Though framed in the language of wealth creation for "investors," the change was actually a scheme to allow the trustees to make highly speculative investment deals with relatively small personal risk. After all, it wasn't their money.

These investments led to catastrophe for formerly enslaved families trying desperately to acquire wealth. Unaware of these investments, account holders were unable to insulate themselves from the inherent risks. And in 1873, when the market failed—and the bank's investments with it— over half of African American wealth in the United States disappeared.[67] Further, unlike White banks, this failure was without hope of redress; Congress closed the bank in 1874, leaving thousands of account holders with nothing to show for either their labor or their trust. All of this, it must be remembered, occurred at a time when the federal government actively enriched former slave owners by allowing them to reclaim all their former wealth *and* paying them reparations for the financial losses of their enslaved "property."[68] African Americans, who for the first time entered American society with the prospect of both land and money before them, found themselves less than a decade later in the position of having neither, even as White wealth continued to grow.[69]

As Reconstruction ended and Jim Crow began, it became clear that the political leaders of the White South were committed to keeping African Americans in that position. The most obvious form of this commitment was the obstruction of African American attempts to own land in the South. This was not new. Southern Whites had long obstructed any attempt by African Americans—enslaved or free—to own land.[70] In the post-emancipation world, this obstruction continued through the systematic refusal of banks to lend money or extend credit to African Americans, and the refusal of White landowners to sell to them. In combination with Whites' refusal to invest in or to patronize Black businesses, this created a context in which many African Americans were economically dependent upon their former masters. Having neither land nor capital, many returned to their former plantations and began new lives as sharecroppers under conditions that felt disconcertingly similar to the lives they sought to leave behind.[71]

This was not true of everyone, of course. One of the unintended consequences of White resistance to Black economic integration was the creation of a powerful parallel ecosystem of Black economic institutions in communities across the nation. This ecosystem included the creation of historically Black colleges and universities (HBCUs), Black banks, Black businesses, and Black business leagues, all ingeniously created and deliberately connected to create new conditions for African American wealth. The effects of this ecosystem were incredibly powerful; cities around the country—from Memphis to Philadelphia, from Tulsa to Durham—saw the birth of vibrant Black economies that became the engines of enormous Black wealth.

In spite of the power and significance of this new ecosystem, however, African Americans were never able to close the wealth gap created by centuries of enslavement. One reason for this was the parallel nature of these separate economies. African American enterprises existed largely outside of mainstream networks of capital investment, licensing, services, and real estate access. Without these networks, all of which were controlled by Whites, Black businesses were inevitably disadvantaged in both local and national markets. But there was another more sinister reason that contributed to this inequity: the menace of White violence. The Tulsa race riot of

1921 is a case in point. In the early days of the twentieth century, African Americans fled the South in record numbers. This Great Migration, the largest peacetime movement of human beings in history, fundamentally transformed cities across the United States.[72] In Tulsa, for example, in just a few years, African Americans came to make up over 10 percent of the population, becoming a powerful economic force and forming a thriving business community known nationwide as Black Wall Street. In 1921, however, a sickeningly familiar series of events unfolded: A White woman accused a Black man of attempted assault. He was arrested and jailed, and a White mob gathered to exact vengeance. But, unlike that of southern communities, the relative economic autonomy of Tulsa's African American community gave its members a sense of strength and self-determination. Some thirty armed African American men went to the jail to protect the prisoner. As the White mob grew to over two thousand people, shots were fired and a rampage of violence began. By the time it ended, White Tulsans burned eighteen thousand Black homes, destroyed $2 to $3 million of Black property, and left nearly three hundred African Americans dead in the streets.[73] These horrible events were not unique. In the late nineteenth and early twentieth centuries, riots targeting Black communities occurred in cities all over the country: New Orleans and Memphis (1866), Pittsburgh (1886), Denver (1887), Omaha (1891), Wilmington (1898), Little Rock and Atlanta (1906), East St. Louis, Lexington, and Philadelphia (1917), Chicago, Baltimore, Omaha, Charleston, and Knoxville (1919), and Little Rock (1927)—to name but a few. Though varied in proximate cause, each of these resulted in the systematic destruction of the institutions of the Black economy. Thus, even as the nation emerged from the Long Depression of the 1870s to the 1890s and entered into the roaring economy of the Gilded Age, African Americans were largely excluded from its benefits.

While the Jim Crow South was a source of incalculable economic harm for Black Americans, the obstruction of Black wealth was not solely a southern issue. It was a national issue. Perhaps the clearest and most consequential example of this reality was the New Deal program implemented by President Franklin Roosevelt in the 1930s. One of the largest financial stimulus initiatives in American history, the New Deal was a response to the Great Depression whose goals were "the three Rs": to provide *relief* to the unemployed, *recovery* for the economy, and financial *reform* so as to prevent such an event from happening again. As part of its broad programmatic reach, the New Deal provided employment through public works initiatives, standardized wages across a number of sectors, and encouraged collective action through unionization of labor. In addition to these financial initiatives, the federal government—through the newly created Federal Housing Administration—sought to create low-cost home ownership for an unprecedented number of Americans. Taken together, these initiatives created a "robust, home-owning, capital creating" middle class.[74] But they did so almost wholly along racial lines. The new middle class, in other words, was a White middle class.

Due to southern political resistance, African Americans were excluded from both wage standardization and labor unions, not only freezing them out of the benefits of those tools but also giving their White counterparts a decided advantage in reaping the financial windfall of the New Deal. The New Deal's housing policies were even worse for African Americans. While Whites received federally subsidized, low-cost loans for home ownership, African Americans were excluded. In a practice that can only be called "White affirmative action," between 1934 and 1968, 98 percent of federally subsidized mortgage loans were given to White Americans.[75] In addition, in order to reduce the risk of these loans, banks developed a standardized system for grading the property values of neighborhoods across the nation. Mortgage applications in neighborhoods deemed "desirable" were given loans, while those in neighborhoods deemed "undesirable" were not. Predictably, the difference between these two designations was closely correlated to the presence of African Americans: the more African Americans present in a neighborhood, the less desirable and thus investable it became. The consequences of this process of redlining were enormous: White Americans increasingly moved into wholly White communities, thus increasing their wealth by that very act, while Black Americans remained trapped in devalued ghettos from which there would be no escape.[76] Due to the policies of the New Deal, by the middle of the twentieth century, when the American economy roared to life in the wake of World War II, the economic inequalities established by slavery and enforced by Jim Crow expanded to become an enduring feature of national life. Indeed, the fruit of these choices defines American economic life to this day.[77]

Seeing Theft

What, then, is the effect of White supremacy on African American life? In short, *theft*. The theft of truth through the romanticization of American history and the erasure of African Americans from that history. The theft of power, of the personal and political agency necessary for effectively challenging White supremacy. And the theft of wealth by extracting it from African Americans and by purposefully obstructing their struggle to acquire it. Understanding each of these forms of theft is crucial, not only because it helps us see the truth about White supremacy but also because it shows us the work that must be done if we are to finally repair the damage wrought by its centuries of plunder.

4

The Call to Own

Where were all the legal and civil authorities of the country, to say nothing of the Christian churches, that they permitted such things to be?

—Ida B. Wells, *Crusade for Justice*

The True Test of Their Faith

On the morning of May 4, 1969, one year after Robert Walker and Echol Cole's tragic accident in Memphis, James Forman dramatically interrupted the eleven o'clock service of New York City's historic Riverside Church. A longtime activist and director of international affairs for the Student Nonviolent Coordinating Committee, Forman had been on the front lines of numerous civil rights campaigns from Selma to Birmingham to the March on Washington. Yet even for him, this was an exceptional occasion. As Riverside's choir and congregation finished singing the opening hymn, "When Morning Gilds the Skies," Forman strode down the center aisle, deflected a few attempts to restrain him, ascended the chancel steps, and turned to face the bewildered congregation. He began to read a statement entitled the "Black Manifesto," which had been authored by Forman and adopted by the National Black Economic Development Conference (NBEDC) just a week earlier. Speaking loudly yet slowly and with a steady voice, Forman declared that White churches owed reparations for their centuries of complicity in the racist plunder of African Americans.

We are therefore demanding of the white Christian churches and Jewish synagogues, which are part and parcel of the system of capitalism, that they begin to pay reparations to black people in this country. We are demanding $500,000,000 from the Christian white churches and the Jewish synagogues. . . . Fifteen dollars for every black brother and sister in the United States is only a beginning of the reparations due us as people who have been exploited and degraded, brutalized, killed and persecuted.[1]

The dauntless proposal of the "Black Manifesto" was that the Christian church must make recompense for its past wrongs and, in doing so, endow the reconstruction of the economic foundations of American society and the healing of its racist roots. But why did it assign the burden of redressing these injustices to the *church*?[2] As Riverside's congregants listened in shock and confusion, Forman went on to argue that "Christianity was used to help enslave us" and that Christians "have been involved in the exploitation and rape of black people since the country was founded." Captured in Africa by violence, he declared, "we were kept in bondage and political servitude and forced to work as slaves by the military machinery and the Christian Church working hand in hand." Thus, the White church's "membership, white America, has profited and still exploits black people."[3] This damning account of history led to a second reason for the manifesto's focus on the church: the church must be held accountable not only for its culpability but also for its unacknowledged contradictions. Forman condemned the church's "hypocritical declarations and doctrines of brotherhood," and he noted that the demand for reparations would be for White Christians "the true test of their faith and belief in the Cross and the words of the prophets."[4] In other words, the manifesto was an indignant demand for Christian integrity; the church must live up to its own lofty convictions and claims. When asked in 1970, "Why did you single out the church?" Reverend Calvin B. Marshall III, chairman of the NBEDC, responded without hesitation: "Because the church is the only institution claiming to be in the business of salvation, resurrection, and the giving and restoring of life. General Motors has never made that kind of claim."[5]

As upsetting as this message was to its White Christian audience, the manifesto's arguments and demands would not be easily ignored. Riverside's minister, choir, and two-thirds of the 1,500 worshipers walked out in protest during Forman's presentation, but the following day the *New York Times* published a front-page article about the incident with the headline, "Black Militant Halts Service at Riverside Church."[6] Other newspapers quickly picked up the story. Within twenty-four hours of his unwelcome visit, James Forman had begun to send shock waves across the country. In the following weeks, the initial jolt of the "Black Manifesto" was further amplified as Forman presented its demands to officials at the headquarters of various denominations and Christian organizations. Additionally, in response to the manifesto's call for grassroots involvement, many local Black groups engaged in "the total disruption of selected church-sponsored agencies" and "active confrontation inside white churches."[7] By the end of July 1969, demands in the name of the manifesto had been made to numerous ecclesial bodies at the local, regional, and national levels—congregations, dioceses, synods, conferences—including nearly every major denomination across the United States. For several months in 1969, reparations had become a public conversation in the American church. Even more remarkable, it was a conversation *about* the American church.

But it was not a welcome conversation in every place. Numerous ecclesial bodies, including some that had not directly received demands, issued public statements that articulated a wide range of sentiments.[8] Many openly expressed their outrage and sharp disapproval of the manifesto's message and methods.[9] Others expressed their shared concern for the problems of racism and poverty but distanced themselves from its rhetoric and ultimately rejected its demands for reparations. Still others offered rebuttals to the manifesto by calling attention to their organization's already existing ministries as proof of their inculpability and need for no further response.[10] Certain groups did, in fact, make financial grants and initiate new church-based programs in direct response to the manifesto's demands.[11] But by the summer of 1970, over one year after his infamous disruption of Riverside Church, Forman reported that less than $300,000—or 0.06 percent of his original goal of $500 million—had been collected by the NBEDC.[12]

In light of this underwhelming financial response, the broader significance of this remarkable, if short-lived, moment in 1969 can easily be overlooked. But the radical demands of the "Black Manifesto" galvanized activists whose confidence in the civil rights movement had begun to falter, particularly after King's assassination just one year earlier. For this reason, the manifesto is often credited with having catalyzed the modern reparations movement in America.[13] Within the church, the manifesto became a gadfly that agitated the soothed consciences of White American Christians. As noted by historian and theologian Gayraud Wilmore, Forman's "dramatic confrontation with one of the historic symbols of White middle class Protestantism has precipitated perhaps the most serious crisis in the American religious establishment since the bitter polemics and antagonisms which divided it prior to the Civil War."[14] This crisis came about because of the manifesto's demand for something more fundamental and more costly than just recompense: it demanded *responsibility*. Forman's words were, after all, an unremitting public rebuke of the church's refusal to take ownership of the sins of its past, and ownership of its creeds, convictions, and claims. The "Black Manifesto," in other words, was far more than a call to pay. It was a call to *own*. And today, over fifty years later, that call still awaits a robust response from the American church.

The Call to Own

Whose responsibility is it to address White supremacy's centuries-long theft of African Americans? Ask anyone this question today and the most likely response will be that this responsibility, if it belongs to anyone at all, belongs chiefly to the US government. This popular focus on the government is understandable. As we learned in chapters 2 and 3, White supremacy could not have been birthed or sustained in American culture apart from the plundering policies, interests, and practices of the state. Any honest account of our nation's racial history will lead to the conclusion that the government bears tremendous moral liability for its perpetration of mass cultural theft.

Notwithstanding the public's broad resistance to the notion of reparations,[15] the government has already proven its willingness and capacity to enact reparations programs. For example, in 1946, Congress created the Indian Claims Commission, which awarded approximately $1.3 billion to 176 tribes and bands for land taken by force or deception. The Alaska Native Claims Settlement Act of 1971 provided Alaskan native tribes with nearly $1 billion along with the return of 44 million acres of land. The Civil Liberties Act of 1988 provided $1.65 billion in compensation to Japanese Americans who were unjustly incarcerated in concentration camps during World War II.[16] And what about reparations for the enslavement of African Americans? Eight months before the signing of the Emancipation Proclamation, the Compensated Emancipation Act of 1862 freed enslaved people in the District of Columbia and, in a troubling twist of irony, compensated *slave owners* who had been loyal to the Union up to $300 for each freed slave. The question is not whether it is legally or economically feasible for the government to enact reparations; history clearly demonstrates that it is. The question is, and always has been, whether the government and the citizens it represents can muster the moral and political will to own our collective past and to devote ourselves to its repair.

Even so, the work of repairing the ravages of White supremacy is not the burden of the government alone. We believe that the Christian church in America bears a singular responsibility to address the historical thefts of White supremacy, for three primary reasons. First, the church's fundamental *mission* should compel God's people to become agents of repair in a world ravaged by theft. Second, the church's complicated *history*, which tells of both its faithfulness and its failure in the face of White supremacy, demands an honest reckoning and furnishes the church with both hope and humiliation before the call to repair. Third, the church's *moral tradition*, particularly its ethics of restitution and restoration, equips it with the spiritual resources with which to address this history and to begin the work of repair. Indeed, we believe that if the church were to wholeheartedly embrace this responsibility, it could serve as a servant, catalyst, and forerunner to other institutions, including the government, that may endeavor to enact reparations. The church, after all, is called in all things to be a "sign, instrument and foretaste of God's redeeming grace for the whole life of society."[17]

Before proceeding, we must briefly clarify what we mean by the "church."[18] In some places throughout this book and particularly in this chapter, we use the term in reference to *congregations*. The church is, at its most basic, a worshiping assembly of God's redeemed people in a particular place. These local communities are devoted primarily to the cultivation of the inner life of the church, nurturing and forming God's redeemed people.

But congregations are also called to be, in the memorable words of Lesslie Newbigin, "a holy priesthood for the sake of the world."[19] They release their members into the world to love their neighbors even as they themselves have been loved by Christ. Whether through the pulpits of proslavery congregations in the antebellum South, or the community organization and spiritual replenishment provided by African American congregations during the civil rights era—from Dexter Avenue Baptist Church in Montgomery to Clayborn Temple in Memphis to 16th Street Baptist Church in Birmingham—America's racial history is replete with examples of the outsized power of local congregations.

In other places in this work, we intend the label "church" to be inclusive of Christian *institutions*: denominations, academic institutions, publications, and other ecclesial organizations and societies that serve a more specialized ministerial purpose than that of local congregations. Some of these institutions operate under the oversight of congregations and their officers, others independently of them. It was not local congregations but parachurch organizations such as the American Anti-Slavery Society in the mid-nineteenth century and the Southern Christian Leadership Conference during the civil rights movement that provided essential leadership to historical movements of Christian resistance against White supremacy.[20] The significance of this institutional expression of the church should not be minimized.

In other places still, we use the label "church" to include the Christian *movement of individuals*. In this sense, we understand the church to be a people not only gathered in congregational life but also scattered and sent to live out their vocations in the world. In the words of Abraham Kuyper, the church thus "individualizes itself" in its members, who are "interwoven with the very fabric of national life" as they exercise an "extra-institutional influence" on society as servants and neighbors.[21] In our view, it is difficult to assess the relationship between American Christianity and White supremacy without properly accounting for this expression of the church. For it is in this capacity that ordinary Christians are encouraged and empowered to work for the repair of our broken world in their daily callings—as citizens and neighbors, as employees and volunteers, as fathers, mothers, and children in their neighborhoods. And it is in this capacity that Christian individuals, by their cumulative vocational power, have promoted or provided shelter for White supremacy—as slave owners, as segregationist business owners, as members of the Ku Klux Klan or Citizens' Councils, or as silent "White moderate" neighbors.[22] Indeed, as we will see, White supremacy's greatest ally in America has not always been the church's formal institutions or congregations but instead its scattered and informally gathered individuals.[23] The neglect of this noninstitutional dimension of the church, we believe, has made it too easy for Christians to disown or distance themselves from the White supremacist words, ideas, and practices of Christian citizens, crowds, and mobs. Nevertheless, this too is an expression of the church, flawed and undesirable as it may be.

Taken together, this is what we mean by the "church." It is composed of congregations, institutions, and individuals, and this beautiful yet broken body, we believe, must own the multigenerational thefts of White supremacy. But why? Our goal in this chapter is to explore the church's *mission* and *history* (we will explore its *moral tradition* in chapters 5 and 6).

We begin, then, with the church's mission.

The Mission of the Church in a World of Theft

When exploring the possibility of the church's engagement in the work of reparations, one tendency is to begin by weighing the church's *sins*—its historical and ongoing failings and flaws. That approach is, of course, crucial to any reparations calculus. However, we believe there is a more compelling starting point: namely, the church's abundant convictions and claims about its relationship with the broken and plundered world to which it has been called—in short, its mission in a world of theft. In what follows we will briefly explore four dimensions of this mission, as well as the various ways it intersects with the demands of racial repair. This includes the church's *identity* as a community of love, its *capacity* for the advancement of its mission, its *calling* to attend to the deepest wounds of its immediate context, and its *civic responsibility* as a participant in democratic society.

Vocational Identity

The first missional reason the church has a fundamental responsibility to respond to the theft of White supremacy emerges from its nature and identity as a community of love. One of the great mysteries of the Christian faith is that the church is the beloved of God. God's people, treacherous and prone to wander, are loved as an adorned bride and cherished as God's treasured possession. Obtained by God's own blood, the church is a community constituted by an act of love. Its first calling, therefore, is to know this God, to abide in his love, and to respond with adoration and reciprocal love.[24]

The beloved church is also a community commissioned for the work of love in the midst of the world. It could not be otherwise, for that which indwells God's people is the love of the manger, the foot basin, and the cross, and so that love must in accordance with its nature be shared, given, and spent. The church must extend the "impoverished power" of self-renouncing love to the tables of its homes and to the streets of its cities.[25] Indeed, the cruciform love with which the church serves its neighbor flows downhill. It seeks the downtrodden and disinherited, those who "live with their backs constantly against the wall."[26] It lifts up the bowed down. It yearns to "comfort all who mourn" and "bind up the brokenhearted." The church should "set at liberty those who are oppressed" and endeavor to "proclaim good news to the poor" and "liberty to the captives."[27]

In other words, the church by its nature exists to be a healer of the very kind of wounds inflicted by the extractor, captor, and oppressor known as White supremacy. The church is called to lift up and love the downtrodden, despoiled, captive, brokenhearted, and oppressed. The church must take seriously the work of repair because, in the most profound way, love is simply who we are.

Transformational Capacity

Second, the church can and must respond to the theft of White supremacy because it is equipped to do the work of love. The church has a unique capacity to effect social healing and transformation, particularly in its local communities. This might seem to be an audacious claim in light of declining church attendance and the percentage of Americans who identify as Christian; indeed, the church appears to be diminishing in influence and relevance in American public life.[28] Even so, the church possesses a significant capacity to do immense good for and with its neighbors. And it could do so in the following four ways.

First, the church's greatest asset is its human capital—its people and the relationships it fosters. After all, congregations are embodied communities of committed members. This basic relational character of the church yields enormous potential for the work of reparations for a few reasons. Reparations, we must remember, is an essentially relational rather than transactional endeavor; it requires the cultivation of communities—and churches are uniquely committed to the nurture of relationships in community. Not only this, churches also consist of people with a diversity of talents, skills, and callings, scattered across various spheres of life; such communities have vast potential for creative enterprises that emerge from the unique vocations and passions of their people. Further, the community-based character of the church facilitates deep and flexible relational networks both within the church and in the local community with neighbors and community partners.

However, in order for these communities to repair rather than recapitulate the devastating wounds of White supremacy, the church must nurture a certain *kind* of community. In other words, it must devote its immense spiritual resources to the transformation of individual lives. This is the second way in which the church is uniquely equipped to do the work of love: it is already in the business of changing lives by the power of God. After all, churches are well suited for the spiritual, even supernatural, work of nurturing inward virtues like honesty, vulnerability, self-renunciation, and other-centered love. As we will demonstrate in subsequent chapters, this inner work is vital to the work of repair.

Third, churches are equipped for the work of reparative love because of their commitment and calling to love their neighbors in a local context. We refer to congregations as *local* churches because they are (or ought to be) rooted in local neighborhoods, towns, and cities. There are several beneficial aspects to this priority of locality. First of all, this commitment affords churches the opportunity to gain an intimate knowledge of the ground-level effects of White supremacy's thefts and the possibilities of local repair. One town might be haunted by its history of racial riots, another by the legacy of lynching, and Christian residents might learn and lament the unique histories of each as part of the call to neighbor love. The local presence of the church also opens avenues for partnerships with neighbors and community organizations. Because a church will not be an expert in all things in its local community—and this is often the case in the work of racial repair—it is called to collaborate with and support those who are. Finally, in being rooted to a particular place and committed to a specific people, the church can persevere in the pursuit of racial healing over the long haul. When others come and go, the church is called to remain. The repair of the ravages of White supremacy in our local communities is an arduous and long-term endeavor; it will require people who will stay.

Finally, the church is uniquely equipped to do the work of love because of the substantial financial resources at its disposal. Reparations is more than the transfer of material goods, but it is certainly not less than that. And the church is a steward of significant wealth. True, not every congregation is wealthy or situated in a flourishing part of town. But, with each community doing its part, the collective church has been blessed with significant resources that it has been called to share, using those resources to love its neighbors. Just as importantly, the church is called by its Scriptures to handle its material resources in a certain way: with a spirit of service, sacrifice, and generosity, eschewing the self-aggrandizement, acquisitiveness, and material arrogance of our age. In short, giving is what Christians do. And in engaging the work of reparations, giving is what Christians must continue to do for the good of our neighbors.

Missional Integrity

Third, the church's responsibility to address the thefts of White supremacy is derived from its vital relationship to its local context. The church is always called to a *particular* work of love, a missional endeavor *somewhere* for the good of *someone*. Its people inhabit real places and parishes, and they minister to the flesh-and-blood afflictions and needs found therein. The unique stories, people, assets, and needs shape and direct how the church devotes itself to and directs its resources toward the love of neighbor. And if this is so, there is one question that beckons serious consideration: *How should churches minister if they are embedded in one of the longest standing White supremacist social orders in the history of the world?*

This is, of course, not a theoretical exercise. If we finally see White supremacy for what it truly is—a terrorizing disorder that has been methodically woven into the moral, social, and cultural fabric of our nation over hundreds of years and, left unacknowledged and unaddressed, continues its plunder even today—how can we deliberately refuse to engage the reality of White supremacy in our churches? And if we discover that White supremacy is a *defining* social reality—not peripheral but integral to the social order in which the American church now dwells, worships, and serves—how can the American church fail to make it a missional priority to repair the ravages of White supremacy?

And if White supremacy as such affects and infects even the demographics of our neighborhoods, the resources we steward and exchange, the workplaces in which we deploy our gifts, the words and ideas our children and our neighbors' children encounter in their schools and local libraries—how can we claim to love our cities or serve our neighbors if we ignore the power and presence of White supremacy in our local contexts? Indeed, the church must take its White supremacist context seriously if its mission is to have any integrity.

Theologian Albert Barnes, writing in 1857, insisted that the church, when it "springs up in the midst of a mass of moral corruption," must actively address any "existing evil within its own geographical limits." This work, he argues, is an essential "part of its mission in the world":

> A church, therefore, located in the midst of slavery, though all its members may be wholly unconnected with slavery, yet owes an important duty to society and to God in reference to the system; and its mission will not be accomplished by securing merely the sanctification of its own members, or even by drawing within its fold multitudes of those who shall be saved.[29]

Even if a church's ministries are flourishing, if it refuses to address the "mass of moral corruption" existing "within its own geographical limits," Barnes suggests, the church is lacking in missional integrity. No less today than in his day, the church "owes an important duty to society and to God in reference to the system" of White supremacy.

Civic Responsibility

The fourth missional reason the church must take up the call to repair emerges from its responsibilities as a participant in a democratic society. While the work of reparations has significant implications for the wholeness of the church and the healing of its neighbors, it is not simply a matter of ecclesial or individual concern; it is also a matter of public concern. The church as an organization in a civil society has a civic obligation to attend to White supremacy as a threat to democratic life in America. And it must do so not for the preservation of Christian interests but for the sake of the common good.

One helpful example of this dimension of Christian civic responsibility is found in an address by Martin Luther King Jr. at a meeting of the Southern Christian Leadership Conference (SCLC) in 1958. At the time, the SCLC was launching a campaign to increase the number of registered voters in the South, and King called upon his fellow Christian citizens to address a particular expression of the theft of power: the systematic exclusion of African Americans from full electoral participation. He declared:

> In the name of God, in the interest of human dignity and for the cause of democracy, I appeal to these millions to gird their courage, to speak out and to act on their basic convictions. In their hearts the white Southerners know the loyalty, the courage and the democratic responsibility of the Negro people. . . . And the South should know that the effort of Negroes to vote is not merely a matter of exercising rights guaranteed by the United States Constitution. The question is beyond rights. We have a duty to perform. We have a moral obligation to carry out. We have the duty to remove from political domination a small minority that cripples the economic and social institutions of our nation and thereby degrades and impoverishes everyone. But beyond this, it is our duty to struggle by non-violence for justice, because we are opposed to all injustices, wherever it exists, first of all, in ourselves.[30]

King warns his audience that the harms of White supremacy extend far beyond the individual Black citizen; rather, it "cripples the economic and social institutions of our nation" and "degrades and impoverishes everyone." Black disenfranchisement, therefore, is a collective concern that requires collective action. Thus King appeals to the duty of American citizens both

Black and White to secure for Blacks their "democratic responsibility"—indeed, their "moral obligation"—to vote.

We recognize that for some Christians this may be an unfamiliar way of speaking about the church's vocation. But, in fact, the underlying ideals are fully resonant with the vision of neighborliness and Christian service found in Scripture. Consider, for example, the oft-cited text Jeremiah 29:7. In this passage, originally delivered to the people of Judah during their exile in Babylon, the prophet urges against religious ghettoization and civic disengagement. Instead, he calls God's people to recognize their basic interdependence with their pagan neighbors and to selflessly commit themselves to the common good in their city: "But seek the welfare of the city where I have sent you into exile, and pray to the Lord on its behalf, for in its welfare you will find your welfare."

When confronted with the despoiling harms of White supremacy, American Christians must seek to guard and promote the welfare of their Black neighbors as an expression of the duties of democratic citizenship. And not primarily because of the damage it inflicts on the church but because White supremacy, to use King's words, "cripples the economic and social institutions of our nation" and "degrades and impoverishes *everyone*." Viewed in this light, reparations is a collective concern that requires collective action. Therefore, when the church repents corporately for its racism, it must do so not as a private act of piety but as a public act that restores, if incrementally and only momentarily, the integrity of Christian institutions. And when the church critiques the cultural disorder of White supremacy, it must do so not simply as a private act of rebuke for its members but as a public act of prophetic repudiation before the citizens of its cities. And when the church forms and equips its members to participate in the work of reparations—selflessly seeking the welfare of their fellow citizens, reimagining the plundered world which they have been called to love, and laboring toward a more just and whole social order—it must do so not only as a private act of Christian faithfulness but as a public act of democratic citizenship.

In sum, in these four distinct yet interrelated ways—vocational identity, transformational capacity, missional integrity, civic responsibility—the church's mission presses the church to address the historic thefts of White supremacy. This alone serves as a powerful motivator, and yet there is a second reason the American church must respond to the call to repair: its complicated history.

The History of the Church in a World of Theft

In 1847, five years before delivering his unforgettable speech "What to the Slave Is the Fourth of July?," Frederick Douglass stood before six hundred spectators in Market Hall in Syracuse, New York, and gave voice to his anguished ambivalence about the American church. With characteristic insight and prophetic passion, Douglass declared:

> I love the religion of Christianity—which cometh from above—which is pure, peaceable, gentle, easy to be entreated, full of good fruits, and without hypocrisy. I love that religion which sends its votaries to bind up the wounds of those who have fallen among thieves. By all the love I bear to such a Christianity as this, I hate that of the Priest and Levite, that with long-faced Phariseeism goes up to Jerusalem and worship[s], and leaves the bruised and wounded to die. I despise that religion that can carry Bibles to the heathen on the other side of the globe and withhold them from heathen on this side—which can talk about human rights yonder and traffic in human flesh here. I love that which makes its votaries do to others as they would that others should do to them. . . . There is another religion. It is that which takes off fetters instead of binding them on—that breaks every yoke—that lift[s] up the bowed down. The Anti-Slavery platform is based on this kind of religion. It spreads its table to the lame, the half, and the blind. It goes down after a long neglected race. It passes, link by link till it finds the lowest link in humanity's chain—humanity's most degraded form in the most abject condition. It reaches down its arm and tells them to stand up. This is Anti-Slavery—this is Christianity.[31]

With these words, Douglass called attention to the complexities and contradictions of American Christianity. He spoke of two antithetical expressions of the church with regard to slavery. One takes off fetters; the other binds them on. One binds up the wounds of the downtrodden; the other leaves the bruised and wounded to die. One is a true embodiment of the Christian Scriptures;[32] the other must be described as "another religion" entirely. If "What to the Slave Is the Fourth of July?" unmasked the immeasurable distance between two Americas, this earlier speech lamented the inestimable chasm between America's *two Christianities*.

These two Christianities, these two painfully incompatible embodiments of the church, are not unique to Douglass's historical moment. They have been present at every point in the long history of the American church's engagement with White supremacy. At times the church has served as White supremacy's adversary, mounting a valiant resistance against despoiling forces; at other times the church has served as its ally, energetically promoting its interests and eagerly sharing in its benefits. The history of the American church is a story of these contradictions—a history of *faithfulness* and *failure*. And we are called to own it all.

A History of Faithfulness

The story of the American church's faithful resistance against White supremacy is an old story, one that predates our nation's founding. As early as 1663, antislavery Mennonites banned slavery in their settlement on the Delaware Bay. By 1688 four Dutch-speaking Quaker immigrants in Germantown, Pennsylvania, had drafted the first organized protest against slavery in the English colonies.[33] In fact, it was Quaker Christianity that inspired the earliest abolition efforts. John Woolman, Anthony Benezet, Benjamin Lay, and other abolitionist "prophets" sought to purge their Quaker communities of human bondage, condemning the practice as "the greatest of sins" and those who practice it as "apostates" of the Christian faith.[34] By the mid-eighteenth century, many Quakers began to free their slaves—some along with compensation—in what came to be known as the "Quaker manumission movement."[35] It was an early preview of the raptures of freedom that were yet to come.

Over the decades that followed, abolitionism developed and matured in the midst of revival, revolution, and rebellion. It was more than a religious movement; to be sure, many of its proponents were driven by Enlightenment ideals rather than Christian conviction. And no less than a complex constellation of forces—political, moral, economic, cultural—catalyzed the push for emancipation. In the end, it was military might that proved conclusive. Even so, from the early days of the Quakers until the ratification of the Thirteenth Amendment, the church served a crucial role in fueling the moral energy of the campaign to abolish slavery in America.

In this regard, the work of public moral persuasion was central to the church's calling. Numerous Christian ministers and laypersons alike argued the case for the dignity of the enslaved, the sinfulness of slavery, the errors of popular proslavery arguments, and the daily realities of slavery's evilness. Antislavery sermons, tracts, newspapers, and books authored by abolitionists both Black and White were disseminated widely.[36] In 1834, the American Anti-Slavery Society distributed 122,000 pieces of literature; by 1840, that number soared to 3 million.[37] And for good reason. As the following excerpt of Theodore Dwight Weld's words demonstrates, the abolitionists' reasoning was powerful, captivating, and in many cases, convincing:

> No condition of birth, no shade of color, no mere misfortune of circumstance can annul the birth-right charter, which God has bequeathed to every being upon whom he has stamped his own image, by making him *a free moral agent*. . . . He who robs his fellow man of this tramples upon right, subverts justice, outrages humanity, . . . and sacrilegiously assumes the prerogative of God; and further, . . . he who retains by force, and refuses to surrender that which was originally obtained by violence or fraud, is joint partner in the original sin, becomes its apologist and makes it the business of every moment to perpetuate it afresh, however he may lull his conscience by the vain plea of expedience or necessity.[38]

But the public presentation of biblical arguments against slavery was not by itself decisive for abolition,[39] nor was it the only work of the church. The polemics of the abolitionists were also accompanied by bold action. Abolitionist convictions bore fruit in local congregations. Some church members began to leave their slavery-accommodating congregations in protest. In a few instances, White churches sponsored the establishment of Black independent congregations. The spirit of abolition also rippled outward, reframing people's private and public lives. Some freed their slaves at the cost of their own personal wealth. Others dared to provide shelter and assistance to fugitive slaves escaping to the north on the Underground Railroad. Numerous abolitionist societies, many with close ties to local congregations, were formed during this time—by 1838, there were 1,346 local antislavery associations with a membership of over 100,000 eager individuals.[40] From these networks emerged new social enterprises, the creation of new institutions, and the reform of existing ones. Schools for slaves and freedpeople were newly established. Stores were brought into alignment with the free-labor movement, which aspired to sell no goods produced by the enslaved. Some engaged the process of political reform. In the face of opposition, charges of heresy, and even occasionally violence, these abolitionists labored tirelessly for the freedom of the enslaved and the dismantling of slavery. And, in the end, their labors proved not to be in vain. Slavery was no more.

But abolition was not a cure-all for the sprawling epidemic of White supremacy, just as chattel slavery was not its only symptom. It soon became clear after the Civil War that many White Christians in the South would devote themselves to the preservation and restoration of a racial hierarchy. What's more, one of the paradoxes of the abolition movement is its failure to address fundamental assumptions about Black racial inferiority that remained fixed in the minds of most White Americans—and not only in their minds but also in their institutions and culture. This was true even within the church. Historian Laura Mitchell observes, "Even the most committed abolitionists often had trouble perceiving blacks as 'beloved' brothers."[41] To the disappointment of many after the war, White Christians who were formerly devoted to abolition placed more emphasis on sectional reconciliation than on the continuing fight against White supremacy.[42] Its plunderous root thus lived on in postbellum America. As intersectional repair took precedence over racial repair, White Christians receded from the scene. And so it was, from Reconstruction through the Jim Crow era, the story of the church's faithful resistance against White supremacy was carried by and large by African American Christians.

During Reconstruction, the church stood "second only to the family as a focal point of black life."[43] Established and led by freedpeople in the decades after the Civil War, Black churches emerged as an increasingly crucial source of social cohesion within the community. In the restoration of political power, Black ministers played a prominent role in politics; 230 Black clergymen came to hold local, state, or national office during Reconstruction.[44] Moreover, African Methodist theologians during this period pursued the possibilities of the repair of truth—namely, the truth of Black history, origins, and identity. They produced a genre of "race histories" with the aim of disputing the racist notions of inherent Black inferiority and imparting instead a dignified—and most of all, *true*—history. Henry McNeal Turner famously defended the continued use of the word "African" in the African Methodist Episcopal denominational title. In a country where Blackness stood for "ignorance, degradation, indolence, and all that is low and vile," Turner urged fellow African Americans to claim their African descent, and to "honor black, dignify it with virtues, and pay as much respect to it as nature and nature's God does."[45]

Importantly, the church also served as a place of refuge in the midst of the threats and degradations of Jim Crow. As Paul Harvey observes, "Black church people used their institutions to blunt racial terror and state-sanctioned segregation and to advance the living, working, and legal conditions of their congregants."[46] Black Protestants often addressed in the pulpit and in print the atrocities of lynching and the racial terrorism of the Ku Klux Klan, and they did not hesitate to denounce both.[47] The same was true with regard to segregation. In response to the claim that African Americans had not in fact suffered from Jim Crow laws, the editor of the *National Baptist Union-Review* countered with an unsettling list of examples: "mob violence, starvation, wages, peonage, shameful educational neglect, Jim Crow laws, enforced segregation, miscarriage of justice in courts, brutal police regulations, inadequate housing, nonsanitary localities, disenfranchisements, mistreatment of our women and girls by a vicious element, signs reading 'Niggers and Dogs Not Allowed' and a hundred other insults."[48] A. W. Jackson, a minister writing in the *A.M.E. Christian Recorder*, proclaimed, "Race Prejudice is the President of our nation, . . . the Priest of every church; the President of every School in the land; and the Chief of all the Railroads, Hotels and all else that rest on American soil."[49] Indeed, the church—that is, Black churches—bore faithful witness to the evils of Jim Crow segregation.

This public witness continued into the civil rights era. One could certainly make the case, as others have, that the Black church provided the "indispensable foundation" for the civil rights movement.[50] For our brief and limited purposes, we will note simply that the Christian church was powerfully *present* in this unparalleled period in history, faithfully resisting White supremacy through its people and publicly bearing witness to the kingdom of God.

Perhaps the church served the movement most profoundly by furnishing God's people with its vast scriptural, theological, and moral resources. Indeed, Martin Luther King Jr. drew from those resources as he formulated his vision for the "beloved community," which in turn invigorated the civil rights movement. As Charles Marsh explains, "The logic of King's dream was theologically specific: beloved community as the realization of divine love in lived social relation. . . . King's concept of love [was] the passion to make human life and social existence a parable of God's love for the world. It was *agape*: the outrageous venture of loving the other without conditions—a risk and a costly sacrifice."[51] This transcendent vision of love was a divine gift to King, and through him it was a gift to the world.

But this was not all that the church was or did. In the struggle for justice, the church was—as it always is—a community of people. People who gathered and organized. People who hoped, wept, and prayed. People who, with courage and discipline, withstood jeers, police batons, and fire hoses. People who did so believing their cause was righteous and would not fail. They were not only activists in the streets but worshipers at local churches—faithful communities that "volunteered space for meetings, housed out-of-town reformers, mobilized congregations for meals and other support, occasionally served as makeshift hospitals, and provided in general the indispensable infrastructure of the movement."[52] Thus, we may conclude with Paul Harvey that "it is impossible to conceive of the civil rights movement without placing black Christianity at its center, for it empowered the rank and file who made the movement *move*. And when it moved, it demolished the system of legal segregation."[53] Behold the church's faithfulness in a world of violence and plunder.

A History of Failure

But if the story of the church in America is one of vocational faithfulness, it is also one of shameful failure. For even as one hand of Christ's body was restoring and healing, its other hand was stealing. James Forman was correct: the church in America stands culpable for its participation in the plunder of African Americans. And yet it was not Forman alone but a great cloud of Christian witnesses who have testified to this. They did so not as enemies of the church, as their opponents often labeled them, but as lovers of Christ and his beautiful yet blemished and scarred body. These witnesses included David Walker, who in 1829, after rehearsing the unparalleled cruelties of White slaveholding Christians, exclaimed: "What kind!! Oh! what kind!!! of Christianity can be found this day in all the earth!!!!!!" In 1836, Angelina Grimké, writing to women of the South, described Christians as "the main pillars of this grand temple built to Mammon and to Moloch," and "the professors of religion" as the "most worthy of blame." In 1842, James Birney pronounced the church the "bulwark of slavery." Albert Barnes likewise declared, "There is no power *out* of the church that could sustain slavery an hour if it were not sustained *in* it." In 1852, Frederick Douglass brought this unmitigated moral charge: "The American church is guilty, when viewed in connection with what it is doing to uphold slavery; but it is superlatively guilty when viewed in connection with its ability to abolish slavery. The sin of which it is guilty is one of omission as well as of commission." In 1910, Francis Grimké confessed in reference to Jim Crow Christianity, "It is a humiliating confession to make, but it is true, the church today is the great bulwark of race prejudice in this country. It is doing more than any other single agency to uphold it, to make it respectable, to encourage people to continue in it. It not only upholds it within its own peculiar institutions, but furnishes an example to the non-believing world, to do the same." And in 1969, shortly after James Forman's first visit to Riverside Church, the National Committee for Black Churchmen declared that White churches in America "undeniably" have been "the moral cement of the structure of racism in this nation, and the vast majority of them continue to play that role today." In every generation, American Christians, both Black and White, have lamented and borne witness to the same observation: the church bears significant responsibility for the evils of White supremacy in America.[54]

But what, more precisely, is the church responsible for? Given the limitations of this book, it would be impossible to present a comprehensive account of the church's historical partnership with racism. We are grateful for the work that has been produced in recent years to bring these realities more fully into public view, and we commend to our readers works such as Jemar Tisby's *The Color of Compromise: The Truth about the American Church's Complicity in Racism* and Robert Jones's *White Too Long: The Legacy of White Supremacy in American Christianity*.[55] Our more focused goal in what follows is to illuminate the church's relationship with White supremacy as characterized in the previous chapter. That is, if the effect of White supremacy is a multidimensional cultural *theft* of African Americans, then we may see the church as having inhabited three different roles in relation to that theft: as *perpetrator*, as *accomplice*, and as *silent bystander*.

The Church as Perpetrator

We begin with an uncomfortable truth, one that Christians today must learn to acknowledge about our collective history. The church in America did not merely lend indirect support to the historical thefts of White supremacy. The church was itself a frequent and active perpetrator of theft, the primary actor in countless instances of Black plunder. A few examples may illustrate this.

The first of these involves the ownership of slaves, which certainly entailed every kind of theft but most especially the theft of bodily agency and wealth. It is a well-established fact that a shamefully large number of Christians were slave owners during the antebellum era. In 1855, abolitionist minister and educator John Fee estimated that ministers of the gospel and members of Protestant churches owned a total of 660,563 slaves whose total market value amounted to about $264 million.[56] (Adjusted for inflation, that sum is the equivalent of about $8 billion today.) However, it was not individual members or ministers of local churches alone but local churches *themselves* that owned slaves.[57] In this perverse and galling practice, congregations purchased slaves who were hired out to the highest bidder on an annual basis. The compensation for the leased labor of the slaves typically paid the ministers' salaries—over the course of one hundred years in one church's case—thereby relieving congregants of the responsibility of contributing personal tithes and offerings.[58] Over time, a church's investment often grew more profitable as the enslaved women bore children.

Take one example: Briery Presbyterian Church in Prince Edward County, Virginia, bought five slaves in the 1760s. By 1841, without making any additional purchases, the church's trustees were overseeing an extended family of over thirty-five slaves. That is not to say the church demonstrated much regard for the sanctity of the family or the innocence of children. On Christmas Day 1843, Briery's trustees hired out nine-year-old Spencer, son of Frank and Vilet, to Reverend Samuel D. Stuart for $4.00 for the year. Three years later, the church auctioned off two more of Vilet's children: ten-year-old "Little" Brister for $2.50 and nine-year-old Catherine for $4.00. The following year Frank and Vilet were hired out to different masters, thus separating the spouses from each other and from their children in order that the church's generously compensated minister could tend to the needs of Briery's White families. In fact, church-owned slavery was infamously cruel. A master typically had a personal financial incentive to protect the well-being of his slaves, but church-owned slaves had no such protection. They were hired out on a temporary basis to individuals who only had the short-term goal of squeezing as much profit from them as possible—skimping on food, clothing, and medical care for the sake of a greater return on investment—before the end of the year's term.[59] For this reason, hiring out slaves was viewed as "a horrid aggravation of the miseries of their condition," according to one observer, and "the worst kind of slavery," according to another.[60] The church was an owner of slaves, an owner of the worst kind.

The church also functioned as an active perpetrator of White supremacist theft in its gross misuse of the Christian Scriptures. These public distortions of biblical truth provided moral cover for the despoiling policies and practices of other institutions (as we will see below), and they served as acts of theft in their own right. On innumerable occasions, Christians vandalized the truth of the ineradicable dignity of Black image-bearers, and in its place they taught and preached profound lies about African American identity. The American church perpetrated the theft of truth.

One example of this type of ecclesial theft entailed the literal pilfering of the pages of Scripture. "Slave Bibles," as they were called, were heavily edited versions of Scripture that removed passages like Galatians 3:28 from the New Testament and 90 percent of the Old Testament, including passages like Exodus 21:16, Jeremiah 22:13, and the narratives between Genesis 45 and Exodus 19.[61] Those deleted chapters tell the story of Joseph's escape from slavery and Israel's liberation from bondage in Egypt. Slave owners feared that these narratives might incite rebellion among slaves; their solution, therefore, was to impose religious control and a theft not only of text but of a fully affirmed dignity.

And yet, because most slaves could not read and many local laws and customs prohibited slave literacy, Christian ministers and slave owners often turned to catechesis—the memorization of doctrine presented orally in question-and-answer format—for the "Christian" formation of their slaves. As the following examples illustrate, the primary goal of these catechisms was not biblical instruction but the maintenance of the existing social order; they were in reality a sacralized pedagogy of control. Consider the following excerpt from an Episcopalian slave catechism issued in Charleston, South Carolina:

Q: Who gave you a master and a mistress?
A: God gave them to me.
Q: Who says that you must obey them?
A: God says that I must.
Q: What book tells you all these things?
A: The Bible.
Q: What does God say about your work?
A: He that will not work shall not eat.
Q: Did Adam and Eve have to work?
A: Yes, they were to keep the garden.
Q: Was it hard to keep that garden?
A: No, it was very easy.
Q: What makes the crops so hard to grow now?
A: Sin makes it.
Q: What makes you lazy?
A: My own wicked heart.[62]

Here is how another catechism explains what the Bible says about the slave's ultimate purpose:

Q: What did God make you for?
A: To make a crop.[63]

In homes and across plantations, enslaved image-bearers were taught despoiling deceptions: that God had ultimately created them for utility, not for God-honoring doxology nor with ineradicable dignity. With the authority of Scripture, their existence and their identity were defined by their labor.

The church's thefts of truth took place not simply in the private lives of its members but also in the public spaces of its assemblies—in the pulpit, in convention halls, and in print. And while the social impact of the church can never be reduced to the words and actions of its most public figures, it cannot be accurately assessed apart from them. Take, for example, Robert L. Dabney, an esteemed southern Presbyterian minister, theologian, Confederate Army chaplain, and chief of staff to Stonewall Jackson. In 1867, shortly after the defeat of the Confederacy, Dabney stood before the Synod of Virginia to argue passionately against the admission of Black men to church office. His commitment to White supremacist ideals was fully transparent in his words:

> I greatly doubt whether a single Presbyterian negro will ever be found to come fully up to that high standard of learning, manners, sanctity, prudence, and moral weight and acceptability, which our constitution requires. . . . I oppose the entrusting of the destinies of our Church, in any degree whatever, to black rulers, because that race is not trustworthy for such position. . . . Now, who that knows the negro, does not know that his is a subservient race; that he is made to follow, and not to lead; and his temperament, idiosyncrasy, and social relation, make him untrustworthy as a depository of power? . . . Do the Bible and our standards require us in consistency to introduce black men into all our Church courts as our equals, and as spiritual rulers of the laity of the superior race? This, Moderator, is the cardinal question.[64]

Obstructing a person's ministerial calling on the basis of race is undoubtedly a form of ecclesial theft. But Dabney's concerns extended beyond the realm of the church. He argued not simply against ecclesiastical equality but against the social and political equality he feared would be the inevitable result. For Dabney, as with White supremacists in every generation, most harrowing of all was the prospect of "amalgamation," the mixing of races by intermarriage:

Now, is any one so fond as to believe still that this can be honestly, squarely done, and yet social equality can be denied? Do you tell me that after you have admitted this negro thus to your debates, your votes, your pulpits, your sick and dying beds, your weddings and funerals, you will still exclude him from your parlours and tables? *Credat Judaeus Apella!* I tell you, Sir, this doctrine, if it does not mean nothing, or if it does not mean Yankee hypocrisy, means ultimately, *amalgamation. . . .* But now, when the negro is grasping political equality, when he is no longer an inferior and in ser-vitude, when his temper is assuming and impudent in many cases, when in many sections he outnumbers the whites, it becomes both Church and civil society to guard this danger with tenfold as much jealousy as when they were our servants.[65]

Dabney's perspective is not idiosyncratic or peripheral; in fact, his words were representative of many churches in this period. And as we will see presently, these deeply held White supremacist convictions would not be easily dislodged from the soul of the American church.

The Church as Accomplice

Certainly, the church was not the perpetrator in every instance of plun-der from African Americans. That principal role was filled at times by individuals or institutions (government, business, academic, civic), with the church serving in a supporting role. In other words, the church has often played the part of *accomplice*—a partner, enabler, and protector of White supremacist theft. And it did so in several important ways.

The church has taken on this role of accomplice by *assisting* and *co-operating* with other institutions in the plunder of African Americans. One notable example from the nineteenth century is the church's part-nership with the academy in propagating the widely embraced fiction that African Americans were inherently—biologically—inferior, even subhuman.[66] For example, in 1851, Samuel Cartwright, a Christian physician in New Orleans, published "Diseases and Peculiarities of the Negro Race" in the Southern agricultural magazine *DeBow's Review*. In the article, which evokes the language of Christian faith, Cartwright writes about "drapetomania," a disease that allegedly caused slaves to run away:

> If the white man attempts to oppose the Deity's will, by trying to make the negro anything else than 'the submissive knee-bender,' (which the Almighty declared he should be) by trying to raise him to a level with himself, or by putting himself on an equality with the negro, . . . the negro will run away; but if he keeps him in the position that we learn from the Scriptures he was intended to occupy, . . . the negro is spellbound, and cannot run away.[67]

The medical advice? Infantilization. "If treated kindly . . . they are very easily governed—more so than any other people in the world," Cartwright explained. "They have only to be kept in that state and treated like children, with care, kindness, attention and humanity, to prevent and cure them from running away."[68]

A far more menacing example is the work of Charles Carroll, a polygenist minister from Missouri, in what is perhaps the most renowned example of the cooperation between scientific racism and the Christian faith. In 1900, in the widely heralded *The Negro, a Beast; or, "In the Image of God,"* Carroll describes the "Negro" as "a beast, but created with articulate speech and hands, that he may be of service to his owner—the White man":

> All scientific investigation of the subject proves the Negro to be an ape; and that he simply stands at the head of the ape family, as the lion stands at the head of the cat family. When God's plan of creation, and the drift of Bible history are properly understood, it will be found that the teachings of scripture upon this, as upon every other subject, harmonize with those of science. . . . Thus the modern Christian, like the atheist, takes man, whom God created "in his own image," and takes the Negro, whom God made "after his kind"—the ape kind—and places them in the same family, as different "races" of one "species" of animal.[69]

According to Carroll's reasoning, race mixing was the moral equivalent of bestiality, an unspeakable violation of divine law. And the offspring of man and "Negro" were nothing more than "monstrosities" that have "no rights social, financial, political or religious that man need respect."[70] Elements of Carroll's argument certainly gave pause to his Christian contemporaries. However, given the enthusiasm with which *The Negro, a Beast* was received even in the church, one may conclude that Carroll's audience took his racist reasoning seriously if not always literally. The effect was clear: the dehumanization of African Americans—the theft of their social identity. In this instance and others like it, the church stood side by side with the academy—along with the state—as pillars of a civilization built on bondage.[71]

At other times, the church served as an accomplice by willingly *benefiting* from White supremacy. The church knowingly harbored stolen goods and received the profit and bounty of despoiling acts. We have already mentioned that Christian members of slave-owning churches in the eighteenth and nineteenth centuries eagerly embraced the personal financial advantages that came from leasing young Black children to local slaveholders. But many other churches that did not institutionally own slaves were endowed by the income of its members and benefactors whose wealth was directly generated from the labor and trade of enslaved Africans. In many cases, their buildings were constructed with slave labor.[72]

Furthermore, Christian institutions, and not individuals and local churches alone, knowingly benefited from the spoils of slavery. After conducting a thorough investigation of its institutional complicity with slavery and the slave trade, Princeton Theological Seminary recently revealed that financial gifts given directly by slaveholders and the interest income it subsequently generated accounted for 15 percent of the seminary's total revenue during the pre–Civil War era. When including donors whose wealth was at least partially derived from slavery, as much as 30 to 40 percent of the seminary's revenue during that period could be tied to slavery.[73] Southern Baptist Theological Seminary conducted a similar internal inquiry, establishing that it, too, had benefited from wealth derived from slave labor and the brutalities of the convict-lease system.[74] These are only two examples; there are surely many other historical Christian institutions that were built on the labor of enslaved persons. After all, as Princeton's report soberly remarks, "No prominent institution from this period could escape its own context."[75]

Still another way in which the church served as an accomplice was by publicly *authorizing* the theft of truth, power, and wealth. By its public handling of the Christian Scriptures, the church provided the moral justification needed for others to successfully accomplish their plunder of African Americans. Appealing to a "plain" and "literal" reading of Scripture, ministers, laypersons, and seminary faculty members alike defended the institutions of slavery and the slave trade with numerous biblical texts.[76] Of course, their efforts were ultimately unsuccessful. Even so, insofar as this exculpatory endeavor persisted for 250 years, the church provided moral shelter for thousands who kidnapped, sold, exploited, abused, raped, tortured, and murdered men, women, and children in the millions. Untold horrors were morally authorized by the Christian church.

As noted earlier, the church's public authorization of White supremacy did not simply cease with the abolition of its most pernicious institutional expression, slavery. After the Civil War, Christian ministers in the South reiterated their convictions that slavery was a God-ordained institution, that the institution had established a well-ordered hierarchy in antebellum life, and that it had allowed savage Africans to be rescued, converted, and trained in Christian civilization. Their point in preaching this was not simply to share reminiscences about an age now past; it was also to warn the church about the moral retrogression of former Black slaves. These congregations were told that, after emancipation, freedpeople had sunk to a morally degenerate condition once the discipline of slavery had been removed.[77] And just as Robert Dabney had publicly called the church to guard against the "dangers" of the equality of "impudent" freedpeople, other ministers of the Lost Cause likewise promoted the fear of alleged "Negro" decline.[78] Their innate nature—bestial, lustful, undisciplined, criminal—was perilously unrestrained. Thus began the urgent search for an adequate substitute for slavery that could restore order, morality, and discipline to southern civilization. It was a search that ultimately found its way to paternalism, rigid measures of control, and public segregation in Jim Crow. And though the activities of the Ku Klux Klan and lynch law were considered by ministers to have crossed the line of acceptability, these ministers and their churches were ultimately sympathetic to the Klan's moral vision—namely, the endeavor to protect southern virtue, restrain Black retrogression, and restore "good moral and civil order."[79] And so, if Lost Cause pulpits did not explicitly support the violence of lynch law and the terrorist activities of the Ku Klux Klan, they certainly did not unequivocally condemn them.[80]

Quite naturally, the church, especially but not exclusively in the South, continued in its role as an ally—*and an accomplice*—of Jim Crow. Churches did not have nearly the same enthusiasm in their defense of segregation as they did in their defense of slavery a century earlier, perhaps in part because the biblical arguments themselves were comparatively weaker.[81] But that is not to say a vigorous defense was not mounted. When the Supreme Court ruled in 1954 that segregation in public schools was unconstitutional, the national leadership of major denominations, including the Southern Baptist Convention and the Presbyterian Church (US), publicly endorsed the decision to the dismay of many of their own members. Thus, it was not always denominational leadership but prominent Christian leaders, local churches, and lay members who allied themselves with segregationist forces and preached against desegregation.

In an address to the South Carolina legislature, W. A. Criswell described the *Brown v. Board of Education* decision as "foolishness" and an "idiocy," criticized desegregation as "a denial of all that we believe in," and condemned those who promoted racial integration as "a bunch of infidels, dying from the neck up."[82] The Tuscaloosa Presbytery of the Presbyterian Church (US) declared that the General Assembly's endorsement of *Brown* would lead to "race mongrelization, which result would become a 'stench in the nostrils' of all true lovers of race purity."[83] On Easter morning in 1960, Bob Jones, president of Bob Jones University, one of the largest and most influential Christian schools in the country, delivered a radio address entitled, "Is Segregation Scriptural?" later published as a widely distributed pamphlet.[84] During his address, Jones labeled desegregationists as "Satanic propagandists" and described desegregation as an effort to "disturb God's established order." Basing his views on Acts 17, Jones declared that "God made of one blood all nations, but He also drew the boundary lines between races." He concluded, "If you are against segregation and against racial separation, then you are against God Almighty because He made racial separation. . . . God is the author of segregation."

The Church as Silent Bystander

Finally, the church has acted not only as an active perpetrator and accomplice but also as a *silent bystander* to the generational thefts of White supremacy. To be clear, bystanders do not bear moral responsibility for a theft or robbery simply because of their physical proximity to it; rather, they are responsible only if they have knowledge of the act, together with the ability and moral obligation to prevent it.[85] But the church was not an "innocent bystander," stumbling upon the scene of a crime, frustrated by its powerlessness. Rather, the church had ample knowledge of the thefts of slavery, Jim Crow, and the racial violence of the Klan and the lynch mob. And it also had the moral obligation, authority, and practical resources to successfully disrupt or prevent these evils, whether in part or in whole. And yet White churches did and said little. Consequently, the church is responsible for its refusals to denounce or prevent White supremacist theft, particularly among its own members and officers. In sum, the church is culpable for its egregious, generational, willful neglect of African Americans.

The church's silence and passivity was not, of course, coincidental. It was undergirded by a long-standing *doctrinal* commitment. We hear an echo of this theology of silence in King's "Letter from a Birmingham Jail," when he says of White clergymen who resisted the civil rights movement, "I have heard many ministers say: 'Those are social issues, with which the gospel has no real concern.'"[86] Those doctrinal commitments held that the church is a "spiritual" institution, that it therefore must not involve itself with social or political concerns, that it must "major on evangelism" and the saving of souls rather than social action; and that matters of public concern must therefore be left to the providence of God.[87] To be clear, our proposal is not that their convictions were entirely absent of merit, but rather that they were unevenly and selectively applied. As Francis Grimké observed in 1900, in spite of the plain evidence of racial terrorism, White ministers remained unconscionably mute about those crimes even as they were verbose about other "social issues":

> We hear a great deal from these same pulpits about the Liquor Traffic, about gambling, about Sabbath desecration, about the suffering Armenians. . . . When the question was up about suppressing the Louisiana Lottery they also had a great deal to say, and many of them rang out in eloquent appeals in favor of wiping out that great gambling scheme, which had done so much to debauch the people. And when the question was raised about opening the Columbian Exposition on the Sabbath, what a tremendous furor it created in these pulpits; the whole land echoed and reechoed with the sound of clerical voices, with the thunders which proceeded from these lofty watch-towers

on the walls of Zion. But when it comes to Southern brutality, to the killing of Negroes, and the despoiling them of their civil and political rights, they are—to borrow an expression from the prophet Isaiah—"dumb dogs that cannot bark."[88]

In practice, *within* the life of the church, this silence entails a refusal to enact church discipline—a vital ecclesial power designed to restrain the proliferation of moral evil within the church. In the era of slavery, some churches excommunicated slaveholding members; most didn't. But as abolitionist John Fee argues in *Non-Fellowship with Slaveholders the Duty of Christians* (1855), when moral corruption is in one's church and fellowship with slaveholding persists in one's midst, Christian duty is not limited to one's personal nonpossession of slaves. Rather, Fee maintains, Christians must refuse to receive unrepentant slaveholders into membership until they put away the sin of slaveholding, or they must subject those slaveholders to discipline, or they must withdraw from the church that has become irreparably corrupt. Otherwise, a person abides in fellowship with slaveholders—indeed, with slavery itself—and becomes complicit with its evils.[89]

This culpable silence and inaction was also practiced by the church in its public life. This is corroborated by the consistent testimony of Christians both Black and White. Our forebears agree: the church was guilty of willful neglect of its plundered African American neighbors. In his widely circulated *The Church and Slavery* (1857), Albert Barnes, minister of First Presbyterian Church in Philadelphia, concluded:

> If each of the great denominations of Christians in the land should first detach itself wholly from the system, and should thus bring the power of its own example to bear upon it, and if, in a proper way, the power of the church, through the pulpit, the press, and the private sentiments and lives of its members, were brought to bear upon it, no one can believe that the system would long exist. It is thus in the power of the church, if it would, to secure, at no distant period, the entire abolition of slavery in this land; and, having this power, it must be held responsible for its exercise. And if it *be* a fact that the church *has* the power, it is a most humiliating and painful reflection that that power is *not* exercised, and that this monstrous system *can* look for its support in any way to the church of God.[90]

In 1879, some years after the end of slavery, abolitionist Oliver Johnson reflected on the church's avoidance of the subject of slavery at the denominational level during the antebellum era:

> The Episcopalian, Presbyterian, Congregational, Unitarian and Universalist churches, with some differences as to method, location, etc., were essentially alike in spirit, in their firm resistance to the anti-slavery movement, and in their refusal or neglect to adopt any efficient measures for the overthrow of slavery. They were alike in exerting their ingenuity to evade the subject entirely; and when this was found to be impossible, they all alike made their action as feeble and meaningless as lay in their power. . . . And when passably satisfactory resolutions were adopted, as they sometimes were, by local ecclesiastical bodies, they became worthless for lack of corresponding action.[91]

Journalist and lynching investigator Ida B. Wells, who once described African Americans as being "accustomed . . . to the indifference and apathy of Christian people,"[92] also wrote about a memorable conversation she had in 1894 with British social and religious leaders. They were stunned to hear about the American church's tepid response to the scourge of lynching in the post-Reconstruction era. Wells explained:

> Again the question was asked where were all the legal and civil authorities of the country, to say nothing of the Christian churches, that they permitted such things to be? I could only say that despite the axiom that there is a remedy for every wrong, everybody in authority from the President of the United States down, had declared their inability to do anything; and that the Christian bodies and moral associations do not touch the question. It is the easiest way to get along in the South (and those portions in the North where lynchings take place) to ignore the question altogether; our American Christians are too busy saving the souls of white Christians from burning in hell-fire to save the lives of black ones from present burning in fires kindled by white Christians. The feelings of the people who commit these acts must not be hurt by protesting against this sort of thing, and so the bodies of the victims of mob hate must be sacrificed, and the country disgraced because of that fear to speak out.[93]

In 1910, Francis Grimké, minister of Fifteenth Street Presbyterian Church in Washington, DC, testified to the proliferation of Jim Crow racism and argued that this was owing to the church's "quiet acquiescence" and cooperation:

That the Christianity represented in white America is spurious, I am not prepared to say. That the church has failed to do its duty, in this matter, I am prepared, however, to say. Had it been true to its great commission; had it lived up to its opportunities; had it stood squarely and uncompromisingly for Christian principles, the sad, the humiliating, the disgraceful fact of which we are speaking, never would have been possible. The fact that in Christian America, in this land that is rolling up its church members by the millions, race prejudice has gone on steadily increasing, is a standing indictment of the white Christianity of this land—an indictment that ought to bring the blush of shame to the faces of the men and women, who are responsible for it, whose silence, whose quiet acquiescence, whose cowardice, or worse whose active cooperation, have made it possible. The first thing for the church to do, I say, is to wake up to the fact that it can do something.[94]

In his "Letter from a Birmingham Jail" (1963), Martin Luther King Jr. famously bemoaned the passivity and laxity of the church: "We will have to repent in this generation not merely for the hateful words and actions of the bad people but for the appalling silence of the good people."[95] Among those who stood by silently, King found Christians, clergymen in particular, to be the chief offenders:

I felt that the white ministers, priests, and rabbis of the South would be among our strongest allies. Instead, some have been outright opponents, refusing to understand the freedom movement and misrepresenting its leaders; all too many others have been more cautious than courageous and have remained silent behind the anesthetizing security of stained glass windows. . . . In the midst of blatant injustices inflicted upon the Negro, I have watched white churchmen stand on the sideline and mouth pious irrelevancies and sanctimonious trivialities.[96]

Surely King would have agreed with his colleague Fannie Lou Hamer, who suggested in 1965 that the church had only "played the role of the church for the past hundred years and failed to do what [the] church should have done."[97] And even fifty five years later, Hamer's spiritual descendants continue to testify to the same failures. Tony Evans writes in 2020,

The evangelical church needs to speak up where it has been silent on injustice and racism. The biggest problem in the culture today is the failure of the church. We wouldn't even have a racial crisis in America if the church had not consistently failed to deal with racism as the severe sin it is. But because the church has historically ignored and downplayed it, the issue still exists. Where the church is called to set an example, we have cowered.[98]

Tragically, the church's legacy as a silent bystander before the robberies of White supremacy appears to be as old and enduring as White supremacy itself.

Owning Our History

What then shall we make of the church's complicated history? This question of course deserves far more consideration than this book could provide, but allow us to offer a few brief comments. First, it is hardly a singularly Christian tendency to read history selectively. But as a people committed to truth, we must resist the temptation to neglect either the story of the church's faithfulness *or* the story of the church's failures with regard to White supremacy. Both are indelible parts of our story: one hand of Christ's body was healing and restoring even as the other was stealing. The American church, in other words, must learn to own its *whole* history: if the church's role in the abolition of slavery, then also its role in establishing and preserving slavery; if the righteousness of Douglass, Wells, and King, then also the unrighteousness of Dabney, Criswell, and Jones; if the moral courage of the Black church in the civil rights era, then also the moral cowardice of the White church during that same period; if the church's faithfulness, then also the church's failures. All of it is ours, an indivisible part of our ecclesial inheritance, and thus all of it must be fully owned.

Second, this history implicates us all. Some may insist that individuals and discrete institutions alone are responsible for the aforementioned failures, but this line of reasoning simply will not do. These sins are *our* sins. Time and again, the Christian Scriptures affirm the principle of corporate or collective responsibility in the church.[99] The church, after all, is one body, and its members are irrevocably bound to one another in Christ by covenant. As theologian John Murray has argued, "We cannot abstract ourselves from the corporate responsibility which belongs to the church as a corporate entity. The corporate witness of the church is our witness and the corporate default of the church is our default."[100] To be clear, corporate responsibility does not violate the principle of personal responsibility,[101] nor does it imply that constituent members of a group are held responsible to the same degree and in the same manner as if they had *personally* committed the evil.[102] Even so, the principle of corporate responsibility does lead us to address corporate sins corporately—not only repudiating the sins of others, and not only lamenting the effects of sin, but also collectively confessing and repenting of sins. This leads us to our final reflection.

Practically speaking, how then must we respond to this complicated history? Just as we must see and own each part of our collective story, we must also respond to each part. On the one hand, understanding the church's history of *faithfulness* is critical because it reminds us not only of the history of the church's labor to resist the power of White supremacy but also of the efficacy of these efforts. The simple truth is that when the people of God collaborate with one another and with their neighbors in redemptive labor, powerful social transformation can occur. On the other hand, seeing the church's history of *failure* is critical not only because it keeps us from proud triumphalism in our labors but also because it demands that we honestly reckon with those failures. In other words, the church's past faithfulness fuels us with *hope* concerning the *possibility* of the church in its work of repair. And the church's past failures fuel us with *repentance* concerning the *culpability* of the church and demand that we engage the work of repair. Indeed, one of the glories of the church is that we are not left alone but are generously furnished with a rich moral tradition that teaches us how to address the culpability and possibilities revealed in the church's complicated history. This is the subject of our next two chapters.

A Call to the Church

It has been fifty years since James Forman ascended the chancel steps of Riverside Church and called the American church to own its missional convictions with integrity, to own its complicity in the racist plunder of Black America, and ultimately to own the work of repair. As we have seen in this chapter, the church in America has a singular responsibility to address the historical thefts of White supremacy. First, because of its mission and calling in the midst of a world of plunder. And second, because of its complicated history of faithfulness and failure. Whose responsibility is it to address White supremacy's centuries-long theft of African Americans? The church. Fifty years ago, when the call to take up this responsibility was issued, most churches demurred. The invitation was declined. The question remains whether in this generation Christians in America will respond differently. Will they—will *we*—finally see and own and respond to the call of reparations as a singular call to the church?

5

Owning the Ethic of Restitution

Blood spilled in violence doesn't just dry and drift away in the wind, no! It cries out for restitution, redemption.

—Ralph Ellison, *Juneteenth*

Blinded with the Love of Gain

In 1684, John Hepburn departed Great Britain and settled down in East Jersey where he made a quiet living as a tailor. He arrived in America as an indentured servant and a Quaker. Both of these attributes, each in its own way, would arouse within him a moral disquietude over the enslavement of Africans—the former by fostering personal empathy for those laboring under lifelong bondage, the latter by embedding him in a religious community on the front lines of the abolition movement. Initially, however, Hepburn's convictions, not to mention his pen, lay dormant.

But year after year Hepburn's disdain for slavery deepened as he studied abolitionist writings from both sides of the Atlantic and witnessed an alarming number of his neighbors purchasing slaves. He also gained firsthand knowledge of the cruelties of the slave trade during frequent visits to Perth Amboy, the port city that became the center of the slave trade in New Jersey. As slavery was increasingly woven into the colony's political economy, and as local slave codes created increasingly unbearable conditions for enslaved Africans, Hepburn grew more troubled in conscience. Finally, after thirty years of waiting silently—mistakenly, he would later confess—he could bear it no longer. Hepburn decided to publicly contend for the truth.[1]

The result was a strongly worded pamphlet, *The American Defence of the Christian Golden Rule*, published in 1715.[2] Writing out of a sense of "Christian duty," Hepburn condemns slavery as "an abominable Anti-Christian practice" and "an Affront upon the ever blessed *Messiah*, and his glorious Gospel." He enumerates the cruelties of slavery, critiques the greed of slave merchants, bemoans the hypocrisy of Christians, and calls slave owners to repentance. But the most remarkable feature of *American Defence* is its argument that the Bible requires a *particular expression* of repentance for the "inriching sin" of slavery—namely, restitution. Not only does slavery "rob men of their *Liberty* and *Labour*"; slavery also, by forcing and compelling God's creatures against their will, entails the "Manifest Robbery" of human agency itself. "Blinded with the love of Gain," enslavers continue this inhumane practice of robbery only in order to "highly inrich themselves by the Bargain." Thus, Hepburn concludes, slave owners not only must repent of these sins but also must return to their enslaved image-bearers all that they had stolen from them:

> *I* am of Opinion, that such Sins cannot be repented of without *Restitution* made to them that they have wronged; for until the *Cause be removed*, *I* know not how the *Effect should* cease. But they that live and dye without making Restitution to them that they have wronged, how they can expect the Forgiveness of God, *I* leave this to the Reader to judge, and then they cannot blame the Writer for a false Construction. . . . It cannot stand with the Justice of God that the Negroes or the wronged shall have no Restitution at all; and seeing then that they must be restored of the Wrongs that they have suffered, it must be restored out of the Property of him that hath wronged them; and this Property is his Interest of Eternal Life; and such a proportion of this as will be equivalent to the Wrongs done unto the Negroes or any others, must go to make up this Restitution; for they will have it.[3]

With these words, Hepburn issued an extraordinary call. Many of his predecessors in print had urged Christian slave owners to treat their slaves kindly and to ensure that they had been evangelized. Some had begun to condemn the evils of slavery and call for the manumission of slaves. But none had publicly argued, as Hepburn did, that the Bible requires not only the emancipation of slaves but also their compensation through restitution. And yet Hepburn explained that the basic argument wasn't original to him. He enthusiastically credits his firm belief in the necessity of restitution to two widely published sermons by John Tillotson, the Anglican archbishop of Canterbury from 1691 to 1694. Entitled "The Nature and Necessity of Restitution," Tillotson's exposition of Luke 19:8–9 defines *restitution* as "making Reparation or Satisfaction to another, for the Injuries we have done him," and restoring "a Man to the good Condition, from which, contrary to Right and to our Duty, we have removed from him."[4] Although Tillotson's study was without specific reference to slavery, Hepburn maintains that the archbishop's teaching could be soundly "applied to the wrongs done to Negroes." He declares confidently, "I have Bishop Tillotson on my side"—by which he meant, of course, he had the bishop's Bible on his side. Hepburn passionately urged Christians who had been "blinded with the love of Gain" not simply to see but to own—to own their self-enriching sin and to own their Scriptures. For it is in those Scriptures that they will—and we will—discover, perhaps for the first time, the call to restitution.

Owning Our Ethical Heritage

Today, over three hundred years since John Hepburn declared that enslaved Africans were owed recompense for their manifold injuries, many Americans mistakenly believe that reparations is a relatively new idea—one that originated perhaps during the height of the Black Power movement in the 1960s. Some have attempted to improve upon this historical error by demonstrating that, while it is true that many White Americans were first introduced to reparations during the civil rights era, the movement dates back to the days immediately after the Civil War when Americans sought to hold the nation to its promise of furnishing every freedperson with land and self-determination. During the Reconstruction era, organized efforts to secure compensation from the federal government soared, even as they gradually evolved into an exclusively Black endeavor. However, as Hepburn's trailblazing tract demonstrates, the belief that slaves were owed restitution was publicized fully 150 years before General William T. Sherman's promise of "forty acres and a mule," and 250 years before James Forman demanded recompense from the American church. Restitution for the thefts of White supremacy is an *old* idea. Indeed, it is older than America itself.

What is more, *American Defence* also demonstrates that the early call for restitution in America, like abolitionism as a whole, was originally a distinctly *Christian* endeavor. That endeavor remained, for the most part, in the realm of pamphlet and pen; only a small number of Christians subsequently compensated their manumitted slaves. Alas, it is also true that Christians would later be among the most vociferous opponents of reparations. Even so, we must recognize that the earliest public cases for reparations in America were made on the basis of the Bible, and thus reparations has a distinct, if forgotten, place in the history of American Christian thought and practice. Over three hundred years ago, our Christian forebears, both Black and White, began to identify a theological kernel that never fully sprouted into mature, collective conviction or action among non-Black (and non-Native) American Christians. For Christians today, reparations begins with a call to return to that kernel, acknowledge its arrested development, and cultivate the Christian idea that restitution is owed to those despoiled by the scourge of White supremacy.

We believe that to construct a Christian account of reparations, it is crucial that we own not only the church's fundamental mission in a world ravaged by theft, and its complicated history in regard to White supremacist theft, but also its scriptural and theological heritage in regard to the ethics of theft. That heritage raises a fundamental question: *What is morally required of those who are guilty of stealing?* And it offers an unequivocal answer: not repentance alone but restitution. Indeed, the two are inseparable.

Our goal in what follows is to introduce our readers to the biblical foundations of restitution, the first of two moral logics of reparations. First, we start with the narrative of Zacchaeus, the Bible's clearest and most compelling example of restitution. We then examine its moral foundations as established by the Hebrew Scriptures, drawing out five essential

elements of restitution. This will lead us, third, to explore how past generations understood and applied those principles—wisdom we sorely need
considering our generation's basic ignorance with respect to these ethics.
Finally, we will briefly consider how Christians in early American history,
like John Hepburn, appealed to restitution in search of a biblical response
to White supremacy.

We begin with the story of one who embodied the necessity and beauty
of restitution perhaps better than any other character in the Bible: Zacchaeus, the infamous tax collector from Jericho whose story is told in
Luke 19:1–10. We would be wise to examine his story, and indeed walk in
his sandals. But in order to fully appreciate the moral significance of the
stunning promise that he makes at the story's climax, we must begin by
recalling his former way of life.

Restitution and Zacchaeus

Zacchaeus was a thief in plain sight. All tax collectors were, at least that's
what everyone in Jericho would have told you. But as a *"chief* tax collector," someone who had advanced in prominence and supervised other
rank-and-file collectors, Zacchaeus was one of the best at what he did. He
was an expert at plundering his neighbors for personal enrichment. Such
ignominious success was achieved by skillfully exploiting the tax collection
system, which operated in the Roman province of Judea in the following
way: Tax collectors would offer to prepay the government the duties and
tolls to be collected in a district for the coming year, and contracts were
awarded to the highest bidders. While they were obligated to deliver no
less than the agreed upon amount, the collectors were also afforded the
liberty to collect a "surcharge" from the people—whomever they could
prey upon and pillage—in order to turn a much larger profit.[5]

As one can imagine, opportunities for abuse and corruption abounded.
Stationed throughout well-traveled cities like Jericho, tax collectors would
regularly overcharge passersby, pocket the surplus, and, if fraud was sus-
pected, confiscate their goods with force and harassment. Statutes that
regulated these practices did exist; and taxation rates were made public
and penalties for corruption were threatened. But these laws were rarely

or unevenly enforced, and tax collectors themselves were "often the only ones with precise knowledge of the relevant statutes."[6] Thus, not unlike oppressive systems in every time and place, the despoiling practices of tax collectors in Judea, while technically illegal, were permitted by uncodified social norms and facilitated by the control of knowledge. Theirs was a dirty job—synonymous with extortion and greed, and suited, according to one ancient observer, only for "the most ruthless of men, brimful of inhumanity."[7]

At this point, one might notice how little our portrait of Zacchaeus harmonizes with the image of the bumbling, even mildly endearing, character that popularly lives in the minds of modern readers—minds all too informed, perhaps, by children's song and storybook depictions of this "wee little man." We tend to imagine Zacchaeus to be something like Joe Pesci's character in the holiday classic *Home Alone*. In reality, he was more like Joe Pesci's character in the mobster classic *Goodfellas*. The ancient tax collection system promoted nothing less than "institutionalized robbery," and Zacchaeus was one of its very best robbers.[8]

This brief sketch of Zacchaeus's life of theft prepares us for two important surprises that are promptly introduced in the narrative. The first is the surprise of Jesus's *radical kindness*. He is expected simply to pass by, but instead he stops, looks up at the "sinner" perched in a tree, and addresses him personally. This is, of course, what divine love does. Love sees, stops, and calls us by name. What is more, Jesus, in a jaw-dropping, countercultural moment, invites himself over to the tax collector's home: "I must stay at your house today" (19:5). In the ancient world, the giving and receiving of hospitality was a sign of intimacy and solidarity, a wholehearted exchange of friendship. Any self-respecting Jew, therefore, would have been far more circumspect with his social commitments than Jesus apparently was. After all, tax collectors were widely regarded "almost as the moral equivalent of lepers"[9]—condemned for their habitual stealing, shunned as ritually unclean because of their regular contact with Gentiles, and loathed for their collusion with Rome. In light of these strongly held social perceptions, it is utterly scandalous for Jesus to associate with so despised a figure with such intimacy and generosity. No wonder the crowd grumbles with sharp disapproval.

And no wonder Zacchaeus's life is so dramatically changed. This brings us to the second surprise, the tax collector's *radical transformation*. Both of these surprises are closely related. As Romans 2:4 and Titus 2:11–12 clearly testify, God's kindness leads us to repentance, and his grace teaches us to renounce ungodliness. Surely it is the kindness and grace of Jesus that leads Zacchaeus to renounce his former way of life and pledge to redress his wrongs. He stands as if to make a public vow and boldly declares, "Behold, Lord, the half of my goods I give to the poor. And if I have defrauded anyone of anything, I restore it fourfold" (19:8). With these remarkable and life-altering words, Zacchaeus makes two astonishing commitments. Acknowledging that he, as a tax collector, stood at the center of an extractive system designed to plunder the most vulnerable members of society, Zacchaeus offers half of his possessions to the poor.[10] What is more, he commits to the monumental task of returning all that he had personally stolen from his neighbors. Once a despised thief, now a beloved son, Zacchaeus promises to make restitution.

Restitution and the Hebrew Scriptures

It is easy, upon hearing the Zacchaeus story, to imagine that this offer of restitution was an example of singular magnanimity, a spontaneous gesture of abundant goodwill. In truth, however, Zacchaeus's response was a conscious act of obedience to the Hebrew Scriptures. So thoroughly infused into ancient Jewish thought and life was the practice of restitution that, in an unplanned moment of repentance, Zacchaeus could recall its norms as effortlessly as we might recall the tip percentage owed to a waiter after a good meal. Numerous examples of restitution are found throughout the Old Testament.[11] But its moral foundation is established primarily by three passages from the law of Moses: Exodus 21:33–22:15; Leviticus 6:1–7; and Numbers 5:5–8.[12] Since each of these are located in a part of the Bible that Christians tend to skim over hurriedly (or, let's be honest, not at all), we would do well to examine them more closely. As we do so, we will discover *five essential principles of restitution*. They can be summarized briefly as follows.

   Realization. Restitution starts with the personal realization of guilt (Lev. 6:4). This, we are told, must also lead to verbal confession of sin (Num.

5:8). Restitution, seeming at first to involve little more than a physical transfer of goods, is thus introduced as a relentlessly spiritual act and a fruit of repentance. But though it begins with confession and apology, it cannot end there.

Return. After realizing their guilt, those in possession of sinfully acquired goods are required to "return" what was taken and "make full restitution" to the injured party (Lev. 6:4–5; Num. 5:7). This must be done even at painful cost to one's own livelihood (Exod. 22:3).[13] In many circumstances, guilty parties must also pay an additional penalty based on the value of the stolen goods—for example, an added fifth of the value (Lev. 6:4–5; Num. 5:7), or a total restitution payment of double (Exod. 22:4, 9), or four or even five times (Exod. 22:1), the original value.[14] These variables notwithstanding, the basic thrust of the law is plain: *If you steal something, you have to give it back.*

This basic command is applied to a wide range of types of stealing: severe forms of sinful taking, such as robbery, extortion, or thefts aggravated by perjury, and also more underhanded expressions of theft, such as taking something entrusted to you by a neighbor, or finding and keeping lost property (Lev. 6:2–4). According to these laws, restitution is required even in cases of indirect causality and negligence—for example, when someone's livestock wanders into a neighbor's field and consumes the produce there or when a fire started by one person damages a neighbor's property (Exod. 21:33–34; 22:5, 6, 14). Thus, it is clear from such examples that Scripture does not portray restitution as a rare and radical response to only the most heinous instances of stealing. Instead, it is a routine response to even the most ordinary instances.

Of course, its proper application is not always obvious in every case. For instance, what if the person to whom restitution is owed cannot be found or has since died? This practical concern is anticipated by the Bible and emerges as our next principle.

Relatives. Consider the special instructions found in Numbers 5:8: "But if the man has no next of kin to whom restitution may be made for the wrong, the restitution for wrong shall go to the Lord for the priest, in addition to the ram of atonement with which atonement is made for him." The clear but unstated implication of the first half of the verse is that if the injured party is deceased, the goods should be returned to his next of kin. And if no such relatives or heirs can be found, restitution should be offered to the priest as representative of God, the rightful and ultimate owner of all things.

Ram. In the law of Moses, restitution itself does not atone for the sin of theft. Instead, the sacrificial ram, given to the priest and presented before the Lord on the thief's behalf, serves as an offering of atonement (Lev. 6:6–7; Num. 5:8). This offering is designated by the Hebrew word *'asham,* which traditionally has been translated in this context as "guilt offering." However, some scholars argue that the word may refer to the *penalty* or *compensation* that, first, renders payment for the sinner's guilt as restitution made unto the Lord (all thefts against God's image-bearers ultimately being thefts against God himself), and second, *repairs* breaches of faith with the Lord. Thus, they conclude, the *'asham* that is the focus of Leviticus 5:14–6:7 may be more accurately called a "reparation offering."[15] Indeed, the ram alone—a bloody, compensatory, substitutionary, reparation offering—makes atonement for every sin of stealing. One of the chief benefits of atonement is, of course, forgiveness, to which we now turn our attention.

Remission. By *remission,* we refer to the forgiveness of sins, which is generously offered to all: "He shall be forgiven for any of the things that one may do and thereby become guilty" (Lev. 6:7). This promise must not be taken for granted: there is no sin of theft or robbery, no matter how egregious, that is beyond the reach of God's mercy. There is a crucial quali-fication, however: Restitution is presented in these passages as a *condition* of divine forgiveness.[16] And the offer of forgiveness does not nullify the need for restitution. This truth is established by the sequence of reparative actions outlined in these passages: first, guilt is realized, then the stolen property is returned, and *only thereafter* is atonement made and forgive-ness declared (Lev. 6:4–7; Num. 5:7–8). This is not because the thief's restitution itself makes or merits atonement for sin but rather because true repentance, as Old Testament scholar Jay Sklar argues, "goes beyond say-ing, 'I'm sorry'" and "extends to correcting the wrong as fully as possible (cf. Luke 19:8–9)."[17] On the exact same day, the returned goods are given to the neighbor while the ram is given to God by way of the priest, who "makes atonement" for the repentant thief and declares him "forgiven" at last (Lev. 6:5–7). Restitution is not meritorious, but it is mandatory for the remission of sins.

Realization, return, relatives, ram, and *remission*: these are the themes and principles that form the moral foundation of restitution in Zacchaeus's day as well as our own. But before we can apply these to our own context, we must establish that it is interpretatively and ethically legitimate to do so. Which aspects of these Old Testament restitution laws, if any, have abiding validity? Which have been abrogated with the arrival of Christ?[18] In short, is restitution an enduring obligation for Christians today, or have they gone the way of pork restrictions and animal sacrifices?

The answers to these questions are not nearly as unsettled as some might suspect. Generations of readers of Scripture across church history have repeatedly affirmed restitution as an enduring Christian responsibility and a foundational expression of God's unchanging moral law.[19] Jesus, after all, did not challenge, qualify, or reject Zacchaeus's appeal to the law of restitution and his promise to fulfill it. He publicly celebrated it. However, Jesus's broad endorsement does not itself imply that every part of the Old Testament laws of restitution remain binding for Christ's followers. Two aspects in particular appear to have been abrogated. The first involves the *penalties* added to the principal. According to the consistent testimony of the church, when making restitution, Christians are no longer required to pay the added fifth of the value (Lev. 6:5; Num. 5:7), or to pay back double (Exod. 22:4, 7, 9) or four or five times the value (Exod. 22:1), as the case may be. Now, in Christ, "simple restitution" will do.[20]

The Old Testament laws of restitution are also no longer binding in their demand for an offering of a *ram* for atonement. As N. T. Wright observes, "What Zacchaeus would normally have obtained through visiting Jerusalem and participating in the sacrificial cult, Jesus gave him on the spot."[21] Jesus himself would be the ram. Gordon Wenham has pointed out that the word *'asham*—which, as we observed earlier, refers to the reparation offering in Leviticus 6 and Numbers 5—also occurs in Isaiah 53:10. There it is said of the Suffering Servant that, in being put to grief and crushed for our iniquities, "his soul makes an *'asham*"—a reparation offering—to the

Lord. Thus, Wenham concludes, "Christ's death, the perfect reparation offering, has therefore made it obsolete, along with the other sacrifices. It is no longer necessary to 'compensate' God for our failure by bringing a ram or a lamb to the altar. Our spiritual debts have been written off in the sacrifice of Christ."[22] Since the advent of Christ, restitution differs from its practice in the Hebrew Scriptures in that *only simple restitution is required and atonement for theft is accomplished in Christ's death*, but its ethical force otherwise remains fundamentally the same. As with Zacchaeus, the basic obligation endures to this day: *If you steal something, you have to give it back.*

Restitution and Christian Tradition

Having identified these foundational principles of restitution in the Hebrew Scriptures, and having established their abiding validity, how do we begin to *apply* them? In seeking to explore this crucial question, we have observed that there is in the church a notable lack of contemporary resources on this topic. Restitution, in our generation, is largely a forgotten and untaught ethic. Thankfully, this has not been the case for every generation of Christians. The Christian church has in fact produced a trove of resources on restitution—*though we need to go back a few centuries to find them*. Prior eras of Christian thought are replete with theological and pastoral instruction on the nature and practice of restitution. In our pursuit of wisdom in applying restitution, our Christian forebears shall be our guide.

It is impossible to do full justice to these historical sources under the constraints of a book of this length. With some notable exceptions, they appear in the sixteenth to the eighteenth century and consist of a wide variety of theological treatises, published sermons, and different authors.[23] What follows is merely a synthesis of these works. Even so, across these works, a consensus clearly emerges regarding the various dimensions of restitution, in particular its *comprehensiveness*, *recipients*, *providers*, and *moral urgency*. And something more begins to emerge: the necessity and applicability of restitution for the multigenerational cultural theft of African Americans. We begin with the far-reaching and comprehensive scope of restitution.

The Comprehensiveness of Restitution

It is the unwavering conviction of our Christian forebears that the practice of restitution should extend into every sphere of life as we seek to rectify every kind of theft. The literature describes the essential comprehensiveness of restitution in three ways. First, restitution is required for *every kind* of stealing—not only the sinful *taking* of what rightfully belongs to another but also the sinful *withholding*, *obstructing*, and *keeping* of those stolen or found items.[24]

Second, when making restitution, the original goods must be returned—or payment of equivalent value must be made[25]—whether they be *material* or *nonmaterial* possessions. With regard to the latter, a considerable amount of attention is given to the theft and restitution of *nonmaterial* possessions—things that are, according to Aquinas, "transitory in reality yet remain in their effect."[26] Examples include the return of dishonor (the stolen honor) of one's parents; the repair of "Spiritual Injuries done to the Souls of Men"; adultery (stolen chastity); and slander, which is viewed as the theft of one's reputation, a good name being "a much dearer possession" than even physical property.[27] Although these sins extend beyond the realm of physical goods, the literature recognizes that *one can take what one cannot touch, and that the robbery of the intangible possessions of one's personhood often entails the most heinous form of sinful taking*. Restitution requires the restoration of these things also. Even when dealing with nonmaterial things, the essential practice of returning and restoring what was wrongly taken still applies.[28]

Third, while the principles of restitution are ordinarily applied to cases involving individuals, older commentators view them as relevant to the theft of groups or corporate bodies as well. Tillotson, for example, recognizes that the injured party is sometimes "a Community or Body of Men." Acknowledging that such cases are typically complex, he teaches that "it is proper to repair the Injuries to Communities or Bodies of Men, by equivalent good Offices, or by some publick good Work, which may be of common Benefit and Advantage."[29] In sum, restitution is comprehensive: it can and must be made for every type of theft, including the unjust taking or keeping of nonmaterial possessions, and it may be presented to groups and corporate bodies.

The Recipients of Restitution

If restitution entails the return of the thing originally stolen, whether it be a material or nonmaterial good, then *to whom* should those goods be returned? According to the early literature, there are three classes of rightful recipients of restitution: *original owners, heirs,* and *the poor.*

Principally, restitution is owed to the *true owner* of anything stolen. Simple enough. The second rightful recipients of restitution are the true owner's *heirs.* The identity of this group, along with that of the next, is based on the "next of kin" clause in Numbers 5:8, introduced earlier. If the rightful recipient—the true owner—is deceased or cannot be located, the consensus is clear that *restitution must be made to his or her descendants— their children, heirs, successors, nearest relations, next of kin, or executors of estate.*[30] Seventeenth-century Anglican divine Ezekiel Hopkins reasons that recompense must be made "to whom it is to be supposed that what thou hast wrongfully detained would have descended and been left by them."[31] The guilty party must return what *would have been* the heir's rightful possession by inheritance had its transmission never been interrupted by the theft. While certainly a complicating factor, the death of those originally robbed—so often raised as an objection to the practice of reparations—is not the insurmountable obstacle it is often believed to be. Indeed, *Scripture itself anticipates this very challenge* and gives us the way forward: restitution goes to the descendants of the deceased.

The final class of recipients to be recognized is *the poor.* A most reasonable question follows after the previous point: What if these heirs, like their predecessor, have also died or cannot be found? Once more, the early commentators are unflinching in their agreement: The ill-gotten goods, according to Numbers 5:8, must be given to God for pious uses or as relief to the poor.[32] If the stolen item is not justly one's own, it must no longer be retained. But since God is "the original proprietor of all things" (Thomas Ridgley) and "the Head Landlord of the World" (William Beveridge), those possessions ultimately belong to him and therefore ought to be "put . . . into God's treasury" (Thomas Watson) for "the use of the highest and principal Owner" (Richard Baxter), *especially in service of the poor*, who are "the Trustees of God, appointed to receive all just Dues, when there is no else to demand them" (White Kennett).[33]

Granting one's sinfully acquired goods to the poor is also the proper course of action when repentant repeat offenders cannot count or recall every past instance of theft or wronged strangers whose identities and whereabouts they do not know. (As some have noted, this may have been the true motivation behind Zacchaeus's distribution of his possession to the poor.[34]) Yet one must be careful not to misconstrue the nature of this act. William Beveridge firmly insists that this provision of restitution to the poor under such circumstances is not alms but the discharge of a debt: "I say pay, not give it, for it is not an Act of Charity, but Justice; they owe it to Somebody tho' they do not know to whom, if they did they ought to pay it to them; but seeing they do not know the Persons to whom they ought to pay it, they pay it to the Poor in their steads."[35]

The Providers of Restitution

If owners, heirs, and the poor are the proper recipients of restitution, who is bound to *make* it? The early commentators speak of three types of providers of restitution: *perpetrators*, *accomplices*, and *heirs*.

Quite naturally, *perpetrators* of theft, those who have sinfully taken, withheld, kept, or obstructed the just acquisition of what rightly belongs to another, are obligated by Scripture to return the ill-gotten goods. If the return of the original possession is not possible, whether because the perpetrators are no longer in possession of it or because it is nonmaterial or unquantifiable, a payment of equivalent value (often referred to as *satisfaction*) must be made. But that is not all. *Accomplices* who participate in the act of stealing, whether directly or indirectly, must also make restitution. On this the writings of Thomas Aquinas, Thomas Boston, and Richard Baxter are worth examining briefly.

In his classic work *Summa Theologiae*, Aquinas provides an elucidating discussion of restitution in relation to the ethics of complicity. Using Romans 1:32 as his starting point, he argues that individuals may be regarded as the "cause of an unjust taking" if they "co-operate with" the perpetrator in one of nine ways: by *command*, by *counsel*, by *consent*, by *flattery* ("praising a man for his courage in thieving"), by *receiving* ("giving him shelter or any other kind of assistance"), by *participation* ("taking part in the theft or robbery, as a fellow evil-doer"), by *silence* ("omitting the command or counsel which would hinder him from thieving or robbing"), by *not preventing* ("omitting to do what would have hindered him"), and by *not denouncing* (closely related to, yet distinct from, the case of silence). Aquinas also stipulates that the one who fails to prevent a theft bears responsibility only if he is "able and bound to prevent him."[36]

He further explains that accomplices of theft are always bound to make restitution in five of these cases: *command, consent, receiving, participation, not preventing.*

> First, in the case of *command*: because he that commands is the chief mover, wherefore he is bound to restitution principally. Secondly, in the case of *consent*; namely of one without whose consent the robbery cannot take place. Thirdly, in the case of *receiving*; when, to wit, a man is a receiver of thieves, and gives them assistance. Fourthly, in the case of *participation*; when a man takes part in the theft and in the booty. Fifthly, he who does *not prevent* the theft, whereas he is bound to do so; for instance, persons in authority who are bound to safeguard justice on earth, are bound to restitution, if by their neglect thieves prosper, because their salary is given to them in payment of their preserving justice here below.[37]

In the four remaining types of cases, he explains, individuals are "not always" bound to restitution; rather, each circumstance must be judged according to its own merits. For example:

> The counsellor or flatterer is bound to restitution, only when it may be judged with probability that the unjust taking resulted from such causes. . . . He that fails to denounce a thief or does not withstand or reprehend him is not always bound to restitution, but only when he is obliged, in virtue of his office, to do so: as in the case of earthly princes who do not incur any great danger thereby; for they are invested with public authority, in order that they may maintain justice.[38]

Baxter contends that "those that concur in the injury, being accessories," are "bound to make restitution or satisfaction." He describes eight different types of accessories to the sin of stealing as follows:

1. Those that teach or command another to do it.
2. Those who send a commission, or authorize another to do it.

3. Those who counsel, exhort, or persuade another to do it.
4. Those who by consenting are the causes of it.
5. Those who cooperate and assist in the injury knowingly and voluntarily.
6. Those who hinder it not when they could and were obliged to do it.
7. Those who make the act their own, by owning it, or consenting afterward.
8. Those who will not reveal it afterward, that the injured party may recover his own, when they are obliged to reveal it.[39]

Similarly, Boston argues that not only thieves but also "partakers with thieves or unjust persons" are guilty of breaking the eighth commandment. He defines these complicit "partakers" as follows:

1. All that encourage and tempt them to it: these directly concur to the guilt.
2. All that receive or harbor stolen goods, Proverbs 29:25. Such are all that join with them to hide what is taken away from their neighbours; such as wittingly and willingly take them from them as gifts, or that buy them from them, because they get a round pennyworth; but they are the dearest ever they bought, if they knew the matter as it is; such as wittingly and willingly receive the profit of them; so the husbands, wives, children, and servants, are guilty of the theft of their relatives in that case. Doubly deceitful and cruel are they who receive the pickeries of children.
3. Such as do not hinder it when it is in their power; when people see a person at that soul-ruining trade, and let them be doing; certainly know them guilty, and yet will not so much as tell them of it prudently; though perhaps they will spread it to others, and then set their foot on it.[40]

Such individuals are transgressors of the eighth commandment, says Boston, and insofar as "partakers in sin may lay their account to be partakers in plagues with the sinner (Ps. 50:18)," they, too, must make restitution.

Finally, early commentators describe a third type of provider of restitution, in addition to perpetrators and accomplices: the *heirs* of deceased thieves. Having inherited the unjustly acquired goods—and being themselves now in possession of them—they must make restitution. Consider

Thomas Watson's articulation of this view. Answering the question, "What if the party who did the wrong is dead?" he writes:

> Mark what I say: if there be any who have estates left them and they know that the parties who left their estates had defrauded others and died with that guilt upon, then the heirs or executors who possess those estates are bound in conscience to make restitution, otherwise they entail the curse of God upon their family.[41]

This responsibility applies *even if the descendants did not personally participate in the original theft, and even if they were not yet alive when it was committed.* How so? Boston clarifies: "Injustice can give no man a title to what is his neighbor's before God; and therefore what you have of him unjustly, is still his, and ye are fraudulent and wrong possessors of it, as well as if ye had directly stolen it."[42] By this logic, the restitutionary responsibility of these heirs is not grounded in a moral transfer of the parent's (or ancestor's) personal guilt to their heir but in the simple yet crucial fact that the stolen possessions, despite now being in the hands of the heir, still belong to the original owner (or that original owner's heir).[43]

The following hypothetical scenario may illustrate the point. Suppose your mother gives you a car on your sixteenth birthday, and for years you benefit greatly from its use. Until one day, a stranger knocks on your door and, much to your surprise, asks for his car back. "What? That car is *mine!*" you say, with astonishment and swelling indignation. "Your mom stole it from me years ago," he explains calmly. "Look in the glove compartment. My name's still on the title: *Mr. Jones.*" Now, in this moment, it would do you no good to reply, "But I didn't steal it," and certainly not, "I didn't know it was stolen." On both counts, your ignorance is beside the point. All that matters is *whose name is on the title*, and it is not your name. You must return the car to him, not because you were the one who stole it but simply because the car legally belongs to—and never ceased to belong to—one Mr. Jones. Restitution must be made by the heirs of thieves.[44]

The Moral Urgency of Restitution

Finally, we bring our survey to a close with the earlier commentators' view of restitution as a matter of great moral urgency. Their demand for immediate action arises from their grave concern for the impact of need-less delays on both *the moral well-being of one who withholds restitution* (its rightful provider) and *the practical well-being of the one from whom restitution is withheld* (its rightful recipient).

Is it sufficient for a perpetrator or accomplice to repent for sins of steal-ing without making restitution? In short, *absolutely not*. Why? To retain ill-gotten goods is itself an expression of unrepentance, a persistence in sin.[45] As Hopkins explains, "As long as you detain what is another's, so long you continue in the commission of the same sin; for unjust posses-sion is a continual and prolonged theft." Beveridge argues that "so long as he hath it in his Hands he still wrongs his Neighbour as much as he did when he first got it. . . . And whatsoever Sin it was whereby ye got your Neighbours Goods at first, ye commit the same Sin every Day, until ye put him again in to the actual Possession of them."[46] By this reasoning, their unsettling yet irrefutable conclusion is this: apart from restitution, divine forgiveness is illusory, for restitution authenticates our repentance for theft. Beveridge continues:

> Till this is done your Sin can never be pardoned, for it is plain, there can be no Pardon without true Repentance; and it is as plain, that there can be no true Repentance without Restitution; for no Man can be said to be truly Penitent for any Sin that still continues in it; but as I observed before, he that sinned in getting his Neighbour's Goods, still continues in the same Sin until he hath restored them to him; for he wrongs him as much by unlawful keeping, as he did by unlawful getting, of them; and therefore it is in vain to pretend that you are sorry for the Sin, until you restore what you got by it.[47]

Centuries earlier, Augustine expressed a similar conviction: "If someone is able to restore the stolen property which was the object of his sin, and does not restore it, his repentance is not real, but a pretense. If, however, he is really repenting, the sin cannot be forgiven before he returns what was stolen."[48] Augustine's unwavering point of view has been summed up in the oft-cited dictum: *Without restitution, no remission.*

Early commentators are quite certain that, according to passages such as Proverbs 21:7, Jeremiah 17:11, and Job 20:12–29, when restitution is forsaken a "secret withering curse" is visited upon the thief, his posses-sions, and his entire household.[49] One of the common manifestations of this temporal curse, according to Watson, is *fear*. He writes, "The thief is a terror to himself, he is always in fear. Guilt breeds fear, if he hears but the shaking of a tree, his heart shakes. . . . If a briar doth but take hold of a thief's garment, he is afraid it is the officer to apprehend him; and 'fear hath torment.'"[50] Calvin rebuts those who suppose that the passage of time may rid them of this terrorized conscience: this "contamination" is "never purged unless the house is well cleared of the ill-gotten gain."[51] Indeed, for those who forestall in making restitution, the personal stakes could not be higher.

But there is a second reason that restitution should be made with a sense of moral urgency: the well-being of the injured party, which must be properly considered in love. In Henry Bullinger's words:

> Thou needest not by thy morrow and over-morrow delays to augment [the injured party's] discommodity and hinderance any longer, from whom thou hast, by thy subtle means and wicked violence, wrested the goods that he hath; considering, that he to his loss hath lacked them long enough, and been without them too long.[52]

Our despoiled neighbor has continued in a state of deprivation and must be restored to their original condition immediately. Just as Leviticus 19:13 says that the unpaid wages of a hired worker "shall not remain with you all night until the morning," Aquinas argues that "neither is it lawful, in other cases of restitution, to delay, and restitution should be made at once."[53] Scripture makes it plain that neither the costs nor the impracticalities of restitution nullify our obligation to fulfill it. For our sake, and for the sake of our neighbors, we must not delay.

Restitution and White Supremacy

While these views of restitution's comprehensiveness, recipients, providers, and moral urgency may seem novel and esoteric to us today, they were in reality commonly held Christian convictions in the sixteenth through eighteenth century. In fact, in the 1662 Book of Common Prayer, the call to make restitution was routinely put before the consciences of worshipers during the administration of holy Communion. After exhorting communicants to examine their lives and "confess your selves to Almighty God," the minister would issue this pastoral warning:

> And if ye shall perceive your offenses to be such as are not only against God, but also against your neighbours; *then ye shall reconcile your selves unto them, being ready to make restitution, and satisfaction, according to the uttermost of your powers, for all injuries and wrongs done by you to any other*; and being likewise ready to forgive others that have offended you, as ye would have forgiveness of your offences at God's hand: for otherwise the receiving of the holy Communion doth nothing else but increase your damnation.[54]

This also indicates to us that restitution was part of the prevailing moral worldview of early American Christians during the same centuries in which White supremacy's reign was established in America.[55] The ethic of restitution, like White supremacy, was *original* in America, woven into the moral fabric of the new nation. And yet, lamentably, most White Christians in this period failed to advocate for slave reparations. Worse still, they stood by silently, and in many cases actively cooperated with and partook of the mass robbery of African Americans. How could this be? The problem, as we have seen, was not that they didn't believe in restitution. The problem was that they didn't believe they had stolen anything—or anyone.[56]

But there was a remnant of Christians who were persuaded that the Bible required restitution for theft, that slavery was a form of theft, and therefore that the Bible required restitution for slavery. John Hepburn, introduced at the beginning of this chapter, was one remarkable champion of these convictions, but he wasn't alone. A modest but valiant chorus of Christians, of both European and African descent, publicly argued that restitution was the proper moral response to the theft of White supremacy. At the same time that Beveridge, Baxter, and Boston were teaching the church about the Bible's laws of restitution, a faithful remnant in colonial America was calling their fellow Christians to fulfill those obligations.

Former slave trader and abolitionist Ralph Sandiford, distressed by the religious hypocrisy he witnessed around him, named restitution as a requirement of "true Repentance" for the sin of slavery.[57] An anonymous abolitionist, whose essay was printed by Hepburn alongside *American*

Defence, wrote in regard to enslaved Africans: "I know of no other way to make them Restitution for the wrong done them (but the Cost of sending them home to be part, if they desire it) and without Restitution (where it is possible and the Wrong known) we know of no Pardon."[58]

In a short antislavery essay, political activist Thomas Paine, writing of "the past treatment of African slaves," asked rhetorically, "Are we not, therefore, bound in duty to [God] and to them to repair these injuries, as far as possible?" And he exclaimed on behalf of White Christians across America, "What singular obligations are we under to these injured people!"[59]

Congregationalist ministers Samuel Hopkins and Ezra Stiles wrote a public letter to raise funds on behalf of two Black missionary candidates as "compensation . . . for the injuries they are constantly receiving by this unrighteous practice, and all its attendants."[60] And in his forceful antislavery tract *A Dialogue concerning the Slavery of the Africans*, Hopkins, appealing to Deuteronomy 15:13–15, directed slave owners not only to remove "the galling yoke from their necks" but also to "give all proper encouragement and assistance to those who have served you well . . . by giving them reasonable wages for their labor if they still continue with you, or liberally furnishing them with what is necessary in order to their living comfortably, and being in a way to provide for themselves."[61]

Likewise, merchant and revolutionary James Swan, also drawing from Deuteronomy 15, argued in his widely circulated *A Disuasion to Great Britain and the Colonies* that slaveholders, upon freeing a slave, must "give him liberally of what the Lord hath blessed them with."[62] Swan called the Christian body politic not only to retrospective payment but also to prospective investment, enabling emancipated slaves to be fully restored to equal status in the nation's life and economy, to enjoy some of the fruit of their labor, and to start anew.

Some years later, in a sermon entitled "The Charitable Blessed," Timothy Dwight IV—a congregationalist minister and grandson of slaveholding theologian Jonathan Edwards—exhorted his listeners to assume responsibility for their ancestors' enslavement of Africans: "*Our* parents and ancestors have brought *their* parents, or ancestors, in the course of a most iniquitous traffic, from their native country; and made them slaves."[63] And what Dwight preached next remains one of the most powerful articulations of the moral necessity of corporate restitution for slavery in early American Christian history:

> When we introduced these unhappy people into this country, we charged ourselves with the whole care of their temporal and eternal interests; and became responsible to God for the manner, in which we should perform this duty. It is in vain to allege, that *our ancestors* brought them hither, and not we. As well might a son, who inherited an ample patrimony, refuse to pay a debt, because it was contracted by his father. We inherit our ample patrimony with all its incumbrances; and are bound to pay the debts of our ancestors. *This* debt, particularly, we are bound to discharge: and, when the righteous Judge of the Universe comes to reckon with his servants, he will rigidly exact the payment at our hands. To give them liberty, and stop here, is to entail upon them a curse. We are bound to give them, also, knowledge, industry, economy, good habits, moral and religious instruction, and all the means of eternal life.[64]

While the most widely publicized arguments for restitution for slavery were articulated by Christians of European descent, their views were resonant with, and in many cases directly based on, the moral outlook of enslaved Africans themselves. Slaves remained steadfast in what historian Lynda Morgan describes as their "stalwart appreciation for the dignity of work."[65] Persuaded of the inherent value of their work, they held firmly to the conviction that "the result of labour belongs of right to the labourer" and concluded, as Black abolitionist David Ruggles later did, that slavery was mass exploitation and robbery, and thus a "flagrant violation" of both the seventh and eighth commandments in the Bible.[66] Indeed, no one knew better than slaves themselves that their labor, along with their bodies, was stolen.

In due time, believing that "God himself was the first pleader of the cause of slaves" (in the later words of Richard Allen and Absalom Jones), Black Christians in bondage began to plead their case in court.[67] During the 1770s in New England, a number of Black freedom petitions were submitted by organized groups of slaves, some of which included requests for compensation for their unpaid labor on the basis of the Bible.[68] One such petition used Swan's *Disuasion* to establish the moral grounds of its argument for restitution. In another, seven "poor Negroes & molattoes" of Dartmouth, Massachusetts, petitioned against being subjected to taxation without the right to vote. Invoking the name of God, they declare that "being Chiefly of the African Extract and by Reason of Long Bondag and hard Slavery we have been deprived of Injoying the Profits of our Labourer or the advantage of Inheriting Estates from our Parents as our Neighbouers the white peopel do."[69] These enslaved Christians were confident in their right to receive compensation for their years of unrequited toil. It was plain to them that they had been dispossessed of economic advantages that their White Christian neighbors regularly enjoyed. In other words, they sought restitution for White supremacist theft.

The public appeal for restitution by African Americans, many of them Christians, would multiply in the nineteenth century. And their advocacy would expand beyond the rights and claims of individuals to those of their entire community. Maria Stewart argued, "We have formed the labor, they have received the profits; we have planted the vines, they have eaten the fruits of them."[70] Henry Highland Garnet exhorted American slaves, "Think how many tears you have poured out upon the soil which you have cultivated with unrequited toil and enriched with your blood; and then go to your lordly enslavers and . . . entreat them to remove the grievous burdens which they have imposed upon you, and to remunerate you for your labor."[71] Delegates at the National Emigration Convention of Colored People called on the federal government to establish a "national indemnity . . . as a redress of our grievances for the unparalleled wrongs, undisguised impositions, and unmitigated oppression, which we have suffered at the hands of this American people."[72] Sojourner Truth would say of the American republic, "Our unpaid labor has been a stepping-stone to its financial success. Some of its dividends must surely be ours."[73] And Callie House declared, "If the Government had the right to free us she had a right to make some provision for us and since she did not make it soon after Emancipation she ought to make it now."[74]

But prior to this later surge in public advocacy for restitution, African Americans, unlike their White abolitionist counterparts, had limited opportunities to make their case by way of speech, petition, or pamphlet. Even so, they would not be silenced or stripped of their hope. As evidenced by well-known spirituals like "Go Down, Moses," enslaved Christians—"the original reparationists"[75]—often clung to their right to restitution by way of song. Gathered together in forest, field, and cabin, they drew hope from a time long past when God's captive people had been freed and furnished liberally with divinely appointed recompense:

> No more shall they in bondage toil,
> Let my people go;
> Let them come out with Egypt's spoil,
> Let my people go.[76]

Their simple, lyrical appeal to the story of the exodus was both profound and subversive. They identified their White Christian masters not with Moses—as the slave owners themselves undoubtedly would have—but Pharaoh. They identified their White Christian neighbors not with Israel but Egypt.[77] They recognized that the Israelites had received, in Ezekiel Hopkins's words, "what was rightfully their own" and "might be well considered in lieu of their wages . . . as a reward for their tedious servitude."[78] They believed they had the same biblical right to restitution, not simply as individuals but as a people. They believed, as Jourdon Anderson later would, that they had waited far too long, toiling "for generations without recompense." And yet they also believed, above all else, that God would one day fulfill their hopes.

The call of reparations, we believe, is to sing this song with these forebears of our faith and, with God's help, to fulfill the demands of restitution at last.

6

Owning the Ethic of Restoration

—

The ultimate solution to the race problem lies in the willingness of men to obey the unenforceable.

—Martin Luther King Jr.

A Good Samaritan of Hunted Flesh and Blood

One day when he was seven years old, Levi Coffin was playing by the roadside where his father was chopping wood. He looked up and saw a gang of slaves trudging toward them along the road. The dark-skinned men were handcuffed and chained in pairs, towed by a long chain that extended between them. And a White man rode behind them on horseback, goading his caravan of human chattel with a long whip whenever their weary and reluctant feet lagged on the long journey. Since neither his parents nor grandparents ever owned slaves—increasingly a rarity in rural North Carolina in the early nineteenth century—this was truly unlike anything the boy had seen before.

As the forlorn procession passed, Levi's father, with his only son at his side, engaged the men and asked about the reasons for which they were chained. With a deep and inconsolable sadness etched on his face, one of them responded with words that would be etched indelibly on the young boy's mind: "*They have taken us away from our wives and children, and they chain us lest we should make our escape and go back to them.*"[1] The thought of this father being stolen from his family—forcibly taken and kept from his children—haunted young Levi that day. With a mix of pained sympathy and childlike curiosity, he asked his father a litany of questions about what he had just witnessed. His father patiently answered each one—about the men, about the slave driver, about the meaning of their chains. But one thing lingered unresolved in the boy's imagination as if he had just awoken from a bad dream: it was *"how terribly we should feel if Father were taken away from us."* In a very real sense, these sentiments would haunt his moral imagination for years to come. He would later describe this life-altering incident as "the first awakening of sympathy with the oppressed" and the beginning of his "hatred of oppression and injustice in every form." And so it was that Levi Coffin, who would become one of the most storied figures of the Underground Railroad, was "converted" at the age of seven to the cause of abolitionism.[2]

In the years that followed, ignited by formative experiences like the one just described and stoked by his Christian faith, Coffin's antislavery convictions would fan into flame. He would condemn slavery as a "system by which, in order to get their labour without wages, the slaves were robbed of everything else."[3] The fugitive slave laws that Coffin would spend his days defying were formulated on the legal principle of restitution; slave owners, it was argued, had the right to recover their lost or stolen property. But Coffin clung to the belief that fugitive slaves were the true victims of theft.[4] He also believed that it was "simply a Christian duty" to restore these despoiled human beings to a condition befitting their identity as "the image of God."[5] And when he moved to Newport, Indiana, in 1826, he would be afforded a singular opportunity to fulfill that very duty.

Soon after settling into his new home in Newport, together with his wife Catherine and their infant son Jesse, Coffin discovered that they were living on a "line" of the Underground Railroad—the clandestine network of safe houses, routes, and people who assisted runaway slaves during their perilous flight to freedom. He also learned that many of the fugitives who passed through Newport were captured by search parties and their packs of "negro dogs," but the White residents in town were reluctant to get involved for fear of reprisal. Their fears, of course, were not unfounded.

Under the law, those who assisted fugitive slaves were subject to heavy fines and imprisonment, and to the harassment and violent threats of slave owners and slave hunters. And Coffin himself would be no stranger to such intimidation. At the height of his involvement in the Underground Railroad, men routinely threatened to burn his house, or worse, shoot him, drag him into the woods, and hang him on a tree.[6] But despite these foreboding dangers, Coffin remained confident that "my life was in the hands of my Divine Master." And not only this, his mind and will were held captive to Scripture's call to "love thy neighbor as thyself."[7] And so Levi and Catherine Coffin eagerly welcomed fugitive slaves into their home.

Their temporary neighbors arrived in groups of two to seventeen, often in the middle of the night and in poor health from exposure and fatigue from their harrowing journey. With humanizing compassion, the Coffins provided them unsparingly with anything they could offer: shelter, rest, food, convalescence, fresh garments, shoes, and supplies for the continuing journey north. As he describes in his autobiography, "It soon became known to the colored people in our neighborhood and others that our house was a depot where the hunted and harassed fugitive journeying northward, on the Underground Railroad, could find succor and sympathy."[8] And after decades of providing shelter to thousands of escapees in Newport, Indiana, and in his later years, Cincinnati, Ohio, Levi came to be known by the unofficial title, "the President of the Underground Railroad."[9]

The honor and flattery of that nickname notwithstanding, if there were a term that best captures the life and work of Levi Coffin, it would be one that came to be widely used among abolitionists for those who aided fugitive slaves: *the good Samaritan*. In fact, the biblical parable from which the term originates was formative to Coffin's personal sense of calling. Ever since childhood, he once explained, appealing to the language of the parable, he had been convinced from the Bible that "it was right to feed the hungry and clothe the naked, and to minister to those who had fallen among thieves and were wounded."[10] When he defended the moral case for aiding fugitive slaves, he often appealed to the good Samaritan. In one edition of his autobiography, the editor introduced him as none other than "the Good Samaritan of hunted flesh and blood, with skin not coloured like his own, under whose roof were sheltered over three thousand fugitive slaves."[11]

But why? Why did this parable resonate with Coffin in this manner? And why was it that even to his colleagues and contemporaries the parable of the good Samaritan so aptly encapsulated his work? Consider: Here was a White merchant who showed restorative compassion to neighbors "with skin not coloured like his own," those of a different—and despised—race. Brutalized and plundered, they had "fallen among thieves." Although the dangers were always greatest for the escapees themselves, in providing them with roadside hospitality amid their long, arduous journey, Coffin also risked personal harm. It was a costly enterprise, too; for decades he funneled the wealth he had amassed from his prosperous retail business into the Underground Railroad. And he did these things not primarily as a response to personal guilt—he, his parents, and grandparents never owned a single slave—but rather, as a simple yet profound response to the Bible's call to love your neighbor as yourself. And so, love he did, extending compassion to countless neighbors who had fallen among thieves on the Jericho roads of antebellum America.

Owning the Vocation of Neighbor Love

In this regard, the abolitionist career of Levi Coffin—as one personal embodiment of the parable of the good Samaritan—powerfully illustrates what we believe is the second dimension of a Christian account of reparations. The first, which we explored in the previous chapter, is based on the principles of *restitution* and begins with a sober assessment of one's culpability for theft. Whatever was unjustly taken, withheld, or kept must be returned to its rightful owner. The second, by contrast, emerges from the basic Christian call to the love of neighbor and is best described as the work of *restoration*. That is, in the face of White supremacist theft, the Bible commands us not only to spare no effort in repairing what was broken and to spare no expense in restoring to our neighbors all that was unjustly taken, but to do so *even if we ourselves are not directly culpable*. This, then, is the second of the two moral logics of reparations: the radical, rehabilitative work of neighbor love.

At this point, it is important for us to acknowledge that reparations is ordinarily conceived in exclusively restitutionary terms. For many of our readers, therefore, a view of reparations that is grounded in any moral basis besides the ethics of culpability will be unfamiliar or even objectionable. We understand this response and remain sympathetic to it. For there are indeed too many across our nation and in our churches who, despite being descendants of perpetrators of Black plunder, and despite leading institutions with long-established histories of complicity in Black plunder, and despite being personal beneficiaries of a nation founded on Black plunder, yet refuse to acknowledge or own our shared responsibility for the incalculable and enduring effects of Black plunder. Truly, the restitution of repentance is long overdue—of this we are deeply persuaded.

Even so, we are also persuaded that, according to the Christian Scriptures, reparations is not less than the logic of restitution, but it is undoubtedly more. We believe that the Bible commands us to return our neighbors' stolen things when we are guilty of their theft, and we believe that the Bible also commands us to restore their stolen things even when we are not. We believe that it is necessary to reckon with our *culpability* in the pursuit of racial repair, and we believe that it is also necessary as Christians to reckon with our essential *calling* in this world—our missional identity, integrity, and responsibility to love our despoiled neighbors as ourselves. This is why, for example, the ethic of restoration and the use of the good Samaritan as its moral paradigm holds an important place in the old and long history of American Christian resistance against the thefts of White supremacy.[12] In other words, we believe that in a Christian vision of reparations, it is crucial that we own the church's scriptural and theological heritage in regard to the call to restorative love as an essential response to the multigenerational, cultural theft of White supremacy.

In what follows, we examine the parable of the good Samaritan and its surrounding narrative of Luke 10:25–37. We will draw out elements of the work of restoration as a Christian response to robbery—its *context*, *essence*, *neglect*, and *work*. In the previous chapter, we met Zacchaeus, the tax collector from Jericho; presently we will encounter a Samaritan on a road to that same city. Earlier we examined the nature and necessity of restitution; now we will show you a more excellent way.

The Context of Restoration

In this parable, the work of restoration takes place against the backdrop of a robbery, a violent and bloody crime against a traveler on the notoriously crime-ridden road that runs from Jerusalem to Jericho. This road was unusually steep, descending thousands of vertical feet over the course of only seventeen miles, and travelers were susceptible to bandits who found no shortage of hiding places in its rocky terrain.[13] It hardly would have been a surprise, though no less tragic for its predictability, for Jesus's listeners to hear that a man on this road had been mercilessly assaulted. Some robbers "stripped him and beat him and departed, leaving him half dead" (Luke 10:30).

What exactly was stolen is not explicitly detailed by Jesus, but his description of the event gives us some important clues. In the predatory perspective of the thieves we see the theft of the truth of the traveler's dignity. To them he was not a human being to be honored but a target to be exploited. In the act of beating, we see the theft of bodily agency, the violation of the man's personal boundaries and power. In the extraction of his possessions—money, clothing, and perhaps transportation—we see the theft of wealth and of the security that this wealth entails. This theft, like that of White supremacy, was a comprehensive act of personal plunder.

Indeed, generations of African Americans have made this connection between the thefts experienced on the Jericho road and the thefts experienced under the conditions of White supremacy.[14] Martin Luther King Jr., for example, saw in the parable's "man" an arresting portrait of "the Negro who has been robbed of his personhood, stripped of his sense of dignity, and left dying on some wayside road." The "evil monster" of segregation—and discrimination, its "inseparable twin"—conspired together to carry out a mass mugging, "stripping millions of Negro people of their sense of dignity and robbing them of their birthright of freedom."[15]

Similarly, in her Pulitzer Prize–winning novel *Beloved*, Toni Morrison refigures and retells the parable in the brutal history of antebellum slavery. In a poignant scene that is at once troubling and tender, Morrison tells the story of a redemptive encounter between a proverbial Samaritan and one who had fallen among robbers. Drained of all her strength, Sethe, the book's nineteen-year-old protagonist, collapses to the ground. She has long been stripped of liberty and dignity by years of enslavement, but now—with her womb burdened by a baby, her back ravaged by a recent beating, and her feet faltering after miles of fleeing toward freedom—Sethe is robbed of all but life itself. Then, by chance, a stranger traveling along a path in the woods not ten yards away happens upon the lifeless body that is "stretched out dead." Her name is Amy Denver. As a White woman, she is an unlikely source of support; as an indentured servant, she is familiar herself with exploitation and abuse. Amy, whose name itself is derived from the French word for "beloved," embraces this interruption to her own journey to Boston. She massages Sethe's swollen feet, applies spiderwebs as balm for the whip-ripped flesh on her back, prepares a bed of leaves as temporary hospice overnight, and even assists with the delivery of Sethe's baby the following day. Amy not only restores life; she quite literally multiplies life in this world. But her compassion is not without cost: by aiding and abetting a runaway slave, she assumes great risk of personal harm, and by doing so secretly, she forgoes potential financial reward. Then, just as suddenly as she appears, the one whose name is *love* departs.[16]

Morrison, like King, unlocks the parable's timeless power as she relates it imaginatively—and prophetically—to the historical plunder of Black Americans.[17] In doing so, she provides the reader with affecting glimpses of the parable's main theme: love.

The Essence of Restoration

Restoration is a work of love. That may not be a word normally associated with reparations; for some, *justice* or even *retribution* might more easily come to mind. But it is crucial that we observe how this story of redemptive repair is in fact introduced by Jesus as an illustration of the call to "love . . . your neighbor as yourself" (Luke 10:27). The topic of love is raised when a "lawyer" inquires—not sincerely, we're told, but to test Jesus— about the path to eternal life. When Jesus invites the man to answer his own question based on his knowledge of biblical law, this legal expert cites Deuteronomy 6:5 ("you shall love the Lord your God with all your heart and with all your soul and with all your might") and Leviticus 19:18 ("you shall love your neighbor as yourself")—two texts that have been described jointly as the "law of love."[18] Jesus affirms this response and exhorts him to fulfill it. When the lawyer begins to probe the limits of the commandment, Jesus introduces the parable as an imaginative exposition of neighbor love, which is the moral essence of the work of restoration.

But what exactly do we mean by *love*? As the narrative unfolds, five characteristics begin to emerge.

Essential

First, love is essential. To love our neighbor as ourselves—to love as the Samaritan loved—is the sum of all that God requires of us according to the consistent teaching of Christ and his apostles.[19] Restorative love is elemental to the Christian life. And Jesus affirms such love as a necessary condition of eternal life: "Do this, and you will live" (Luke 10:28). With this Jesus was not suggesting that salvation can be obtained by one's successful obedience to the law of love; his point, rather, was that a sustained lifestyle of restorative love tests and proves the authenticity of one's faith. Jesus simply intended what James meant when he wrote that faith without deeds is dead. And John when he taught that those who close their hands and their hearts against the needs of their brothers reveal that God's love does not abide in them. And Jesus himself when he declared that only those who welcome the stranger, clothe the naked, feed the hungry, care for the sick, and visit the incarcerated will enter into eternal life.[20]

Because of this nonnegotiable character of neighbor love, abolitionist John Fee could invoke the language of the good Samaritan and speak of the restoration of slaves as an essential mark of "the religion of Christ" and the identity of a Christian. As he wrote in 1849,

> The religion of Christ, as illustrated by himself, makes it not our duty to pass by on the other side, as the priest and Levite did, but to go to the suffering man, pour into his wounds the oil and the wine of comfort, place him upon our own beast, take him to the inn, a place where his wants can be supplied, thrust our hands into our pockets and defray expenses, until the robbed and bruised man is healed. This is the religion of Christ. Hence Jesus said, "Love thy neighbor as thyself." Hence John said, "Whoso hath this world's goods (money, food, privilege of voting and changing laws in church or state, freedom of speech, &c.,) and seeth his brother have need,

and shutteth up his bowels of compassion from him, how dwelleth the love of God in him?" How can he be a Christian? Wherefore: "My little children, let us not love in word, neither in tongue; but in DEED and in truth."[21]

Indeed, when we encounter victims of robbery on life's roadsides, our response of love is not an act of charity but covenantal fidelity. It is not optional but essential.

Universal

Closely related to the essentiality of the work of restoration is its universality—the unrestricted reach of the call to serve as agents of neighbor love. Every reader of the good Samaritan parable is implicated in the beauty and boundlessness of this love. Every image-bearer is beholden to their "duty" (as both Coffin and Fee describe it) to fulfill the second great commandment. And every Christian, without exception, is constrained by the Samaritan's example to take up the mantle of repair and to "go, and do likewise."

After all, the Samaritan happened upon the wounded man as he journeyed to Jericho, making these two complete strangers, free of debts or personal obligations to one another based on prior encounters. The Samaritan's magnificent display of love emerged not out of a sight and sense of his guilt but of a sight and sense of his neighbor's downtrodden glory, an image-bearer whose healing and wholeness he passionately pursued. In no way was the Samaritan the personal cause of the man's pain, yet he eagerly sought to heal the wounds of theft. He gladly obligated himself to his neighbor's rehabilitation for love's sake alone.

Personal

Still another characteristic of restorative love is that it is personal rather than transactional. When preaching on the good Samaritan in 1951, minister and civil rights leader Howard Thurman cautioned against the temptation to relate exclusively to our neighbor's need. When pursuing our neighbor with Samaritan-like love, Thurman stressed, "we are related to him. To him!" Later in the same sermon, he again emphasized the vitally personal character of neighbor love: "The primary thing is that when I say,

'I love,' it means that I'm involved in an encounter that leads from the core of me to the core of you."[22] King reasoned similarly when he wrote that "pity may represent little more than the impersonal concern which prompts the mailing of a check, but true sympathy is the personal concern which demands the giving of one's soul."[23] Reparations as actuarial calculations simply will not do. The work of restoration demands, in the end, the giving not of a check but of one's soul—the giving of one's very self.

This personal quality can be seen vividly in the way the Samaritan chose to love with his eyes, his heart, and his hands. The work of restoration fundamentally begins with a different way of seeing. The priest and Levite saw the same facts on the road, but the Samaritan, we're told, saw the man—*he saw a man*—and immediately owned his plundered condition. The eyes of his heart ignited a street-level compassion and mercy. "Compassion" is a visceral word. It means to be moved in one's *bowels*, the bowels being thought of in the ancient world as the seat of love. Compassion is suffering *with* a person; it involves feeling someone else's pain in your gut. "Mercy" is a closely related term that refers to compassion blossoming into *action*. Mercy means kindness toward those who suffer, joined with a readiness to do whatever possible to relieve their suffering. This merciful neighbor "decided not to be compassionate by proxy," in King's words; to the contrary, he bound up the man's wounds, pouring on oil and wine as a healing balm and antiseptic. Having already drawn near in his heart, the Samaritan went to him physically—with extended arms, bended knee, bloodied hands, and, after the long journey to the inn, sore feet. His love was personal.

Sacrificial

In describing the richly personal nature of the Samaritan's love, we have already begun to speak of its next characteristic. Restorative love is *sacrificial* in that the Samaritan's actions were both costly and risky. King memorably describes the costliness of neighbor love as an "excessive altruism."[24] Having already allowed a stranger's suffering to interrupt his journey, the Samaritan placed the stranger on his own animal and resumed the trek on foot. He brought the wounded man to an inn where he took care of him overnight, tending to his every need. And on top of this exorbitant expense of time and energy, he also covered the monetary cost of the man's care in its entirety, effectively handing the innkeeper a proverbial blank check. "Whatever more you spend," he promised without condition or qualification, "I will repay you when I come back." In doing so, the Samaritan embraced the possibility of being stuck with an exorbitant tab. In the ancient world, the price of one's stay at an inn was typically unfixed, and innkeepers were "invariably untruthful, dishonest and oppressive."[25] The Samaritan would have known this, of course, but that is how restorative love speaks, with near-reckless generosity: *charge it to me.*

The Samaritan's decisions and deeds were also risky. When preaching the good Samaritan, King would often linger over the risks entailed in such love. He extolled the Samaritan's "dangerous unselfishness,"[26] seen clearly in the way he exposed himself to the lurking robbers and other hazards of the Jericho road. Fear by its nature drives us toward self-preservation, but, King argues, this risk-absorbing commitment to neighbor yields a fundamental redirection of focus from self to other:

> I imagine that the first question which the priest and Levite asked was: "If I stop to help this man, what will happen to me?" But by the very nature of his concern, the good Samaritan reversed the question: "If I do not stop to help this man, what will happen to him?"

He concludes, "The true neighbor will risk his position, his prestige, and even his life for the welfare of others."[27] Understood in this manner, restorative love is inescapably a call to self-renunciation. Even in the case of Zacchaeus, as we saw, it was not only a literal tree branch from which he descended but also a perch of supremacy in his heart. By giving half of his possessions to the poor, Zacchaeus chose—for the first time perhaps—to make himself a servant to his neighbors. The chief collector chose to disinherit himself for the sake of the disinherited. Like the Samaritan, he chose submission, which lies at the heart of the love that reverses the question, tilting the balance of concern in favor of one's neighbor and away from oneself. Rightly understood as a response to God's prodigality toward sinners, restorative love is nothing less than a call to risk-assuming, reckless, self-renouncing sacrifice on behalf of our plundered neighbors.

Supernatural

This leads us to a final characteristic of restorative love. The sacrificiality described above, practiced consistently over time, proves to be, humanly speaking, impossible. It is in many respects supernatural—wrought in human hearts and institutions by a process of profound spiritual transformation. According to Thurman, if we are to be remade into Samaritan-like neighbors in true community, the life of God in us must move to the center of our awareness, and God himself must "invade the normal processes of life."[28] Only by such a spiritually invasive procedure will our eyes be opened to see not only the realities of White supremacy but, more than that, the faces of our neighbors. Only then will our hands, once limp with reluctance or despair, be invigorated for the wholehearted embrace of street-level love.

King likewise acknowledges the necessity of this deep work of God. Speaking of the Samaritan's singular example, he notes that "no law in the world could have produced such unalloyed compassion, such genuine love, such thorough altruism." To the contrary, this superlative neighborliness could only be produced by an "inner law," a "higher law" etched on the human heart; the Samaritan was "obedient to that which could not be enforced" externally or coercively. Though elusive, its potential for social repair is immense: true racial healing and the overthrowing of the "dark and demonic" forces of White supremacy, King argues, will only be achieved by "true neighbors who are willingly obedient to unenforceable obligations."[29] Indeed, the work of reparations assumes a uniquely Christian character when it is a willing response to the unenforceable obligations of love. The moral power that restores our robbed neighbors even at great cost originates far beyond the reach of the laws, customs, and coercions of society, and even the demands of the church. It begins within. And it begins with God.

These are the five characteristics of neighbor love according to the good Samaritan: it is *essential*, *universal*, *personal*, *sacrificial*, and *supernatural*. This love, in turn, is the essence of restoration, its moral foundation and power. In regard to its practice, however, there is a reality that we must come to grasp: we are by nature resistant to the call to love and restore. Overcoming this struggle begins with learning to recognize our moral reluctance. And so we now turn to the unconscionable neglect of our plundered neighbors.

The Neglect of Restoration

As the man lay beaten, robbed, and left for dead, two religious professionals traveled down that same way to Jericho: first a priest, then a Levite. Each saw the human wreckage on the road. Each "passed by on the other side" (Luke 10:31–32). With this disconcerting sequence of events, Jesus dramatically portrays the avoidance and willful neglect of the call to restoration. In all likelihood, he intended for the lawyer to see in these characters a glimpse of himself. No doubt he intends for every one of us to see glimpses of ourselves too.

The struggle to love is basic to the human condition. Even if persuaded that it is essential, universal, and morally beautiful, we regularly circumnavigate real opportunities to love our neighbors as ourselves. This impulse seems to be especially pronounced in our response to the mass robberies of White supremacy. *Why is the work of restoration commonly left undone, even when the effects of theft are in plain sight?* In what follows, we explore four noteworthy answers to this question that are found in the parable and its surrounding narrative: *anxiety*, *casuistry*, *invisibility*, and *hostility*.

Anxiety

The road had a reputation. Everyone knew to watch out for the craggy terrain—the dark corners, blind spots, and caves where marauders would often lie in wait for unsuspecting travelers. When the priest and Levite came upon the crime scene, perhaps they too were gripped by the fear of being ambushed by the same robbers who might still be lurking in the shadows. They *knew* better than to hang around. And so, with eyes darting anxiously about scanning for any sign of danger, they briskly passed by on the other side of the road.

If we are to understand why the call to restoration remains unheeded in our lives and across our nation, we must learn to recognize the deterring power of fear. The Samaritan's example clearly indicates that the work may be exceedingly costly. The same was true of Zacchaeus, who surrendered well over half of his personal assets and, with it, a share of his social wealth and stature. When we perceive the demands of love that restores those so violently despoiled, we recoil at reparations' prospective costs. The threat to our personal identities, histories, and aspirations. The cost to our cultural inheritance. The loss of power and possessions. We might even begin to wish we hadn't seen the ravaged Black bodies in the first place, succumbing perhaps to the temptation to resolve quietly to look no more. All because we are anxious and afraid.

We must be honest about this reality: Reparations remains largely unconsidered not merely because we are unpersuaded by its moral propositions but because we feel threatened by its personal implications. King was right: "If I stop to help this man," we immediately ask, "*what will happen to me?*" And with one more nervous glance about, we step around the half-dead body and continue on our way.

Casuistry

Having been confronted with the costly call to the love of neighbor, the lawyer replies, "*And who is my neighbor?*" (10:29). The question at first appears innocent enough. His reasoning seems to be sensible, and because of its interest in the meaning of scriptural words, even sophisticated and biblical. But Luke provides divine intelligence on its underlying motives: evidently the lawyer desires only "to justify himself." Which is to say, he asks for a more precise definition of neighbor "not so much to determine to whom he must show love, but so as to calculate the identity of those to whom he need *not* show love."[30] He did this in order to vindicate his past failures, as well as his present refusals, to love those around him. Using the parable as a response, Jesus exposes a common way of neglecting the work of restoration: *casuistry that masquerades as moral curiosity.* With pedantic equivocation and oversubtle reasoning—that is, casuistry—we seek to release ourselves from the simple demands of love.

Over the years, when we have spoken on the topic of reparations in both private and public settings, we have been met with a series of questions: *Who will be paid? For what? How much? By whom? How?* Of course, inquiry itself is legitimate and necessary. We wouldn't be writing this book if we did not believe this were so. But the lawyer's example cautions us against inquiry that arises from a self-justifying mind—that is, out of the sole aim of establishing one's innocence and release from personal responsibility. Not all questions seek understanding; not all yield the fruit of obedience. Some questions are veiled attempts at passing by on the other side of the road. We must beware of the self-justifying pedantry that, with fine-sounding arguments and questions, expends great energy in limiting Christian concern for reparations exclusively to those whose culpability as direct descendants of slaveholders can be verified by Ancestry.com. We must be vigilant against the dishonesty and deceptions of the oft-wielded clarifying question.

In raising this question, the lawyer was attempting to manipulate the definition of *neighbor* itself. True, certain Jewish traditions read Leviticus 19:18 in such a way that excluded foreigners (Samaritans among them) from the category of neighbor, and so the debate as to the definition of *neighbor* was in full swing in Jesus's day.[31] In this sense, the lawyer could have defended the question as being biblically legitimate. But legitimacy is not the pressing issue. It's honesty. The text makes it clear that his true motive was to redefine the meaning of *neighbor* in a way that justified his exclusion of certain kinds of people from the reach of neighbor love.

The elaborate contortions of redefining and justifying are not limited, of course, to the designs of one individual lawyer in a distant land two thousand years ago. In 1667, the colony of Virginia passed an act declaring that Christian baptism did not exempt a person from bondage and slavery.[32] What was that declaration but a fundamental redefinition of *neighbor* that justified the continued enslavement of Africans after their baptism? And what was Black animalization, demonization, and infantilization but a fundamental redefinition of *neighbor—from image-bearer to nonperson*—that justified not only the enslavement of Africans but also the subjugation of their descendants in the Jim Crow era? And are we not tempted to do the same even today? Carefully redefining *neighbor* so as to justify our refusals to love? Contorting our words and ways of thinking so as to create a new ethical category, the "non-neighbor"?[33] And having done this redefining, we might pity such individuals when their injuries become visible to us. We might wish it were not so. Yet we feel no enduring responsibility for these non-neighbors or for the healing of their wounds. Indeed, we have made certain that we don't.

Invisibility

The priest and Levite see, but they do not perceive. They are morally blind. They recognize the fact of a problem but fail to behold the face of a person. Still another reason the call to restorative love is neglected is that our neighbors, along with the plain evidence of their plunder, are invisible to us. In previous chapters, we explored the social invisibility of African Americans as one of the most enduring effects of White supremacy in America. The Bible illustrates the spiritual and moral dynamics that undergird that history, and it cautions us against sheltering that invisibility. Left unacknowledged, the "willed forgetting" of our neighbors will continue to serve as a powerful barrier to the vital work of restoration in our time.

According to Jesus's telling of the parable, why did the priest and Levite pass by on the other side? We have already examined one important consideration: fear. Another is that they embodied a unique sociocultural identity marked by ritualism, elitism, and tribalism, which rendered their neighbor invisible to them. By *ritualism*, we mean that they were supremely concerned with maintaining ceremonial purity. It is possible that they refused to help the stripped and beaten man out of concern for religious customs that regulated contact with a dead (or near-dead) body.[34] By *elitism*, we mean that priests and Levites represented a "privileged group in Jewish society."[35] According to Joel Green, they "shared high status in the community of God's people on the account of ascription—that is, not because they trained or were chosen to be priests but because they were born into priestly families."[36] And by *tribalism*, we have in mind the manner in which priests and Levites scrupulously maintained "circumspect boundaries between clean and unclean, including clean and unclean people," thus epitomizing "a worldview of tribal consciousness, concerned with relative status and us-them cataloguing."[37]

These three aspects of their worldview combined to create a fundamental *separateness* from others that was vital to the preservation of their status and identity. And maintaining this *human distance* not only took precedence over the well-being of their neighbor but also rendered certain types of people—the "sinners," the "unclean," "Gentiles," "foreigners"—as socially *invisible* in their eyes. Those people were regarded as threats to purity, and they were to be avoided as nonpersons and violations of boundaries.

They were reduced to a near-subhuman status, no longer neighbors to love. In the words of King, "The priest and Levite saw only a bleeding body, not a human being like themselves. But the good Samaritan will always remind us to remove the cataracts of provincialism from our spiritual eyes and see men as men."[38]

The invisibility of African Americans is a central feature of our racial history. It remains a significant reason why we persist in our collective neglect of their restoration. As we proposed in chapter 3, the goal of White supremacy is not fundamentally to hate African Americans. Its goal is to instrumentalize them, and then, having exploited and exhausted their utility, to render their humanity and its claims upon White Americans utterly invisible. One feature of this comprehensive erasure is the callous normalization of Black carnage, the camouflaging of plundered bodies against the backdrop of White flourishing. We neither see it nor feel it. Though we glance repeatedly at the evidence of the brutality of White supremacy on the roads of American culture, we yet pass by on the other side. Alas, we cannot love what we do not see.

Hostility

Jesus, perceiving the lawyer's desire to limit the scope of neighbor love, casts a Samaritan in the role of the roadside rescuer. In doing so, he thrusts into the narrative spotlight a final reason that the work of restoration is commonly neglected: racial hostility.

The Jews and Samaritans in Jesus's day shared a fierce animosity and a "reciprocal implacable hatred" that occasionally boiled over into outright violence.[39] These hostilities, like the tribal hostilities of our own time, were deeply rooted in the facts and mythologies of their cultural history. Samaritans claimed direct descent from the patriarchs, yet Jews refused to accept them as blood relations. They were believed to have married pagan peoples introduced to the region during the exile, and thus they came to be reviled as "half-breeds" and "foreigners" whom Jewish fathers forbade their children to marry. They also rejected many of the most treasured religious traditions of the Jews—their rituals, their Scriptures, their deepest hopes—and established their own.[40] Samaritans were therefore flatly condemned by Jews as degenerate fools, heretics, and idolaters who were ultimately destined for hell.[41] And the Samaritans returned the favor.

In light of this bitter and complicated history, Jesus's introduction of a Samaritan—*of all people*—as the paragon of neighborly virtue would have scandalized his audience to the utmost. It was a choice in storytelling "as deliberately shocking as if a Southern preacher before the Civil War had set up a black hero to shame the pillars of white society."[42] The story was crafted in this manner, it appears, because Jesus perceived that a Samaritan was *exactly* the sort of person the lawyer sought to exclude from the duty of neighbor love.

In our observation over years of pastoral ministry and study, White Christians have tended to read the good Samaritan parable as being focused primarily on "benevolence" or "mercy" ministry, with the Samaritan's stunning identity as an ancillary feature of the story. Viewed in this light, the parable's lesson is that we should help anyone in their time of need, the poor in particular, and that we should do so by minimizing social difference and "transcending" the barriers of race and religion.[43] But let us remember that the parable was taught in direct response to the lawyer's refusal to recognize people like the Samaritan as neighbors deserving his love. *And Jesus's purpose was to expose how bigotry treats certain plundered neighbors as unworthy of restorative love.* His point was to correct the neglect of the work of restoration on the basis of our hostilities, and to call us to love *in particular* those whom our hostilities condition us not to love. R. T. France argues that what we have in the parable of the good Samaritan is "not primarily a call to universal benevolence." To the contrary, "this parable, properly understood, is one of the most powerful challenges to racism in the Bible."[44]

For the Jewish members of Jesus's audience, the lawyer among them, to love as the Samaritan loved would have required them to reckon with their own hearts, repenting of their refusals to love. To go and do likewise would have required them to reckon with their history of "implacable hatred." After all, when the Samaritan dismounted his donkey to embrace his generationally forsworn enemy, he did not simply "transcend" that long and sordid history of hostility. With open eyes, he walked straight into it. He thrust his healing hands right into it.

The Work of Restoration

Even so, such hostility is not easily overcome. So unyielding is the lawyer's contempt, he can't even bring himself to say "Samaritan" when asked to name the parable's true neighbor. Yet not even he can deny the extraordinariness of the Samaritan's deeds. And what were those deeds? Earlier we proposed that the story portrays his restorative love as essential, universal, personal, sacrificial, and supernatural. We turn our attention presently to the work itself. What did the Samaritan's love actually *do*, and what does the work of restoration endeavor to accomplish? In short, restoration engages in *cultural resistance*, *comprehensive repair*, *mutual neighboring*, and *collective witness*.

Cultural Resistance

To readers both ancient and modern, the Samaritan is an astounding figure—and not simply for his unexpected ethnicity and acts of moral beauty but also for the way his "excessive altruism" and "dangerous unselfishness" stand in spectacular contrast to every other character (besides Jesus) in Luke's narrative. The pedantic evasions of the lawyer. The violent rapaciousness of the robbers. The heartless inhospitality of the priest and Levite. In other words, Jesus presents the Samaritan—a paragon of redemptive, neighborly love—as an *alternative way of living* in a social order that can only be described as antineighbor. Loving his neighbor to the hilt, he represents a form of *cultural resistance*.

This portrayal of neighbor love as countercultural force is found across the Christian Scriptures. The law of Moses, within which Leviticus 19:18 is located, set Israel apart as "self-consciously distinctive from surrounding nations."[45] Jesus often set his teaching on love in deliberate contrast to the norms of his day: "You have heard that it was said: 'You shall love your neighbor and hate your enemy.' But I say to you, Love your enemies and pray for those who persecute you" (Matt. 5:43–44). The apostles likewise preached about love against the backdrop of the misguided "wisdom of this age" (1 Cor. 2:6). According to the Bible, maturity in love entails the ability to recognize love's counterfeits and to resist love's enemies.

In a culture of antineighborliness, then, love calls God's people to be agents of "neighborly rehabilitation." It means seeking to live a life of giving in a world of rapacious taking. It means disengaging from an economy of extraction and embracing in its place "an economics of abundance that is grounded in divine generosity."[46] The parable of the good Samaritan opens with violence, extraction, rapacity, and neglect—with no neighbors in sight. Then along comes an unexpected agent of restoration, the bearer of bandages and balm, offering powerful alternatives to a predatory culture: self-justification is countered with self-denial; fear is countered with risky sacrifice; acquisitiveness is countered with generosity; self-enrichment is countered with sacrificial service; tribalism is countered with magnanimity; invisibility is countered with seeing; superiority is countered with submission; robbery is countered with restoration.

The work of restoration says *no* to antineighborliness and *yes* to neighbor love. Restoration begins with resistance.

Comprehensive Repair

A second dimension of restoration's work is found in love's call to *repair*. The Samaritan's deeds were oriented toward a particular end—it was not the kindly offer of charity, nor the mere alleviation of a man's misery, but the rehabilitation of a wounded and plundered neighbor to his original good condition. The Samaritan repaired the ruinous effects of a violent robbery, binding up the wounds of the traveler's broken body, broken belongings, and broken spirit in order that his stranger-neighbor might be made whole. With submission and sacrifice, the Samaritan generously returned to the neighbor that which had been unjustly taken from him. In the way that the traveler was seen, embraced, and honored as a person to be loved rather than a problem to be avoided, we see the restoration of the stolen truth of the man's dignity. In the healing of his wounds and the rehabilitation of his physical strength, we see the restoration of his stolen bodily agency and power. In the generous supply of fresh garments, transportation, and monetary resources—satisfying a debt not his own—we see the restoration of the traveler's stolen wealth. Indeed, rehabilitative love reverse engineers the harm that has been done at every point. It is not less than economic and material restoration, but it is undoubtedly more. Its reach is comprehensive. The work of restoration entails a thoroughgoing repair of a thoroughgoing theft.[47]

This holistic character of reparations is illustrated vividly in the life of Levi Coffin. During his twenty years in Newport, he and his wife hosted an annual average of one hundred fugitives, a volume that earned their home the nickname "Grand Central Station" of the Underground Railroad. But Coffin's antislavery work also included other efforts that, despite being less well known, should be no less admired. In his early years, for example, he established a Sunday school through which slaves were taught to read the Bible. In his personal businesses, Coffin often employed free Blacks in preference to Whites "because I knew that they were often unjustly refused and neglected."[48] He did this also in part to enable them to purchase and manumit enslaved relatives. In 1847, Coffin moved to Cincinnati to open a wholesale warehouse that sold goods made exclusively by free (non-slave) labor.[49] In 1854, he helped establish an orphanage for African American children. During the Civil War, he assisted with the collection of food for distribution to former slaves in the North. After the war, Coffin sought to help freed slaves to obtain an education and establish their own businesses. He lobbied the federal government for the creation of the Freedmen's Bureau and raised funds for the Western Freedmen's Aid Society, which created hundreds of schools for freedpeople in the South. Through Christian ministry, private enterprise, employment practices, food distribution, education initiatives, political advocacy, fundraising, and not least, radical hospitality in his home, Coffin's entire life was devoted to the repair of the ravages of White supremacy. His work entailed not only the short-term work of humanitarian relief but also the long-term work of investment in individual lives and the institutional work of creating and reforming various agencies and organizations focused on the restoration of freed slaves. It involved not only assisting the plundered traveler on the Jericho road but also what King described as the work of clearing the Jericho road of its robbers and changing "the conditions which make robbery possible."[50]

The point here is not that faithfulness demands that every individual personally take up *every* dimension of racial repair. Rather, we simply propose that Coffin's life, in a vivid and compelling way, gestures toward the far-reaching range of possibilities and many spheres in which restorative love can and must be expressed in the life of the church. After all, the call of reparations is not merely for a check to be written or for a debt to be repaid but for a world to be repaired.

Mutual Neighboring

In speaking of the comprehensiveness of reparations, we are inevitably confronted with the moral and practical complexity of the work. To be sure, a multidimensional and multigenerational theft requires a multidimensional and multigenerational process of healing. And yet it is important to observe that a simple invitation lies at the heart of the parable of the good Samaritan: the call to be a neighbor. Being a neighbor means, in the first place, identifying as a "we." It means embracing the kind of covenantal solidarity that Archbishop Desmond Tutu had in mind when he spoke of the conviction that "my humanity is caught up, is inextricably bound up, in yours."[51] It means being accountable to one another, responsible for one another, and spurred to collective action with one another, not least when one of "us" is robbed. This notion of *neighbor* is, in a sense, profoundly simple. And yet, in the antineighborly culture in which we now live, nothing is harder than to "go and do likewise."

After all, this commitment to the "we" of neighboring is alien to American priorities; it is a threat to our hyperindividualist mindset. We might think, *The despoilment of African Americans is unfortunate but not ultimately my problem—it is their problem*. Alas, with Cain, we retort, "Am I my brother's keeper?" But the voice of his blood cries from the ground. Indeed, I *am* my brother's keeper. His burdens are *mine*. Her injuries and losses are *mine*. Because of our common, image-bearing humanity. Because of covenantal solidarity. Because we are "we."

Reparations is, at its most basic, a call to be a neighbor.

Collective Witness

The final dimension of the work of restoration directs our attention not outward but, in a sense, upward. Jesus's portrait of the good Samaritan offers a richly compelling, if challenging, model of neighbor love. We must "go and do likewise." But it also offers something even more extraordinary.

Earlier in Luke's Gospel, the words *mercy* and *compassion,* both of which are used in reference to the good Samaritan (10:33, 37), are also used of divine prerogatives and divine action.[52] *Mercy* is ascribed to Israel's God: he lifts up the lowly, fills the hungry, helps the helpless, rescues from the hands of one's enemies, and restores light to those living in the shadow of death. The word is also used in reference to Jesus.[53] The same can be said of the word *compassion,* which is mentioned only two other times by Luke: one in reference to the father of the prodigal son, a clear figure of God, and another in reference to Jesus's response to a grieving woman.[54] Thus, when we imitate the Samaritan, engaging the work of restoration, *we in fact imitate God,* representing his character and embodying his story before the watching world. We offer public glimpses into the very heart of God.

In his powerful study on divine generosity, *God So Loved, He Gave,* Kelly Kapic demonstrates how the Christian story of redemption can be retold according to the motifs of generosity and theft. In the beginning, God gave. Then came the fall of humanity, a story of theft: rejecting the generosity of God, the man and woman took what had not been given. The tragedy of the human condition is that this thieving impulse continues in every fallen heart today: "We take what is not given."[55] But if sin is a ruthless taker, God is a relentless giver, and the story of divine generosity climaxes in just this way: "God has reestablished our belonging to him not by taking, but by giving. . . . For God so loved, he gave."[56]

As recipients of God's self-giving love, God's people are called to participate in this story, reflecting God's pattern of working and living as agents of his generosity.[57] When we embrace the risks and costs of neighbor love, we make visible the very life of Jesus, who himself, in King's words, "willingly traveled hazardous roads."[58] When we endeavor to live in obedience to the unenforceable obligations of love, we give public glimpses of Calvary, "history's most magnificent expression of obedience to the unenforceable."[59] When we go to great lengths to restore broken communities, placing the interests of our neighbors before our own, we become visible agents of the cross of Christ, which King described as "an eternal expression of the length to which God is willing to go to restore a broken community."[60] And when we expend ourselves on behalf of our despoiled neighbors, repairing the ravages of White supremacy, we testify to a God of boundless giving in a world of illicit and insatiable taking.

Reparations, in other words, bears witness not simply to our love for our neighbors but to the very love of God for the world.

Owning Restoration

The parable of the good Samaritan, set against the backdrop of the multi-generational cultural theft of White supremacy, makes a crucial contribution to a Christian account of reparations. It reminds us that the work of restoring all that was unjustly taken from our neighbors is the calling not only of the culpable but of all who seek to live a life of love in the world. Because of this, the church in America, a community whose very purpose is love, must own the ethic of restoration and give itself to this work of healing. Indeed, it is the church's vocation both to dress wounds and to redress wrongs.

The American church is called to the work of reparations. This truth is established by the church's fundamental mission in a world ravaged by theft, its complicated history of faithfulness and failure, and its rich moral and scriptural tradition. Yet the question remains: What does this work look like practically? How can churches become communities of repair, taking up the work of reparations in our own communities? It is to these critical street-level questions that we must now turn.

7

The Call to Repair

Tell them that reparations is ultimately redeeming for everyone, both those who give and those who receive; it is an opportunity for all of us to finally be healed.

—Justin Merrick

Toward the Promised Land

On the morning of April 3, 1968, nearly two months into the sanitation workers' strike, Martin Luther King Jr. boarded a plane to Memphis. Few people in his inner circle wanted him to go. Some were concerned about his chronic exhaustion; over the past several years King was hospitalized for exhaustion on four different occasions, and as recently as February he had canceled his engagements and retreated into desperately needed rest. Others were concerned about this being a distraction for him. Earlier in the year King initiated his most ambitious undertaking: the Poor People's Campaign. The goal of this campaign, which reflected King's growing concern about economic inequality, was to gather millions of poor people from across America in Washington, DC, to illustrate the problem of poverty and to advocate for change. In light of such an undertaking, King's aides viewed his trip to Memphis as a distraction at a time when his full energies were required. But perhaps above all, they were concerned about his safety. Just a week before, King was in Memphis to lead a crowd of nearly fifteen thousand people in a nonviolent march from Clayborn Temple to city hall. However, violence erupted as they made their way up Beale Street. As marchers broke store windows, police retaliated with tear gas, beatings, and the shooting of an unarmed Black teenager named Larry Payne with a shotgun at point-blank range. Fearing for King's safety, march leaders swept him into a hotel room where, standing at an upper-story window, he watched police chase his fellow marchers through the streets. In the days since that march, as grief over Payne's death merged with the overwhelming stress of the strike, many Memphians—indeed, many Americans—saw King as the cause of it all. This meant, as both he and his aides well knew, that in addition to being exhausted and distracted, King was also a target.

But he had to go. After all, he reasoned, the sanitation workers' strike was entirely consistent with his goal of the Poor People's campaign. He hoped that it might illustrate the need for such a campaign and catalyze others to join it as well. King also understood that the violence of the last march was being used as a pretext for people to question both the integrity and the efficacy of his commitment to nonviolence. Watching television coverage of the march, King said, "This is terrible. Now we'll never get anybody to believe in nonviolence."[1] Only by returning to Memphis and leading a nonviolent march could he demonstrate the possibilities of love. Without this, King believed that both the sanitation workers' strike and the Poor People's Campaign would fail. Most importantly, however, King believed that his friends in Memphis and the sanitation workers needed help. He well remembered the long and discouraging days of the Montgomery bus boycott over a decade earlier and how important such outside support was to him. He believed that he, like the good Samaritan, was morally bound to bring such support to others in need. As he put it in a speech the night of his arrival, "The question is not, 'If I stop to help this man in need, what will happen to me?' The question is, 'If I do not stop to help the sanitation workers, what will happen to them?'"[2] And so he went.

The details of the following two days are horribly familiar. King spent the better part of April 3 at the Lorraine Motel seeking assurances from local leaders that the march would, in fact, be nonviolent. Later that evening, King went out into a storm to address a crowd of thousands gathered at Mason Temple. As he had done thousands of times over the years, he encouraged his hearers to continue in the struggle for justice, consoled them that, though there would be "some difficult days ahead," they "as a people will get to the promised land," and assured them that as he considered their struggle, "mine eyes have seen the glory of the coming of the Lord." They were the last public words he would ever speak. The following day, April 4, as he stood on the balcony of the Lorraine Motel joking with friends, an assassin shot Martin Luther King Jr. in the face.[3]

The years following King's murder were unkind to Memphis, and especially unkind to the neighborhoods that once nurtured the sanitation workers' strike. Many Black Memphians moved away. Many who stayed were herded into public housing projects created in the urban renewal movements of the 1970s and 1980s. White Memphians fled to the eastern part of the city, taking their money and institutions with them. As a result, the Black neighborhoods in the heart of downtown Memphis, neighborhoods that once boasted the nation's first Black millionaire, began to disintegrate. The zip code that birthed one of the most important struggles for economic justice in the twentieth century became, in a few short years, the poorest zip code in the entire state of Tennessee. And it remains so today. Memphis, a city with a 64 percent Black population, is the poorest metropolitan area of its size in the nation. Its workers, like the sanitation workers, continue to struggle with wages that are significantly lower than in other parts of the country. And the median household income (to say nothing of wealth) of Black Memphians remains half that of Whites. King may have seen the promised land, but Memphis has yet to see it.

One poignant illustration of the fate of Memphis is Clayborn Temple. This church, home to the sanitation workers' strike and located in the very heart of downtown Memphis, was once the largest church south of the Ohio River and the critical center of a thriving Black community. But after King's murder, as the economy of downtown Memphis failed, and with it the institutions that sustained the Black community, Clayborn Temple closed its doors and fell into almost total ruin. Its organ was silenced. Its pews were removed. Its windows were boarded up. Its ceiling and floors succumbed to moisture and mold. Its entrance was blocked by a large wooden fence. And its surrounding streets, once vibrant with thousands of people seeking social transformation, were largely abandoned.

In July 2018, Anasa Troutman—a brilliant and charismatic African American woman in her mid-forties—moved to Memphis to lead an organization dedicated to the restoration of Clayborn Temple and its service to Memphis's Black community. After nearly twenty years working as a leader in the music industry and in movement building, Troutman instinctively understood both the creative possibilities and the strategic importance of a renewed Clayborn Temple in reviving the heart of downtown Memphis. But as a person, a human being longing for justice, her draw to Clayborn was much more personal. It was a calling. As she put it, "When I walked into the building for the first time I saw so much magic, so much history, and so much possibility. I saw all of the stories the building was holding, that the building was still alive, that she wanted to be able to serve our community."[4] To that end, Troutman became executive director of Historic Clayborn Temple and, after a year of grueling labor, led the organization's successful purchase of the building and, with a team around her, began the long-awaited work of restoration. "I can't explain what that did for me, to purchase a building that was sacred black space to be returned to and used for the liberation of black people in Memphis. I've never done anything more important than that," she says through tears, "and I might never."

Troutman's important work at Historic Clayborn Temple is multifaceted: it includes historic preservation, health and wellness programs, community engagement, economic development, and artistic production. But at its heart, her work is about one thing: reparation. Her work aims to comprehensively repair a community ravaged by White supremacy and abundantly return all that was taken away.

Centering Other Voices

Our goal over the past six chapters has been twofold. First, to persuade our readers that because of the nature of American White supremacy, we need reparations in order for healing to be possible, not merely personal repentance, relational reconciliation, or institutional reform (although each of those is also needed). Second, to call churches to embrace this work of reparations, and to do so as an expression of its historical culpability, moral heritage, and missional calling. To support churches in this work, our goal for this final chapter is to gesture toward some steps in this direction. To do that we must begin by centering voices other than our own.

In the introduction to this work we noted that, by its very nature, the conversation around reparations includes two parties: those who owe reparations and those to whom reparations are owed. Our part in this conversation is the first. We see it as our responsibility to acknowledge the truth of our collective history and our own culpability in it, to surface ethical resources in the Christian tradition that can help us engage the consequences of this history, and to call others in the church to take up the work of reparations in their own communities. However, the specific shape that reparations ought to take, and the concrete ways in which the American theft of truth, power, and wealth is to be repaired, is properly the work of those on the other side of the conversation. In this conversation, we believe that our place, as people who have not suffered the deprivations of White supremacy as African Americans have, is not to lead but to follow, to let our voices give way to the voices of others.

One of the most important (and rewarding) parts of this project has been the work of listening—through personal interviews, panel discussions, and lectures—to creative and inspiring African Americans, like Anasa Troutman, who are working to repair the ravages of White supremacy. This chapter is a synthesis of the ideas explored in this book, using interviews and conversations with African American leaders in various communities throughout the United States. We will be drawing insights from these leaders, who include Anasa Troutman, Taj James, David Bailey, Justin Merrick, and Nwamaka Agbo. In various contexts around the country, each of these women and men share some core convictions that bear powerfully on both the theory and the practice of reparations. Each, for example, believes that the work of reparations is *comprehensive*, that it requires redress of truth, power, and wealth.[5] They see, in other words, that reparations is most truly understood as multidimensional cultural repair. Each also believes that reparative work is fundamentally *local*, that reparations ought to privilege the ideas and agency of local communities. This is not to say that they fail to see larger institutional, national, and multinational horizons for this work. But in each case, their principal commitment to local empowerment and their practical commitment to getting things done gives each a decidedly place-based character. Last, each views reparations not merely in structural or material terms but in deeply *spiritual* terms. Each believes that reparations is an act that requires, and actually enables, personal transformation and healing—both for those who give and for those who receive. For these reasons—their commitment to comprehensive repair, local action, and spiritual transformation—we believe that these women and men are perfectly positioned to serve as guides to Christian institutions committed to the work of repair. In what follows, our hope is simply to introduce our readers to those voices and to ask our readers to listen and, in the end, to follow them on the way.

In doing so, however, we are conscious of a certain tension. It might seem strange, in a book that calls for reparations *to* African Americans, that our primary examples are of work done *by* African Americans. Indeed, this initially felt strange to us. Yet we nonetheless decided to proceed for two reasons. First, and most important, is that doing so was the explicit and consistent advice of the African American leaders with whom we discussed this work. They felt, and we feel, that in taking up the work of reparations, White Americans ought to look not simply to their own instincts but to the instincts of African Americans, to not simply set out on a path but to walk on a path set for them by others. In doing this, White Americans take the first and foundational step of the work of reparations: the renunciation of control. Our decision to highlight the work of African American leaders, then, is best understood as an attempt to center the repeated advice and the reparative work of African Americans as a pattern for our own work of reparations. Second, examples of White Americans—and certainly White churches—self-consciously involved in the work of reparations are few and far between. Those few that have taken up this work, while important, do not always reflect the *comprehensive* (truth, wealth, and power), *local* (serving a specific community), and *spiritual* (emphasizing the necessity of spiritual transformation) priorities emphasized by our African American colleagues. Because of this, our intention is to elevate the work of these colleagues in hopes that churches across the United States will take up the burden of becoming a people of repair.

A People of Repair

White supremacy, though complicated in its expression and incalculable in its harm, is nonetheless reducible, as all evil things are, to a small and dark singularity: the failure to love. It is not just a social system but a spiritual sickness, a way of being human that poisons everything it touches: minds, hearts, bodies, cities, worlds. This way of being has, in one way or another, poisoned each of us individually and all of us together. Because of this, the work of reparations requires us not simply to restructure our social worlds but fundamentally—and perhaps more painfully—to restructure our inner worlds as well.

In saying this, it is not our intention to suggest that the work of reparations is primarily a work that happens inside of White people for the sake of their spiritual good. We insist, however—as all our collaborators have— that *reparations, if it is to be fully itself, must be rooted in a new way of being that expresses itself in a new way of living.* As Anasa Troutman puts it, "Reparations is a way of being a person that honors your connection to another. . . . It is an expression of love." The call to reparations, in other words, requires us to make different kinds of choices and to be different kinds of people, to be people of repair.

But how do we become such people? How do we, in the midst of "a world organized around violence, domination, and extraction," heal from this sickness? How do we become people capable of and committed to the reparative work of love? In asking this question to our colleagues, we learned that the poison of White supremacy can only depart our bodies— and our body politic—if we give ourselves to four spiritual commitments: *the vulnerability of community*, *the humiliation of truth*, *the renunciation of control*, and *the revaluation of wealth*.

The Vulnerability of Community

"White supremacy is built on two lies," says Taj James, "separation and supremacy." In James's account, the first of these tells us that we differ from one another in nature, and the second tells us that we differ from one another in value. As we have seen, these lies are deeply embedded in American culture, and their power is evident everywhere: in enslavement, segregation, and the legacy of estrangement that shadows us all. Through his work as a partner at Full Spectrum Capital Partners, James pursues another world "built on resilience, regeneration, and—perhaps above all—interdependence."[6] It is a world fundamentally defined not by bellicose otherness but by a mutuality that is at once sacrificial and abundant. James points to one of the foundational characteristics of a people of repair: a commitment to the vulnerability of community.

Community is difficult in any circumstance; to create and sustain it is an achievement worthy of honor. But it is especially difficult in the context of an American nation marked by a legacy of pervasive multigenerational theft perpetrated by one group against another, a context in which the manifold harms of theft are alive among us. In this context, it is tempting to go with the grain of White supremacy and to remain within the familiar, though pathological, boundaries it creates between us. The work of reparations, however, requires more than this. It requires a people who are willing to step beyond the borders of White supremacy and step toward one another into an unfamiliar world. And it requires a people willing to labor together to create a new space whose boundaries run not *between* us but *around* us in a new circumference of community.

This work, however, can feel deeply vulnerable. For many White Americans, this vulnerability primarily takes the shape of fear, born of an almost total absence of deep relationships with Black communities: The fear of not knowing what to think, say, or do. The fear of doing something wrong. The fear of looking foolish. The fear of anger. The fear of shame. The fear of rejection. The fear of feeling out of control. These powerful fears often lead White Americans to overcompensate, to shut down, or to simply remain apart. For many Black Americans, there is a vulnerability that expresses itself primarily in exhaustion. This exhaustion, born of a constant exposure to the vicissitudes of White culture, has many forms: The exhaustion of the mere fact of the conversation. The exhaustion of explaining the obvious, yet again. The exhaustion of being used as a tool for assuaging White guilt. The exhaustion of being retraumatized. The exhaustion of impending disappointment. The accumulated exhaustion of years.

Neither White fear nor Black exhaustion is wrong. Both reflect the very real risks of community; the fears will sometimes come true, the exhaustion will sometimes compound. And there are times in everyone's life in which the prospect of pain is simply too much, when the vulnerabilities are too, well, vulnerable. In such times, it is wise and loving to step away from the risks of community and to take the time necessary to work, rest, and heal. And we must give one another both the grace and the space to do so. Even so, if the work of reparations is to succeed, this time of healing, rather than being a rejection of community, must finally be in the service of it, must ultimately lead us back toward the vulnerability of community that love requires. As Anasa Troutman puts it, "Reparations begins with the acknowledgment that we are all connected, that we harm and are harmed, that we need to restore the other person, do the work to help make them whole so that they have the same access to love, wealth, and choices that we have. Reparations is fundamentally relational work."

One of the most important roles churches can play in the work of reparations is the cultivation of communities of vulnerability. This work calls the church to cultivate a *spirituality of vulnerability*. The church can nurture a way of living with ourselves, with God, and with others where our deepest wounds are not concealed by but centered in the life of faith. Sadly, for many Christians, formed to conceive of the Christian life as a defensive display of strength, this emphasis on vulnerability may seem embarrassing, unsettling, or dangerous. The truth, however, is that this kind of life—a life in which we refuse to armor our vulnerabilities but instead open them in love to God and to one another—is precisely the life that faith, hope, and love open to us. This life frees us from the fear of being seen, from the inability to listen, and from the addictive need to be right. Because of this, if churches are to participate in the work of reparations, they must—in sermon, in song, in spiritual care—equip people with the theological vision, emotional capacity, and formative practices necessary to live with others in mutual vulnerability.

In another equally important respect, the vulnerability of community calls churches to create *structures for community*. As we have seen, the Christian church in America exists in a cultural context whose very DNA is estrangement, a context in which generations of personal and institutional habit conspire to keep us apart. Sadly, many Christians seem either locked in their own worlds and unaware of this estrangement or simply resigned to its power. The Christian faith, however, founded as it is on the eternal communion of the Father, Son, and Spirit, renounces estrangement and pursues reconciliation. Indeed, the church is a community whose very life is anchored in and modeled on the one in whom all things are reconciled. Because of this, churches have a moral responsibility and a missional opportunity to create structures—liturgical, sacramental, educational, recreational, convivial—that seek directly and deliberately to overcome the estrangements of White supremacy through a renewal of Christian community. Taj James reminds us that it is only in community that we "can experience the spiritual transformation of release from the lies of separation and supremacy." Only in relationship with others can the work of reparations begin.

The Humiliation of Truth

In addition to being a sickness of the spirit, White supremacy is also an account of the world. This account proposes that human beings are fundamentally defined by race, that Whiteness, by virtue of an alleged personal and moral capacity, is the superior race, and that the benefits of the social order ought to reflect this reality. This account is rooted in violence, justified by romantic myth and deliberate erasure, and embedded in both our private imaginations and our common life. This account is everywhere around us: in the speeches of our leaders, in the statues on our corners, in the practices of our institutions, and in the habits of our hearts. And it is also an utter lie.

In the Church Hill neighborhood in the East End of Richmond, Virginia, David Bailey—along with his friends and neighbors—spends his days seeking to free people from the power of this lie. Through his work with Arrabon and Urban Doxology, Bailey gives talks, leads seminars, and produces material designed to equip communities with the historical knowledge and emotional capacity necessary for the work of repair.[7] Bailey's work points to the second characteristic of a people of repair: a willingness to brave the humiliations of truth.

The ability to open one's self to truth, especially when the truth is painful and requires change, is a hard-won skill of the heart. The challenge is greater when one's nation, and even church, embraces romanticized autobiographies that obscure the truth. And it is a still greater challenge when one's identity, like the church's, is firmly and publicly rooted in the presumption that we are devoted to truth. When threatening truths bear down on us, it is tempting to take shelter inside our consoling half-truths and to close our eyes to everything else. The work of reparations, however, requires people who are committed to seeing beyond the warm glow of romanticized mythology and willing to live in the full light of the truth about themselves and about the world. And it requires people who are willing to labor to deconstruct the lies that serve the dark.

This work, however, is humiliating—especially for many in the White community. As we noted in chapter 1, the truth calls into question some of our most instinctive individual assumptions about our identities, our histories, and our aspirations. And it also calls us to the extremely difficult and ongoing work of reframing our understanding of our lives and living in light of this new frame. Even under the best of circumstances, this work is inevitably marked by overwhelming confusion, shame, and grief. All who walk this path must be prepared for this experience. Bailey notes, "This is hard work because a lot of Christian communities don't have tools to handle the emotional challenges that come from facing the truth." Even so, it is important that, in spite of this pain, we remain open to the truth and let ourselves be healed by it. And not only ourselves but the world around us. Reparations, after all, is not driven by the bondage of shame but by the freedom that comes from living in light of the truth.

In the work of reparations, churches can cultivate a relentless commitment to the truth, even when it is painful. As with the work of community, this has both a spiritual and a structural horizon. Spiritually, the church must deliberately cultivate the *capacity for humility*. This is not as easy as it may seem. In spite of the American church's broad affirmation of humility as a spiritual virtue, the painful fact of the matter is that one of the most broadly evident characteristics of the American church is pride: an intellectual pride that refuses to listen; a moral pride that hastens to condemn; and a political pride that beguiles us with the conviction that we are on the right side of history. Each of these forms of pride are not merely characteristics of a particular demographic or generation. In our experience, they are broadly characteristic of the church as a whole. The peril of this pride is that it blinds us to the truth and closes us off from the interrogations of reality and the inconveniences of love. The remedy for this pride is the deliberate cultivation of a deep humility of the mind and heart—a willingness to stop, listen, consider, and change. As Nwamaka Agbo puts it, "In order to bring about healing and wholeness we need to pause, reflect, and understand the patterns that got us here and then begin a place of having conscious choice about doing something different."[8]

Structurally, this requires the church to create *contexts for truth*. The Christian church in America exists in a cultural context that is predicated upon self-deceit. The foundation of the Christian faith, however, is the unwaveringly true word of God made known in Jesus, and this faith's precondition is the falling of scales from dishonest eyes. Churches ought to reflect this reality by creating deliberate contexts for truth telling. Naturally, this will include preaching, worship, and education. But without deliberate effort, even these activities can simply become venues for telling ourselves what we want to hear. Thus churches also ought to create contexts in which they can listen to speakers, writers, and neighbors who are willing to tell us those truths that we desperately need to hear. As David Bailey reminds us, reparations cannot truly take shape until we are "spiritually formed and emotionally transformed" into a people who embrace the truth.

The Renunciation of Control

White supremacy's central impulse and most urgent need is control. From its very beginning, it has sought to control bodies, labor, wealth, land, and heaven itself. White supremacy is, quite simply, a social order driven by the pathology of its own omnipotence whose destinarian ambitions to control the world amounted to little more than the metastasization of vice. One of its most evident social results is the concentration of every kind of power into the hands of a few and the correlative disempowerment of the many.

As Justin Merrick leaves his apartment in racially mixed midtown Memphis and drives the two miles to his office in the historically Black neighborhood of Binghampton, he sees the ways in which this uneven distribution of power takes concrete form. "Because of the disempowering effect of white supremacy," he says, "many people in my community do not have access to the social and political power necessary to change their lives. Honestly, many of them can't even really imagine a world in which such power, or such change, is possible." Merrick, however, can imagine such a world. When he looks at his community, he sees an enormous amount of talent, beauty, and energy that simply needs support. In his role as executive director of the Center for Transforming Communities in Memphis, Merrick and his team—through community meetings, events, and workshops—help people in neighborhoods around Memphis to "see and grow their ability to make decisions that impact their own lives and to create contexts in which they can meaningfully share in the process of shaping their own communities."[9] When asked what his community most needed from political, business, philanthropic, and ecclesial leaders who, though living largely outside of these communities, nonetheless exert enormous influence over them, his answer was simple: "They have to share power." This points to the third foundational characteristic of a people of repair: the commitment to renounce control.

As with the vulnerability of community and the humiliation of truth, this commitment to the renunciation of control is extremely difficult. It is difficult individually: many of us have spent our lives pursuing the illusion of control and seeking to force our will on everything, from our bodies to our children to our vocational lives. Indeed, there is often a great deal of shame associated with appearing to lose control. This commitment is even more difficult communally. Many of us are part of a church community that reinforces this illusion in both the rhythms of its life and its posture toward the world. And so we are tempted to close our hands more tightly in an attempt to maintain some semblance of control. The work of reparations, however, requires people who give themselves to the emancipatory work of renunciation, out of a deep confidence in God, a humble trust in others, and an honest assessment of the limits of our own agency.

Another important role for the church—a role that, again, expresses itself both spiritually and structurally—is the work of renunciation. Spiritually, this role requires deep attention to our language—even our theological language—and to the ways in which we use it to take over others. It requires sustained exploration of our emotions and of the inner places we go when our sense of control is threatened. It requires the development of practices—reading, praying, confessing, and absolving—to which we submit as a part of our transformation. And it requires the cultivation of spiritual relationships in which we submit to one another in love and follow one another as guides along the way. Structurally, this requires churches to think seriously about our models of leadership, about our processes of decision-making, about the people who we include or exclude in these spaces, and about the missiological import of sharing power in our common life. It also requires us—as a community—to think about the ways in which we seek to exert our control over our neighbors and our larger communities. In doing this, we will not only form ourselves into people who, through our renunciation of control, bear integral witness to the sovereign care of God; we will also create a context in which we can truly—and collaboratively—participate in the work of reparations. Taj James reminds us, "The essence of reparations is giving up control."

The Revaluation of Wealth

White supremacy, as we saw in chapter 3, is rooted in a fundamentally objectifying and extractive view of the world in which goods are held by right, accumulated by power, and held in exclusive perpetuity by those who are White. This view of the world is the headwaters of both the unimaginable wealth and the unending poverty of our communities. Nwamaka Agbo, however, views the world and its wealth differently. In her view, the world is not simply a resource to be extracted but a gift to be stewarded with others. Further, the obligations of this stewardship are not fundamentally defined by one's ability to accumulate but by one's responsibility to collaborate with others for the well-being of all. She calls this vision a "we economy," and it animates her work to support communities in the movement, "from extraction to regeneration and from accumulation to shared prosperity." This is the heart of what Agbo describes as "restorative economics." Her work points to the fourth commitment of a people of repair: the commitment to revalue wealth.[10]

Revaluing wealth means deliberately reframing the way in which we understand its meaning and purpose. Doing so requires us to question what wealth is, why we have it, why we have the amount of it that we do, and what love asks us to do with it. And then we must transform our lives in a way that accords with the answers. For Agbo, this means a fundamental shift away from White supremacy's conception of wealth as an object of extraction and toward a vision of wealth as a tool for the well-being of ourselves and our neighbors. As with the other commitments, this call to revalue wealth is difficult to embrace. It is difficult on an individual level because our identities, our relationships, and our visions of our lives and our children's lives are all deeply bound to the wealth we possess. The call to rethink wealth and to conceive of its value differently can seem deeply threatening. This sense of threat is only compounded by the fact that we live in the wealthiest society in the history of the world, and this society was built on and remains embedded in the logic of extraction. It becomes easy for us to simply stay within the material script we have received, to never seriously reflect on the real meaning of wealth, and to never let that reflection change how we live in the world.

The work of reparations, however, requires this revaluation. Indeed, this work cannot be possible without it. If the church is to be a people of repair, it must deliberately take up the work of revaluing wealth in its communities. Spiritually, this requires us to attend to the rich Christian scriptural and theological tradition regarding wealth, to undertake honest self-reflection about our own habits of extraction and accumulation, and to cultivate foundational practices of having transparency about our wealth and giving that wealth to others so that they might be whole. Unless we become the kind of people who, in Taj James's words, understand that "giving wealth is a spiritual practice," we will never be a people of repair. Structurally, this revaluation means that churches as a whole need to create regular spaces for Christian teaching, not just on money management but on the deep meaning of wealth and its role in the works of love. It also requires churches to have transparent deliberative processes for the accumulation and distribution of wealth, keeping this part of its life open to God and to one another. Perhaps most importantly, all of our colleagues suggest that revaluation requires churches to give in ways that, rather than prioritizing our pet projects, actually prioritize the needs of "communities most impacted by economic disinvestment and political disenfranchisement."[11] Churches must give in ways that deliberately target the damage wrought by White supremacy. For it is only as we do these things that we can become a people capable of taking up the practices of repair.

The Practices of Repair

Faced with these spiritual commitments necessary to become a people of repair—the vulnerability of community, the humiliation of truth, the renunciation of control, and the revaluation of wealth—one might understandably wish to end the conversation here. We have often wished for this reprieve in our own lives. The problem is that we have not yet arrived at the actual work of reparations. After all, the goal is not simply to be a people capable of reparative work. We want to be a people who actually do this work in the world. *Becoming a people of repair and engaging the practices of repair are to be done simultaneously.* Troutman says, "Taking care of other people can't simply wait on personal growth; we can't sit by and allow people to starve and die while we sit in our book clubs. Self-transformation and service are parallel to one another." We turn now to an exploration of the practices of reparations.

Before we do, there are two important caveats. First, this book frames both theft and reparations in terms of three distinct categories: truth, power, and wealth. Though this distinction is historically true and useful practically, the fact of the matter is that each of these is in practice indivisible from and dependent on one another; they exist in a symbiotic system. For example, it is common practice today for ecclesial and philanthropic communities to invest significant resources into Black communities. This work is important, but these resources and the process for determining their use are largely controlled by White people living outside the community. While these resources may be useful in repairing wealth, the process by which they are distributed inadvertently reinforces the theft of power.[12] Those who take up the work of reparations must work diligently to address all of these: truth, wealth, and power. To do less is to subvert the work of repair.

The second caveat: because each of these areas of redress is complex, and even more complex in aggregate, what follows is best understood not as a step-by-step guide to reparations, and certainly not as anything approaching a plan, but simply a framework. There are resources that propose explicit plans for reparations, and we believe that churches should read and reflect on them.[13] Because the reparations conversation is only minimally understood in the American church today, we (and those we interviewed) believe that the most important task of this book is to gesture toward the types of moral and practical instincts necessary for such steps to emerge naturally and to be carried out effectively. In what follows we seek simply to provide church communities with categories for reflection and trajectories for action. The work of living into these categories and following these trajectories is work we must finally do together.

Repairing Truth

As you walk up the sidewalk toward the gate of the National Memorial for Peace and Justice in Montgomery, Alabama, both you and the people walking beside you instinctively grow quiet. You are on the threshold of something sacred, and you know that silence is, in its own way, a form of telling the truth. As you enter, a long walkway stretches before you, showing you the path you must walk. It is filled with large brown metal rectangles hanging from the ceiling and greeting you at eye level. "Look," they seem to say. Leaning in, you notice words: states, counties, names, dates. These are the people murdered by lynching in America, and these are the places where these murders took place. You know that place. Wait, you know that one too. But you can't wait. Sensing a line forming behind you, you walk forward, passing pillar after pillar, name after name, place after place, too many to take in, too many not to take in. Realizing you can't read every one, you decide to touch them instead: maybe that will be enough. Soon you notice that the floor has begun to slope downward. With every step you take the pillars begin to rise above you, your progress causing their rising. You stop. You walk backward hoping, absurdly, that if you walk far enough, they might come down again. But they cannot come down. You can only walk forward. Soon they are high above, the names, places, and dates passing overhead in rows that bear down on you with infinite force. Seeking the refuge of open air, you follow a path to what looks like a garden on a hill in the middle of the memorial. You clamber up the stairs and look around. They are all here, on all sides. You see, for the first time, all of them at once. All of these men and women whose bodies were seized, hanged, burdened, torn apart, and discarded are now raised before you in fixed and immovable solidity. They bear witness. You bear witness. Your silence gives way.

This memorial, erected by the Equal Justice Initiative in 2018, is an important illustration of the work of repairing the truth in the wake of American White supremacy, and it suggests that there are three tasks for all who wish to take up this work as their own.

Acknowledging the Truth

As we noted in chapter 3, White supremacy is rooted in and nourished by cherished myth sustained by a romanticized self-conception and the willful erasure of difference. Because of this, one of the first acts of the repair of truth is simply acknowledgment. Acknowledgment is an act of repudiation, an act of purposefully saying "no, this isn't true" to the allure of our own mythology. But perhaps more importantly, acknowledgment *speaks* the liberating, if terrible, truth about ourselves and about the people we are.

This is what the EJI memorial does: it repudiates the lie that these people didn't matter and so could be murdered with impunity, and it embraces the truth that they had dignity and deserve justice. Churches can do this as well. In our sermons, our songs, our prayers. In congregational statements. In the work of leading citywide initiatives to formally, publicly, and fully tell the truth about the reality of White supremacy in our midst. We can and must do it. Neither we nor our neighbors will ever be free from the lie until we do. As Anasa Troutman puts it, "We have been lying to ourselves about the totality of our core values. Yes, we can make an argument for brotherhood and freedom, but if you look back at the history of our country, at its founding, this country doesn't exist without genocide, destruction, and subjugation. In order to make the leap from who we are to who we want to be we have to deal with that."

Recovering the Truth

The lie of White supremacy was not simply one lie but an assembly of lies gathered and bound together across the centuries to fashion the world we see. This means that *the work of repairing the truth is a lifelong process of recovery, not a one-time act of acknowledgment.* This approach is modeled in the memorial. For years, researchers and volunteers labored to recover the names, places, circumstances, and even the soil from the lynching of Black Americans. And they continue to do so to this day. Likewise, the church can be a community that labors to recover truths hidden by White supremacy. We can labor to recover the truth about Black leaders in the history of our own faith, men and women who have been largely forgotten because of years of indifference and neglect. We can labor to recover the truth about the history of Black churches in our own communities. One of the sad realities of American Christianity is that because of the legacy of White supremacy, many White Christians know more about the church in Iran than they do about the Black church down the street. One of the most important ways to overcome this deficiency is to learn, for the first time, the powerful histories of our Black brothers and sisters in our own communities. Last, we can collaborate with our neighbors and our city leaders to recover the history of the Black community in our cities, much of which has been lost through the careless disregard that has marred so much of our urban development. In this we can participate in the long, painful, but ultimately redemptive process of listening to voices long buried and letting them speak again.

Memorializing the Truth

Perhaps most importantly, however, we must give ourselves to the work of memorializing the truth, of creating stories, spaces, and structures that bear living witness to the resurrection of a long crucified history. Memorialization is at the heart of Troutman's own approach, which she calls "cultural strategy," the use of storytelling for social transformation. She says, "Healing requires that we create new stories for people to step into and new ways for us to see ourselves more clearly. Our work is to interrupt the dominant narrative and replace it with something new. The stories we tell ourselves are the basis of it all." David Bailey agrees: "We have to use storytelling to create a new imagination for the world we are trying to build." This approach is clearly evident in the memorial: having recovered the truth of these murders, it tells the victims' stories in books, photographs, film, and ultimately a deliberately structured space for encounter and contemplation.

Churches, too, can participate in memorialization. Having recovered truths, we can collaborate to make these truths known in a host of ways. In addition to telling these stories in our sermons and liturgies, we can sponsor artists—filmmakers, musicians, painters—who can tell these stories. Further, we can collaborate with others in our community to build actual memorials, enduring expressions of public art that can transform our civic landscapes into theaters of truth, bearing permanent witness against the lie.[14] This is just the beginning of what is possible. Churches must give themselves to this work as a fundamental act of healing our world from the original and enduring lie of White supremacy. As Taj James reminds us, "if people stop believing the stories, the systems based on the stories will collapse."

Repairing Power

On a recent spring evening in Memphis, a group of about two hundred people made their way into a church fellowship hall. They sit at round tables decorated with flowers, stocked with notepads and pens, and rimmed with eight chairs each. To the side are other tables filled with food and drinks and tended by welcoming hosts. This event, cosponsored by Historic Clayborn Temple and the Center for Transforming Communities, is a community meeting, in which people from neighborhoods across the city gather to talk with one another about how they might collaborate to create, in King's words, "a new Memphis." After a brief introduction, the attendees—women and men, White and Black, wealthy and poor—sit at tables talking and listening to one another. They write down ideas. They share them with the group. They collectively agree on next steps. And they walk one another to cars where they share rides home. This is in very many ways an ordinary event, one that takes place in cities around the country every week. But it is also a powerful reminder of the specific types of work needed to repair power.

Seeing Power

One of the essential features of White supremacy is the determination not to see, or to pretend not to see, the reality of Black power. Indeed, much of the history of America has been the history of either denying or demonizing that power, even while exploiting it for personal gain. This practice continues to this day. Many White communities—including churches—because they are not in deep relationships with Black communities, continue to think of those communities primarily in diminished terms, to fail to see their power. One of the most important tasks for White Americans is to learn to see Black communities anew and, in the words of Taj James, to "honor their capacity for self-governance and self-direction." This is what was happening at the community meeting: White Memphians sat at tables listening to and learning from Black Memphians. In doing so, they were able to see what history had conspired to hide: the beauty, brilliance, creativity, and power of their Black neighbors. This is what churches must do as well. Many largely White churches in America have a heart for serving local Black communities. But sadly, many do so in a way that reflects utter ignorance of the strengths—the assets—that exist there. This ignorance is not without consequence: because we do not know the true character of Black communities, we often act in ways that are more damaging than helpful, even as we sincerely intend otherwise. As Justin Merrick notes, "No matter how well-intentioned the work, when churches come with a savior lens, it actually inhibits healing in the community. Shared decision-making is foundational to human healing." Churches can overcome this by beginning missional conversations with Black leaders at the table, listening to their voices, and following where they lead.

Bringing Power

For many White communities, the fear of being paternalistic is so strong that it can lead to a form of disengagement. Unable to take the typical place of leadership, and afraid to do harm, we simply drift away. This impulse, though understandable, misses the mark. The work of repairing power does not mean withholding it in fear but instead bringing it with a commitment to equality and collaboration. Because of the history of White supremacy, and the inequitable distribution of power that resulted from it, Black communities, though having real power resident within themselves, can nonetheless benefit greatly from the resources and networks that White communities take for granted. To withhold these is to compound the harm. We need the willingness to bring power in a different way. Churches have a responsibility to bring our various forms of vocational, relational, and financial power to our Black neighbors, and to do so in a spirit of deliberate and equitable collaboration so that our power is both under the direction of others and used for their good.[15]

Enabling Power

One of the most debilitating elements of White supremacy is how it enables and requires the active diminishment of Black agency in the world. This diminishment has expressed itself in a host of ways: chains of bondage, structures of exclusion, and habits of marginalization. Because of this, the work of reparations must cultivate the sustained and deliberate process of enabling Black empowerment. This is precisely the work of community meetings such as the one that took place in Memphis: while there were many different people in the room, the clear purpose was the aggregation of agency in the interest of those disempowered by White supremacy. And this is the work of churches as well. Churches that wish to engage in the work of repair must understand that our work is deliberately to undertake the work of empowering those whom White supremacy has harmed. We must ask ourselves, as Anasa Troutman puts it, "What kind of infrastructure is necessary to empower black people?"[16] Internally, this calls churches to reflect not only on the people we hire and the leaders we nurture but also on the voices we invite and the initiatives we support. Externally, it requires us to prioritize partnerships with the historically disempowered and to enter into these partnerships with a disciplined commitment to following their lead and enabling their aspirations. This might express itself in a number of ways: affordable counseling,[17] leadership development,[18] community organizing, voting registration, and other forms of political and institutional empowerment.[19] Although many churches may be unfamiliar or uncomfortable with this type of work, for reasons that need to be examined, we must undertake it. For it is only as we do so that we will see communities weakened by White supremacy finally empowered to thrive.

Repairing Wealth

In a small borrowed conference room, Taj James, along with his colleagues Ruben Hernandez and Stephanie Gripne,[20] listens carefully as Black neighborhood leaders from around the city meet for a day-long summit on the work of economic repair. This critical part of the process of healing from White supremacy creates economic stability and an "opportunity for low-income communities to live dignified lives," as Agbo notes.[21] Sleeves rolled up and a marker in hand, James asks questions, reads data, looks at maps, and listens to community ideas for economic development. Over the course of the day as chairs grow hard and coffee cups empty, the whiteboard fills and the rudiments of a plan become clear. People smile, take pictures of the whiteboard, and, after a long dinner together, leave for some well-earned rest. Over the next few days, James, Hernandez, and Gripne visit economic leaders across the city and ask them to join in a community-derived, threefold process for economic repair: building the capacity for wealth, removing obstacles to wealth, and transferring wealth.

Building Capacity for Wealth

James and his colleagues are clear-eyed about the fact that a healthy economy rests upon healthy economic capacity—leaders, infrastructure, and institutions collaborating for the healthy growth and faithful stewardship of wealth. He says, "We have to create an infrastructure for community wealth, an infrastructure that will enable black communities to become capital stewards on a much larger scale. This means more than giving people access to the large economy; it means transforming the economic structures themselves." A new infrastructure is necessary because, as Agbo notes, "the current economy was created by four very powerful forces: extraction, exclusion, accumulation, and control."[22] As a result, local communities often lack the internal capacity required to have real agency in the development of their own communities. The foundation of economic repair is to nurture that capacity. For example, James supports organizations and schools that train local community members to be effective catalysts, recipients, and stewards of financial capital.[23] He also seeks to work with local foundations, banks, and investment groups to create the institutional and infrastructural systems that will serve as the structural foundation for building Black wealth. This work of building that capacity is an obvious place for churches to participate in repairing Black communities from the economic ravages of White supremacy. At both the institutional and individual levels, churches can work with neighborhood leaders and local economic institutions to assess, identify, and cocreate the capacity necessary for local economic thriving.

Removing Obstacles to Wealth

And yet this capacity for agency is not enough for economic renewal because White supremacy has created such enormous obstacles to Black wealth building. Because of this, repairing wealth must entail working with communities to remove these obstacles. For James, indeed for all of our collaborators, the strategy for removing these obstacles is varied and includes, among other things, *overcoming the obstacle of debt by simply buying or forgiving it, overcoming obstacles to lending by creating low-interest loans for businesses and homes, overcoming obstacles to investment by creating investment vehicles that value local efficacy over scalability, overcoming obstacles in philanthropy by easing the process of application and expanding the duration of grants,*[24] *and overcoming obstacles to land ownership by reframing land-acquisition strategies and real estate development.*[25] The goal of each of these is to remove unnecessarily obstructive barriers to Black economic development. Once again, churches are naturally positioned to participate in such work. For example, rather than simply giving money to organizations to remedy the effects of economic inequality, churches could instead use their resources to create strategies for growing Black wealth. This would be more effective long-term in addressing wealth inequality, and it would directly participate in overcoming White supremacy's long history of extracting and obstructing Black wealth.

Transferring Wealth

Perhaps the most important aspect of the work of repairing White supremacy's unjust plunder of Black wealth is the act of transferring wealth— taking wealth that currently resides in White households, churches, and institutions and transferring that wealth into vehicles designed exclusively to create wealth in Black communities. This language of "transfer," though slightly jarring, is both intentional and important. It signals that we are not talking about using White-controlled resources to "help" Black communities. Instead, we want to transfer these resources into contexts that are wholly owned and wholly governed by Black communities. Simply put, until this happens, Black communities will remain in a position of culturally created dependence, never fully able to take the important step from receiving wealth to owning and deploying it. As Taj James notes, "The goal is not simply receiving funds but receiving funds in a way that creates new enterprises that are community owned, new jobs that are community generated, and new investment in vetted, home-grown solutions with income-generating potential. This is what provides a foundation for long-term resilience and economic power."

Transferring wealth will require a significant change of mindset and practice among churches. It will require, most of all, trust. In many churches there is a real, if unspoken, concern that Black communities, if given control, will misuse wealth. Many institutions, in the name of "stewardship," prefer to remain in control even as they give. This suggests an overly romanticized view of the White community's capacity to use wealth in a virtuous way (thereby employing a double standard), and it suggests the lingering presence of diminished conceptions of Black identity. As Anasa Troutman pointedly puts it, "If your concern is 'What if black people spend the money unwisely?' you are living in white supremacy. Is it possible that it will be spent unwisely? Yes. But that's not black—it's human. And that happens in every economic transaction every day everywhere in the world, including those made by white folks. Consider the amount of money that white men have blown over the history of this country. Why do they get to be frivolous, punitive, and wasteful and, at the same time, treat black communities with suspicion? They answer is, they don't. They have to let go. They have to begin to trust." These words require penitent and prayerful reflection.

Transferring wealth will also require churches to cultivate new practices, specifically ceding authority. In many churches the model for economic support is that money is given away, but the terms, amount, and frequency remain largely determined by White institutions. While this is both understandable and conventional, it is not yet reparative. It might alleviate certain forms of Black suffering, but it is not yet creating Black wealth. In light of this, we call churches, as an expression of reparations, to enter into deliberate relationships with Black households, institutions, and communities and—having collaborated to build capacity and remove obstacles—to take the ultimately reparative step of transferring wealth into a context of Black ownership and Black control. Until we do this, the economic legacy of White supremacy and the economic diminishment of our brothers and sisters and their children will remain.

The Possibilities of Repair

Seeing Clayborn Temple now, it is difficult to imagine what it once was. Initially it was a White church, Second Presbyterian Church, the architectural jewel of Memphis's nineteenth- and early-twentieth-century White religious society. By the 1940s, due to White flight and the concentration of Memphis's Black community created by the New Deal, it became a Black space and was renamed Clayborn Temple. In the 1960s, it was the center of Memphis's civil rights struggle, a space alive with weekly—sometimes daily—gatherings. And it was the home of a Black congregation seeking to love God, one another, and their neighbors. All of this is gone now. Clayborn Temple is quiet, empty, braced with scaffolding, boarded up, and waiting.

But Anasa Troutman sees. Walking through the sanctuary, she conjures the past and invites you into that past: Here is where James Lawson preached. Over there is where the "I AM A MAN" signs were printed. Right here is where the sanitation workers left on their daily marches. Over there is where Martin Luther King Jr. came into the building. Here sat the coffin of Larry Payne, the unarmed sixteen-year-old murdered by a police officer. Over there is where Coretta Scott King began her silent march through the city in continuation of her husband's dream. And right here is where the sanitation workers' strike was finally resolved. She sees what it was.

But more importantly she sees what it will be one day: Here is where the artist's studios will be. This will be the performing arts center. This will be the space for education and community meetings. Walking outside, she continues: Out here will be the business incubator, financial services offices, and community kitchen. That land over there will be part of a community-owned cooperative. On and on she goes, pointing and imagining as far as the eye can see. And what future does she see? She sees a world healed from the ravages of White supremacy. A world in which we are emancipated from its lies to live in the freedom of truth. A world in which we are delivered from White supremacy's control so that we can live together in the fullness of our shared power. A world whose wonders are shared by all and stewarded for the good of everyone. A world in which people don't spend their lives laboring for justice but have the opportunity to move beyond justice and into joy. What she sees, in short, is reparations. Reparations. Reparations is the cry of the ages. This is the opportunity of the moment. And this is the call of the church.

EPILOGUE

In September 1865, one month after Jourdon Anderson dictated his famous letter, his former master Colonel Patrick Anderson was driven by debt to sell his estate. Two years later, Colonel Anderson died at the age of forty-three. Jourdon Anderson, by contrast, remained with Mandy and his children at his new home in Dayton, Ohio, until his death at age eighty-one. There is no record that his letter was ever answered.[1]

This book is a call to listen to Jourdon Anderson. It is a call to hear his poignant criticism of White supremacy and the ways in which it stole from him and his family. It is a call to hear his pointed demand for reparations, for concrete acts to repair White supremacy's theft of truth, power, and wealth. But we must listen not only to Jourdon Anderson.

This book was written largely in the spring of 2020, when people around the world experienced the emergence of the COVID-19 pandemic, which disproportionately affected communities already ravaged by White supremacy. And we all beheld the terrible murders of Ahmaud Arbery, Breonna Taylor, Rayshard Brooks, and George Floyd. In response to the accumulated weight of these injustices, the accumulated weight of years, we witnessed protests in cities around the world demanding the end of White supremacy and the construction of a society that values, honors, and protects Black life. As we listened to these protestors and marched with them through tears, we heard, more than we ever imagined, an echo of Jourdon Anderson's cry. We heard our brothers and sisters calling out for reparations.

We believe that the racial healing so desperately needed in our nation—in White and Black communities—will be found not merely in personal repentance, relational reconciliation, or institutional reform but in the work of reparations. We therefore call the church to listen to these voices and to answer them. We call specifically the Christian church in America to embrace reparations as central to faithful Christian mission in this culture. This is a call to renounce White supremacy, fully and finally. It is a call to consciously devote ourselves to the repair of the immeasurable harm—to truth, power, and wealth—that White supremacy has wrought in this world. Only as we do this can we bear witness to the God who makes all things new. Only as we do this can we answer, in concrete ways, the cry of our neighbors. Only as we do this can we become the community we were created to be: a community of repair.

ACKNOWLEDGMENTS

The idea of writing this book together was first conceived in the green room of a conference we both attended in Nashville nearly three years ago, when we began discussing our convictions about reparations as a moral imperative and our shared passion to see the church embrace its work. Since that time, we have benefited immeasurably from the support of many and accrued countless debts along the way.

We owe gratitude to the editorial and marketing team at Brazos Press—in particular, Bob Hosack, Eric Salo, Jeremy Wells, and Kara Day. First for their insightful, hands-on editorial support and encouragement, and second for their forbearance as we endeavored to complete this project in the midst of 2020—a year that, with its racial violence, political instability, and health pandemic demonstrated both the necessity of and the obstacles to the work of reparations. This is without question a better book because of their tireless labor.

As this book focuses on the church's vocation, we also express our sincere thanks to the local congregations that we've had the honor of serving, and being served by, for many years—Grace Meridian Hill in Washington, DC, and Trinity Church in Charlottesville, Virginia. It is there that many of the convictions articulated in these pages were first taught and tested. We're grateful for the encouragement—and challenge—that we have received from members of these communities.

We would also like to thank the many colleagues and friends who read portions of the manuscript and provided invaluable feedback. On more than a few occasions, their probing questions and ideas prompted a decisive turn in the direction of a section or chapter. Of these, we wish to express our particular gratitude to our various African American colleagues and friends who walk with us not only in this work but also in our lives. We are deeply grateful for your wisdom, your trust, your criticism, your friendship, and your love. Although this book is many things, it is perhaps above all an expression of our own love for you in return. Reparations is, in the end, simply the work of love.

Finally, we wish to mark our gratitude for our families. Perhaps more than anyone, our children (Elena, Jeremiah, Noelle, Caroline, Margaret, Annie Mac, and Hal) and our wives (Paula and Courtney) encouraged us in this work even as they bore its costs. We are deeply grateful to be on this journey of reparations with each of you and daily find our own repair in the generosity of your love. Thank you.

NOTES

Introduction

1. Available at https://lettersofnote.com/2012/01/30/to-my-old-master.

2. For more on this see, Bruce Baum, *The Rise and Fall of the Caucasian Race: A Political History of Racial Identity* (New York: NYU Press, 2006).

3. For important accounts of the treatment of Native peoples by the United States, see David Treuer, *The Heartbeat of Wounded Knee: Native America from 1890 to the Present* (New York: Riverhead, 2019); and Jonathan Lear, *Radical Hope: Ethics in the Face of Cultural Devastation* (Cambridge, MA: Harvard University Press, 2006).

4. For more on ADOS see www.ados101.com.

5. For example, Ta-Nehisi Coates, "The Case for Reparations," in *We Were Eight Years in Power: An American Tragedy* (New York: One World, 2017), 163–208; Boris Bittker, *The Case for Black Reparations* (New York: Random House, 1973); and Katherine Franke, *Repair: Redeeming the Promise of Abolition* (Chicago: Haymarket, 2019). As Bittker puts it, "This preoccupation with slavery, in my opinion, has stultified the discussion of black reparations by implying that the only issue is the correction of an ancient injustice. . . . But to concentrate on slavery is to understate the case for compensation, so much so that one might almost suspect that the distant past is serving to suppress the ugly facts of the recent past and of contemporary life. In actuality, slavery was followed not by a century of equality but by a mere decade of faltering progress, repeatedly checked by violence." Bittker, *Case for Black Reparations*, 9, 12.

6. See, e.g., John Tateishi, *Redress: The Inside Story of the Successful Campaign for Japanese American Reparations* (Berkeley: Heyday, 2020).

Chapter 1: The Call to See

1. Joan Turner Beifuss, *At the River I Stand* (Memphis: St. Luke's Press, 1990), 37.

2. This account is taken from a series of personal interviews with several sanitation workers and their families conducted by the author in 2019.

3. For more information on the Memphis sanitation strike of 1968, and on the Memphis civil rights movement generally, see Beifuss, *At the River I Stand*; Michael K. Honey, *Going Down the Jericho Road: The Memphis Strike, Martin Luther King's Last Campaign* (New York: Norton, 2007); Michael K. Honey, *Southern Labor and Black Civil Rights: Organizing Memphis Workers* (Urbana: University of Illinois Press, 1993); G. Wayne Dowdy, *Crusades for*

Freedom: Memphis and the Political Transformation of the American South (Jackson: University Press of Mississippi, 2010); Aram Goudsouzian and Charles W. McKinney Jr., eds., *An Unseen Light: Black Struggles for Freedom in Memphis, Tennessee* (Lexington: University of Kentucky Press, 2018); Laurie B. Green, *Battling the Plantation Mentality: Memphis and the Black Freedom Struggle* (Chapel Hill: University of North Carolina Press, 2007).

4. The term *racism*, as used in this book, has three elements to it. First, classifying human beings into distinct "races" due to presumably fixed and hereditary physical characteristics. Second, assigning notions of inferior mental or moral capacities correlated to those physical characteristics. Third, pushing the people who are seen to have those physical, mental, and moral qualities to the margins of a given social order. For more on this, see Bruce Baum, *The Rise and Fall of the Caucasian Race: A Political History of Racial Identity* (New York: NYU Press, 2006).

5. See, for example, the work of artists Hank Willis Thomas and Glenn Ligon.

6. The claim that White America suffers from a form of moral blindness when it comes to race is a long-standing and virtually universal theme in African American intellectual history—ranging from the early abolitionists of the eighteenth century, to the radical Abolitionists of the nineteenth century, to the Harlem Renaissance, Black Nationalists, and civil rights leaders of the twentieth century, and the Movement for Black Lives of the twenty-first century. For a brilliant contemporary exploration of this theme, see the critically acclaimed documentary-series by Ava DuVernay, "When They See Us."

7. See *Washington Journal*, C-SPAN, August 18, 2016, available at http://www.c-span .org/video/?c4618001/user-clip-caller-admits-racism-gently-advised.

8. This is not to suggest that McGhee views it exclusively in this way. To the contrary, she is consistent in claiming that American racism is much more than a personal prejudice. For more on McGhee and her approach to healing race in America, visit www.demos.org.

9. These strategies, though radical for the time, also proved problematic. This is because in many instances efforts to demonstrate the humanity of African Americans tended to measure that humanity largely in terms familiar to White Americans. Such a tension was, for example, a constant struggle for Frederick Douglass, who was praised by White audiences for his learning, "articulacy," and lighter skin—all characteristics that made him, in their eyes, more "White" and thus more human. For an exploration of these early strategies in dispositional change, see Holly Jackson, *American Radicals: How Nineteenth Century Protest Shaped the Nation* (Crown: New York, 2019); Manisha Sinha, *The Slave's Cause: A History of Abolition* (New Haven: Yale University Press, 2016); and David W. Blight, *Frederick Douglass: Prophet of Freedom* (New York: Simon & Schuster, 2018).

10. Langston Hughes, *Vintage Hughes* (New York: Vintage Books, 2004), 12.

11. Taken from the back cover of Chris Rice and Spencer Perkins, *More Than Equals: Racial Healing for the Sake of the Gospel* (Downers Grove, IL: InterVarsity, 1994).

12. Miroslav Volf, *Exclusion and Embrace: A Theological Exploration of Identity, Otherness, and Reconciliation* (Nashville: Abingdon, 1996).

13. For an important account of the role of faith-based communities in the work of reconciliation, see Charles Marsh, *The Beloved Community: How Faith Shapes Social Justice, from the Civil Rights Movement to Today* (New York: Basic Books, 2006); and Peter Slade, *Open Friendship in a Closed Society: Mission Mississippi and a Theology of Friendship* (New York: Oxford University Press, 2009).

14. Bryan Stevenson, "We Need to Talk about an Injustice," TED Talk, March 2012, https://www.ted.com/talks/bryan_stevenson_we_need_to_talk_about_an_injustice.

15. This is not to suggest that any of the thinkers mentioned here—Heather McGhee, Spencer Perkins, Chris Rice, or Bryan Stevenson—have a limited view of race or that the

works referred to here comprise the whole of their reflections on the matter. To the contrary, each of them share the much broader view of race that we develop below. We have used these examples simply to illustrate common distinct emphases within American understandings of race and the responses to these understandings.

16. Ta-Nehisi Coates, *Between the World and Me* (New York: Spiegel and Grau, 2015).

17. Ta-Nehisi Coates, *The Beautiful Struggle: A Memoir* (New York: Spiegel and Grau, 2008); and Coates, "The Case for Reparations," *Atlantic*, June 2014, https://www.theatlantic.com/magazine/archive/2014/06/the-case-for-reparations/361631.

18. Coates, *Between the World and Me*, 8.

19. Coates, *Between the World and Me*, 8–9.

20. Coates, *Between the World and Me*, 111, 115.

21. For an insightful criticism of Coates's "political fatalism," see Melvin Rogers's review of Coates's *We Were Eight Years in Power* in Rogers, "Keeping the Faith," *Boston Review*, November 1, 2017, http://bostonreview.net/race/melvin-rogers-keeping-faith.

22. Sinha, *Slave's Cause*, 77.

23. David Walker, *David Walker's Appeal, in Four Articles; Together with the Preamble, to the Coloured Citizens of the World, But in Particular, and Very Expressly, to Those of the United States of America* (New York: Hill and Wang, 1965).

24. Henry Mayer, *All on Fire: William Lloyd Garrison and the Abolition of Slavery* (New York: Norton, 1998), 188.

25. Blight, *Frederick Douglass*, 179.

26. Ida B. Wells, *The Red Record* (1895; repr., Frankfurt, Germany: Outlook Press, 2018), 6.

27. Malcolm X, "Racism: The Cancer That Is Destroying America," *Egyptian Gazette*, August 25, 1964.

28. Martin Luther King Jr., "I've Been to the Promised Land" (speech, Memphis, TN, April 3, 1968), in James M. Washington, ed., *A Testament of Hope: The Essential Writings and Speeches of Martin Luther King, Jr.* (San Francisco: HarperCollins, 1986), 280.

29. Each of these saw America not as an empire of liberty with unfortunate but incidental racist entailments but as a culture that was itself deeply bound to racism from the moment of its birth. As Manisha Sinha puts it, "Orations on the abolition of the slave trade in 1808 reveal African American abolitionists' concerted effort to endeavor to construct a counternarrative of slavery and freedom to the dominant national story of freedom inaugurated by the American Revolution . . . and their main motif is . . . [that] the United States was a land of captivity, of slavery, and the discovery of the New World represented not the founding of the shining city on a hill but the start of the crime against Africans." Sinha, *Slave's Cause*, 150.

30. In using the language of *repair*, we do not mean to suggest that there was some pristine form of American life to which we must return. As we will show in the following chapters, we do not believe this to be true. What we do mean to suggest is that because racism goes "all the way down" in American culture, something much more than mere individual, relational, or discrete institutional solutions is called for. The culture itself must be remade.

31. W. E. B. Du Bois, *The Souls of Black Folk: Essays and Sketches* (Chicago: A. C. McClurg, 1903), 1.

32. For a study of the coastal theft in the nineteenth century, see Willie Lee Rose, *Rehearsal for Reconstruction: The Port Royal Experiment* (Athens: University of Georgia Press, 1999); and Katherine Franke, *Repair: Redeeming the Promise of Abolition* (Chicago: Haymarket, 2019). For a study of how this practice continued into the twentieth century, see Andrew W. Kahrl, *This Land Was Ours: How Black Beaches Became White Wealth in the Coastal South* (Chapel Hill: University of North Carolina Press, 2016).

33. Maurie D. McInnis and Louis P. Nelson, eds., *Educated in Tyranny: Slavery at Thomas Jefferson's University* (Charlottesville: University of Virginia Press, 2019).

Chapter 2: Seeing the Reality of White Supremacy

1. David W. Blight, *Frederick Douglass: Prophet of Freedom* (New York: Simon & Schuster, 2018), 229.

2. For a complete critical text of the speech, see Frederick Douglass, "What to the Slave Is the Fourth of July?," in John R. McKivigan, Julie Husband, and Heather L. Kaufman, eds., *The Speeches of Frederick Douglass: A Critical Edition* (New Haven: Yale University Press, 2018), 55–92.

3. Douglass, "What to the Slave Is the Fourth of July?," 57, 58.

4. Douglass, "What to the Slave Is the Fourth of July?," 58.

5. Douglass, "What to the Slave Is the Fourth of July?," 64.

6. Douglass, "What to the Slave Is the Fourth of July?," 67, 68.

7. Douglass, "What to the Slave Is the Fourth of July?," 69.

8. Douglass, "What to the Slave Is the Fourth of July?," 72.

9. Blight, *Frederick Douglass*, 236.

10. US Census Bureau, 2020 Census Survey, https://my2020census.gov.

11. For an important exploration of this phenomenon, see David R. Roediger, *Working toward Whiteness: How America's Immigrants Became White, the Strange Journey from Ellis Island to the Suburbs* (New York: Basic Books, 2005).

12. Although even this tendency to identify people's origins in national terms is itself a relatively recent development.

13. W. E. B. Du Bois, "The Souls of White Folk," in *Darkwater: Voices from within the Veil* (1920; repr., Millwood, NY: Kraus-Thompson, 1975), 29–30.

14. By the middle of the sixteenth century, almost all of the European imperial powers (Portugal, Spain, Italy, the Netherlands, England) used some version of the word *negro*, meaning black, to refer to Africans in general and to enslaved Africans in particular. For more on this, see Bruce Baum, *The Rise and Fall of the Caucasian Race: A Political History of Racial Identity* (New York: NYU Press, 2006), 44. For more on the history of Blackness as an organizing social category, see Thomas Holt, *Children of Fire: A History of African Americans* (New York: Hill and Wang, 2010); David Brion Davis, *Inhuman Bondage: The Rise and Fall of Slavery in the New World* (New York: Oxford University Press, 2006); Davis, *The Problem of Slavery in the Age of Emancipation* (New York: Knopf, 2014); and J. Kameron Carter, *Race: A Theological Account* (New York: Oxford University Press, 2008).

15. As early as the fifteenth century, European explorers such as Christopher Columbus and his brothers Bartholomew and Diego were enslaving Native peoples to provide labor and money for Spanish colonial ambitions. In 1495 alone, the brothers shipped more than five hundred Native Americans to Spain for sale, casting into the sea the bodies of those who died en route. They were not alone. From the late fifteenth to the early seventeenth century, hired traders from every major European colonial power engaged in the trade of enslaved Native peoples. For an account of European enslavement of Native American peoples, see David Treuer, *The Heartbeat of Wounded Knee: Native America from 1890 to the Present* (New York: Riverhead, 2019).

16. Physical characteristics (such as dark skin) were part of this early logic of enslavement. But crucially, these physical characteristics were largely seen as indicators of religion or culture rather than of race per se. The notion of race as an acultural, biological category did not yet exist. It was, rather, forged in the furnace of this inexorable link between slavery and Blackness.

17. For an important discussion of the explicit movement in the American colonies from religious and cultural justifications of slavery to racial justifications, and the way that this transition was codified in law, see Baum, *Rise and Fall of the Caucasian Race*, 45–57.

18. "Slavery produced racism, in the sense that the negative stereotypes that had been applied to slaves and serfs since antiquity, regardless of ethnicity, were ultimately transferred to black slaves and then to most people of African descent after bondage became almost exclusively confined to blacks." David Brion Davis, "The Culmination of Racial Polarities and Prejudice," *William and Mary Quarterly* 54 (January 1997): 762, quoted in Baum, *Rise and Fall of the Caucasian Race*, 49.

19. We will return to this discussion in chapter 3 below. For a more extensive treatment of the history of the transformation of Black identity, see Davis, *Problem of Slavery in the Age of Emancipation*, 3–35; Winthrop D. Jordan, *The White Man's Burden: Historical Origins of Racism in the United States* (New York: Oxford University Press, 1974); and Winthrop D. Jordan, *White over Black: American Attitudes toward the Negro, 1550–1812* (Chapel Hill: University of North Carolina Press, 1968).

20. "The term white came into wide use across England's American colonies after about 1680, which marked a further step in the elaboration of racial discourse and race consciousness." Baum, *Rise and Fall of the Caucasian Race*, 48.

21. Baum notes, "The available evidence supports [the] conclusion [that] the very idea of distinct races, along with systematic racism, emerged largely in the transition from religious and cultural justifications for slavery to distinctly racial justifications for it. . . . The racialization of slavery thus involved the de facto invention of a pan-European white race. . . . European elites created a new system of social stratification based on the idea that human beings are divisible into distinct types (i.e., races) comprising inherited physical characteristics that correspond to different and unequal characters and abilities." Baum, *Rise and Fall of the Caucasian Race*, 45, 48, 49.

22. Matthew Frye Jacobson, *Whiteness of a Different Color: European Immigrants and the Alchemy of Race* (Cambridge, MA: Harvard University Press, 1998), 33.

23. Edmund S. Morgan refers to the dominant role of Whiteness in the new world as an "aristocracy of skin." Morgan, "Slavery and Freedom: The American Paradox," *Journal of American History* 59 (June 1972): 28. Baum also notes, "This racialized 'ennoblement' was different from that characteristic of the earlier European feudal hierarchies: 'white' racialized identity, like ennoblement within the *ancien regime*, 'was a basis for claiming full political rights, for claiming to be subordinate to none.' At the same time, unlike the hereditary status hierarchy of feudalism, the new racialized status hierarchy was embedded within an emerging class structure that promised opportunities for equal citizenship, economic and political independence, and social mobility but reserved these prerogatives exclusively for members of the white race. . . . Moreover, the new system of racialized domination secured a virtual monopoly of political power and material resources and opportunities for members of the white race." Baum, *Rise and Fall of the Caucasian Race*, 48–49.

24. Davis, *Inhuman Bondage*, 146.

25. Holt, *Children of Fire*, 97.

26. For an expansive treatment of early African American resistance to White supremacy, particularly enslavement, see Manisha Sinha, *The Slave's Cause: A History of Abolition* (New Haven: Yale University Press, 2016), chap. 5. For a reflection on the untold stories of Black abolitionists, see Darryl Pinckney, "The Invisibility of Black Abolitionists," in Andrew Delbanco, *The Abolitionist Imagination* (Cambridge, MA: Harvard University Press, 2012), 109–33.

27. For an important exploration of the complex relationship of the American Revolution and American slavery, see David Brion Davis, *The Problem of Slavery in the Age of Revolution, 1770–1823* (New York: Oxford University Press, 1975).

28. For a detailed exploration of the history and meaning of these manumissions, see Orlando Patterson, *Slavery and Social Death: A Comparative Study* (Cambridge, MA: Harvard University Press, 1982), 209–96.

29. Davis, *Inhuman Bondage*, 146.

30. Quoted in Holt, *Children of Fire*, 104.

31. "Although he found it impossible to summon intellectual or moral justifications for the continuation of slavery . . . Jefferson never managed to . . . separate himself from his slaves." Holt, *Children of Fire*, 104.

32. For a detailed historical treatment of the logic and practice of colonization, see Davis, *Problem of Slavery in the Age of Emancipation*, chaps. 3–6.

33. "Shortly after the Revolution, Americans began haphazardly but with detectable acceleration to legislate Negroes into an ever-shrinking corner of the American community. . . . For ten years after the war there were some signs of relaxation, but then came a trend which included tighter restrictions upon slaves and especially free Negroes, separation of the races at places of social gathering, and the founding of all-Negro churches. The American interracial mold was hardening into its familiar ante-bellum shape." Jordan, *White over Black*, 403.

34. These privileges included the ability to make contracts, give evidence in court, and the right to due process. For more on how these privileges were understood, see Eric Foner, *The Second Founding: How the Civil War and Reconstruction Remade the Constitution* (New York: Norton, 2019), 55–92.

35. It is important to remember that White supremacy has never been merely a southern phenomenon. To the contrary, though it has taken different shapes in different places, it is fundamentally an *American* phenomenon. In the memorable words of James Baldwin, "There's no difference between the North and the South—it's just a difference in the way they castrate you, but the fact of the castration is the American fact." Baldwin, *I Am Not Your Negro*, ed. Raoul Peck (New York: Vintage, 2017), 109.

36. W. E. B. Du Bois, *Black Reconstruction in America* (repr., Piscataway, NJ: First Transaction, 2013), 26.

37. For an important account of this often-overlooked violence and of Parks's role in resisting it, see Danielle L. McGuire, *At the Dark End of the Street: Black Women, Rape, and Resistance—A New History of the Civil Rights Movement from Rosa Parks to the Rise of Black Power* (New York: Vintage, 2010).

38. For a helpful account of the struggle against White supremacy in the pre–civil rights movement, Jim Crow era, see Glenda Elizabeth Gilmore, *Defying Dixie: The Radical Roots of Civil Rights, 1919–1950* (New York: Norton, 2008).

39. For a more detailed (though still incomplete!) account of the broad array of post-1968 civil rights resistance to White supremacy, see Michelle Alexander, *The New Jim Crow: Mass Incarceration in the Age of Colorblindness* (New York: New Press, 2010); Jeff Chang, *We Gon' Be Alright: Notes on Race and Resegregation* (New York: Picador, 2016); David L. Chappell, *Waking from the Dream: The Struggle for Civil Rights in the Shadow of Martin Luther King, Jr.* (New York: Random House, 2014); Randall Kennedy, *For Discrimination: Race, Affirmative Action, and the Law* (New York: Pantheon, 2013); Manning Marable, *Race, Reform, and Rebellion: The Second Reconstruction and Beyond in Black America, 1945–2006*, 3rd ed. (Jackson: University Press of Mississippi, 2007); and Alexander Polikoff, *Waiting for Gautreaux: A Story of Segregation, Housing, and the Black Ghetto* (Evanston, IL: Northwestern University Press, 2006).

40. This is not to say that White supremacy has maintained the same strength across American history, nor that real gains against it have not been made. It is simply to say that, with respect to the valuation of human beings and the practices of cultural institutions, White supremacy remains a powerful presence in American life.

Chapter 3: Seeing the Effect of White Supremacy

1. "Jefferson's Gravestone," Monticello.org, accessed September 17, 2020, https://www .monticello.org/site/research-and-collections/jeffersons-gravestone.

2. In Jefferson's own words, the mission of the new university was to "form the statesmen, legislators and judges on whom public prosperity and individual happiness are so much to depend." Quoted in Jon Meacham, *Thomas Jefferson: The Art of Power* (New York: Random House, 2012), 469.

3. Maurie D. McInnis, introduction to *Educated in Tyranny: Slavery at Thomas Jefferson's University*, ed. Maurie D. McInnis and Louis P. Nelson (Charlottesville: University of Virginia Press, 2019), 5.

4. Happily, this is changing. Over the past decade, the University of Virginia has taken important and deliberate steps both to acknowledge this history and to take responsibility for its implications. In 2020, for example, a large memorial to enslaved laborers was completed and opened to the public. For more information on the university's ongoing response to its White supremacist past, see https://slavery.virginia.edu.

5. Benjamin Ford notes, "History also documents that the segregated black and white burial grounds had two distinctly different trajectories and fates. Whereas university records show an intensified focus on the care of the white cemetery by faculty committees and the Board of Visitors in the late nineteenth century, in that same period the university's enslaved cemetery was unnamed and unacknowledged in university policies and left physically unmaintained." Ford, "The African American Burial Ground," in McInnis and Nelson, *Educated in Tyranny*, 241. Recently, reckoning with its past, the University of Virginia has placed a small historical marker informing visitors of the existence of the African American cemetery.

6. This is not to suggest an absolute distinction between the theological and the social forms of identity. Indeed, in the Christian tradition, the theological is the basis of the social. We are simply saying that in the case of the White supremacist social order, the social identity of African Americans was denied.

7. For a brilliant reflection on White supremacy's construction of African American identity, see Toni Morrison, *The Origin of Others* (Cambridge, MA: Harvard University Press, 2017).

8. David Brion Davis, *The Problem of Slavery in the Age of Emancipation* (New York: Knopf, 2014), 17.

9. For more on the role of science in justifying American racism, see especially Gregory Michael Dorr, *Segregation's Science: Eugenics and Society in Virginia* (Charlottesville: University of Virginia Press, 2008); and Harriet A. Washington, *Medical Apartheid: The Dark History of Medical Experimentation on Black Americans from Colonial Times to the Present* (New York: Anchor Books, 2006).

10. See, e.g., Charles Carroll, *The Negro, a Beast; or, "In the Image of God"* (St. Louis: American Book and Bible, 1900). We explore the role of the church more fully in chapter 4.

11. For more on the popular portrayal of African Americans, see Henry Louis Gates Jr., *Stony the Road: Reconstruction, White Supremacy, and the Rise of Jim Crow* (New York: Penguin, 2019), 159–84; Thomas Holt, *Children of Fire: A History of African Americans* (New York: Hill and Wang, 2010), chap. 5; and esp. John Strausbaugh, *Black Like You:*

Blackface, Whiteface, Insult and Imitation in American Popular Culture (New York: Jeremy P. Tarcher, 2006). For perhaps the clearest (and, at the time, most socially influential) example of this account, see D. W. Griffith's 1915 film *The Birth of a Nation*. For more on the racial presumptions of the film, see Gates, *Stony the Road*; and especially the brilliant study by Amy Louise Wood, *Lynching and Spectacle: Witnessing Racial Violence in America, 1890–1940* (Chapel Hill: University of North Carolina Press, 2009).

12. Speaking before Congress in support of the Thirteenth Amendment in 1865, Henry Highland Garnet, a prominent Black Presbyterian minister and abolitionist in Washington, DC, said that slavery was guilty of "snatching a man from the high place to which he was lifted by the hand of God, and dragging him down to the level of brute creation, where he is made to be the companion of the horse and the fellow of the ox." Garnet, *A Memorial Discourse, by Henry Highland Garnet, Delivered in the Hall of the House of Representatives, Washington, D.C. on Sabbath, February 12, 1865* (Philadelphia: Joseph M. Wilson, 1865). For more on animalization, see David Brion Davis, *The Problem of Slavery in the Age of Emancipation* (New York: Knopf, 2014), 3–44; and Mia Bay, *The White Image in the Black Mind: African-American Ideas about White People, 1830–1925* (New York: Oxford University Press, 2000).

13. On the development of these blood myths, especially in light of race-based pseudo-scientific theories of polygenesis, see David Brion Davis, *Inhuman Bondage: The Rise and Fall of Slavery in the New World* (New York: Oxford University Press, 2006), 73–76; and Orlando Patterson, *Slavery and Social Death: A Comparative Study* (Cambridge, MA: Harvard University Press, 1982), 228–34.

14. On these theological justifications, see Davis, *Inhuman Bondage*, 64–73.

15. For an explanation of these social norms, see Sally Mitchell, *Daily Life in Victorian England*, 2nd ed. (Westport, CT: Greenwood, 2009).

16. The moral quality of this convergence was the energy behind southern fulminations against miscegenation and amalgamation. For southern White supremacists, the stakes were not simply the civic order but the alleged divine natural order that served as its foundation.

17. This fear of predatory Black males was used to justify a season of racially motivated riots and lynchings that spanned from the 1890s to the Great Depression in such places as Wilmington, North Carolina (1898), New Orleans (1900), New York (1900), Atlanta (1906), Springfield, Illinois (1908), Tulsa, Oklahoma (1921), as well as the trials of the Scottsboro Boys in 1931 and the Groveland Boys in 1949, the state execution of George Stinney in 1944, and the murder of Emmett Till in 1955. Because of the moral stakes of the alleged offenses, these acts of racial violence were carried out with impunity and celebrated in rituals of juridical exoneration as expressions of divine righteousness. For more on this, see Wood, *Lynching and Spectacle*; James Allen, Hilton Als, John Lewis, and Leon F. Litwack, eds., *Without Sanctuary: Lynching Photography in America* (Santa Fe, NM: Twin Palms, 2005); and Gilbert King, *Devil in the Grove: Thurgood Marshall, the Groveland Boys, and the Dawn of a New America* (New York: Harper Perennial, 2012).

18. Stanley M. Elkins, an incisive expositor of the infantilized ideal, captures the essential point: "Sambo, the typical plantation slave, was docile but irresponsible, loyal but lazy, humble but chronically given to lying and stealing; his behavior was full of infantile silliness and his talk inflated with childish exaggeration. His relationship with his master was one of utter dependence and childlike attachment: it was indeed this childlike quality that was the very key to his being." Elkins, *Slavery: A Problem in American Institutional and Intellectual Life*, 2nd ed. (Chicago: University of Chicago Press, 1968), 82, quoted in Patterson, *Slavery and Social Death*, 96. For a clear portrayal of this infantilization framework, see the 1915 film *The Birth of a Nation*.

19. For important accounts of the post-war process to rebuild America, see Jackson Lears, *Rebirth of a Nation: The Making of Modern America, 1877–1920* (New York: Harper, 2009); and Louis Menand, *The Metaphysical Club: A Story of Ideas in America* (New York: Farrar, Strauss & Giroux, 2001).

20. We are using the word *myth* in the sociological sense of an organizing story that articulates and perpetuates the collectively held meaning and values of a given community.

21. Ethan J. Kytle and Blain Roberts, *Denmark Vesey's Garden: Slavery and Memory in the Cradle of the Confederacy* (New York: New Press, 2018), 123.

22. "By the turn of the Twentieth century, the loyal slave trope had become a national phenomenon. Plantation authors . . . portrayed the Old South as a place of moonlight-and-magnolia romance and loving bonds between master and servant." Kytle and Roberts, *Denmark Vesey's Garden*, 126–27. See also Grace Elizabeth Hale, *Making Whiteness: The Culture of Segregation in the South, 1890–1940* (New York: Vintage, 1999), 62.

23. For a reflection on this shift, see the introduction to Ta-Nehisi Coates, *We Were Eight Years in Power: An American Tragedy* (New York: One World, 2017).

24. For an influential example of the southern account of Reconstruction, see Claude G. Bowers, *The Tragic Era: The Revolution after Lincoln* (Cambridge, MA: Riverside, 1929).

25. This language is a deliberate reframing, from the mythic point of view, of Booker T. Washington's influential 1903 volume, *The Negro Problem*, in which Washington, W. E. B. Du Bois, and others produced a series of essays regarding the process of integrating African Americans into post-war America. For an account of the way in which this notion of "the Negro Problem" took powerful shape in twentieth-century political realities, see Joseph Crespino, *Strom Thurmond's America* (New York: Hill and Wang, 2012); and Darren Dochuk, *From Bible Belt to Sun Belt: Plain Folk Religion, Grassroots Politics, and the Rise of Evangelical Conservatism* (New York: Norton, 2011).

26. For an important account of this process of public memorialization, see David W. Blight, *Race and Reunion: The Civil War in American Memory* (Cambridge, MA: Belknap, 2001); and Kytle and Roberts, *Denmark Vesey's Garden*, 4–116.

27. Henry Louis Gates refers to this as the "visual rhetoric" of White supremacy. See Gates, *Stony the Road*, 106.

28. Gates, *Stony the Road*, 82.

29. Ta-Nehisi Coates refers to this romanticized and racially sanitized account of American history as "the dream." For more on this, see Coates, *Between the World and Me* (New York: Spiegel and Grau, 2015), 102–4.

30. Bruce Baum, *The Rise and Fall of the Caucasian Race: A Political History of Racial Identity* (New York: NYU Press, 2006), 8.

31. This language of "hunting" is not metaphorical, nor is it limited to the plantation posses sent to capture runaway slaves. In 1850, the federal government passed the highly controversial Fugitive Slave Act (modeled on an earlier 1793 version), requiring American citizens in both the South and the North to pursue, capture, and return fugitive slaves back into slavery. The passage of this law not only accelerated the work of the Underground Railroad, it also served to deepen the sectional divisions that ultimately led to the Civil War. For more on this, see Andrew Delbanco, *The War before the War: Fugitive Slaves and the Struggle for America's Soul from the Revolution to the Civil War* (New York: Penguin, 2018).

32. For a chilling collection of these images, see Allen, Als, Lewis, and Litwack, *Without Sanctuary*.

33. For an essential account of this system, see Douglas A. Blackmon, *Slavery by Another Name: The Re-enslavement of Black Americans from the Civil War to World War II* (New York: Anchor Books, 2009).

34. Much has been written recently regarding the ways that the United States continues to subjugate Black bodies by means of the criminal justice system. For important treatments of this theme, see William Stuntz, *The Collapse of American Criminal Justice* (Cambridge, MA: Belknap, 2011); Michelle Alexander, *The New Jim Crow: Mass Incarceration in the Age of Colorblindness* (New York: New Press, 2012); and Bryan Stevenson, *Just Mercy: A Story of Justice and Redemption* (New York: Spiegel and Grau, 2015).

35. For an extended and elegiac reflection on the role of the Black body in America, see Ta-Nehisi Coates, *Between the World and Me*.

36. In making this distinction we do not intend to suggest a stark anthropological dualism in which the body and the mind are somehow fundamentally separate. We are simply using a conventional and experiential distinction between the physical and the psychological.

37. "Slavery is one of the most extreme forms of the relation of domination, approaching the limits of total power from the viewpoint of the master and of total powerlessness from the viewpoint of the slave." Patterson, *Slavery and Social Death*, 1.

38. King, address before the First Annual Institute on Non-Violence and Social Change, December 1956, Montgomery, Alabama, in James M. Washington, ed., *A Testament of Hope: The Essential Writings and Speeches of Martin Luther King, Jr.* (San Francisco: HarperCollins, 1986), 135.

39. For a definitive history of voting in America, see Alexander Keyssar, *The Right to Vote: The Contested History of Democracy in the United States* (New York: Basic Books, 2001).

40. This was also true for women—both White and Black. Women did not receive the right to vote in America until the passage of the Nineteenth Amendment in 1920.

41. Eric Foner, *The Second Founding: How the Civil War and Reconstruction Remade the Constitution* (New York: Norton, 2019), 111.

42. For an account of the process and consequences of the reversal of African American enfranchisement, see the magisterial work of political scientist Ralph J. Bunche, *The Political Status of the Negro in the Age of FDR* (Chicago: University of Chicago Press, 1973).

43. For a study of Freedom Summer, see Charles Marsh, *God's Long Summer: Stories of Faith and Civil Rights* (Princeton: Princeton University Press, 1997); and Wesley C. Hogan, *Many Minds, One Heart: SNCC's Dream for a New America* (Chapel Hill: University of North Carolina Press, 2007).

44. By 1965, the right to vote had become the goal of nearly every major element of the civil rights movement. Groups as diverse as the Southern Christian Leadership Conference, the Student Nonviolent Coordinating Committee, the Congress of Racial Equality, the nascent Black Power movement, and the Nation of Islam each placed the right to vote at the center of their work. In the words of Martin Luther King Jr., voting rights had become "Civil Right No. 1." King, "Civil Right No. 1: The Right to Vote," *New York Times*, March 14, 1965, in Washington, *Testament of Hope*, 182–88.

45. For a history of the Civil Rights Act of 1964, see Clay Risen, *The Bill of the Century: The Epic Battles for the Civil Rights Act* (New York: Bloomsbury, 2014). For a study of the Voting Rights Act of 1965, see Gary May, *Bending Towards Justice: The Voting Rights Act and the Transformation of American Democracy* (Durham: Duke University Press, 2014).

46. Bernard Grofman and Lisa Handley, "The Impact of the Voting Rights Act on Black Representation in Southern State Legislatures" *Legislative Studies Quarterly* 16, no. 1 (Feb. 1991): 111.

47. We are conscious of the fact that in choosing to focus on personal and political power, we have not given sufficient attention to the reality of (nonpolitical) institutional power. This is in part due to the fact that the personal and the political are, in some sense, the most fundamental expressions of power, on which other institutional forms of power

depend. But it is also due to the constraints of space and the need to prioritize. Our hope is to address some of the issues related to institutional power (e.g., admittance to and leadership of cultural institutions) in the following section and in chapter 7. It is our further hope that others will take up this topic (as well as those we have addressed) and offer fuller treatments than we ourselves have been able to do.

48. This is not to suggest a linear development of the three. Though we distinguish them conceptually, they were coexistent historically and intertwined institutionally.

49. In this discussion of wealth, we are heavily reliant on the critical distinction between *income*, the money that one takes in, and *wealth*, the assets under one's final control. On this, see Melvin L. Oliver and Thomas M. Shapiro, *Black Wealth/White Wealth: A New Perspective on Racial Inequality*, 10th anniv. ed. (New York: Routledge, 2006).

50. Willie James Jennings, *The Christian Imagination: Theology and the Origins of Race* (New Haven: Yale University Press, 2010), 63.

51. Jennings, *Christian Imagination*, 43, 75.

52. Edward E. Baptist, *The Half Has Never Been Told: Slavery and the Making of American Capitalism* (New York: Basic Books, 2014), 96–97.

53. On the meaning and uses of branding in enslavement, see Patterson, *Slavery and Social Death*, 59.

54. Patterson, *Slavery and Social Death*, 160.

55. Sven Beckert, *Empire of Cotton: A Global History* (New York: Vintage, 2014).

56. "Between the 1790s and 1820, the United States acquired a near-monopoly on the world's most widely traded commodity, and after 1820, cotton accounted for a majority of all US exports." Baptist, *Half Has Never Been Told*, 113.

57. Baptist, *Half Has Never Been Told*, 113.

58. Baptist, *Half Has Never Been Told*, 91–92.

59. Historian David W. Blight notes, "By 1860 there were more millionaires (slaveholders all) living in the lower Mississippi Valley than anywhere else in the United States. In the same year, nearly 4 million African American slaves were worth some $3.5 billion, making them the single largest financial asset in the entire US economy, worth more than all manufacturing and railroads combined." Blight, "The Civil War and Reconstruction Era, 1845–1877" (course), March 2008, Yale University, https://oyc.yale.edu/history/hist-119, cited by Ta-Nehisi Coates, "Slavery Made America," *Atlantic*, June 24, 2014, https://www.the atlantic.com/business/archive/2014/06/slavery-made-america/373288.

60. Baptist, *Half Has Never Been Told*, xxv.

61. William A. Darity Jr. and A. Kirsten Mullen argue, "Land reform was a vital plank in the Radical's vision for Reconstruction." Darity and Mullen, *From Here to Equality: Reparations for Black Americans in the Twenty-First Century* (Chapel Hill: University of North Carolina Press, 2020), 157. See also Katherine Franke, *Repair: Redeeming the Promise of Abolition* (Chicago: Haymarket, 2019), 58.

62. On this, see Franke, *Repair*, 19–80, esp. 35–53. See also Eric Foner, *Reconstruction: America's Unfinished Revolution, 1863–1877* (New York: Harper Perennial, 1988), 69; and W. E. B. Du Bois, *Black Reconstruction in America, 1860–1880* (New York: Free Press, 1935), 386–87.

63. Franke, *Repair*, 58.

64. Franke, *Repair*, 61; Foner, *Reconstruction*, 247–51; Du Bois, *Black Reconstruction in America*, 74; Darity and Mullen, *From Here to Equality*, 157–60.

65. For a crucial account of the Freedman's Savings Bank, and of Black banking in general, see Mehrsa Baradaran, *The Color of Money: Black Banks and the Racial Wealth Gap* (Cambridge, MA: Belknap, 2017).

66. Baradaran, *Color of Money*, 26.

67. Baradaran, *Color of Money*, 30.

68. On this, see Dorothy S. Provine, *Compensated Emancipation in the District of Columbia: Petitions under the Act of April 16, 1862* (Westminster, MD: Heritage Books, 2009).

69. "W. E. B. Du Bois went so far as to claim that 'not even ten additional years of slavery could have done so much to throttle the thrift of the freedmen as the mismanagement and bankruptcy of the series of savings banks chartered by the Nation for their special aid.'" Baradaran, *Color of Money*, 31, citing Du Bois, *The Souls of Black Folk: Essays and Sketches* (Chicago: A. C. McClurg, 1903), 37.

70. Baradaran, *Color of Money*, 11.

71. Baradaran, *Color of Money*, 38.

72. For a history of the Great Migration, see Isabel Wilkerson, *The Warmth of Other Suns: The Epic Story of America's Great Migration* (New York: Vintage Books, 2010); and Nicholas Lemann, *The Promised Land: The Great Black Migration and How It Changed America* (New York: Vintage, 1991).

73. Baradaran, *Color of Money*, 59–62.

74. Baradaran, *Color of Money*, 103.

75. Baradaran, *Color of Money*, 100, 108.

76. For more on this critically important issue of America's racialized housing policy, see Richard Rothstein, *The Color of Law: A Forgotten History of How Our Government Segregated America* (New York: Liveright, 2017); and Ta-Nehisi Coates, "The Case for Reparations," in *We Were Eight Years in Power*, 163–208.

77. Journalist Trymaine Lee Jones notes, "Though black people make up nearly 13 percent of our nation's population, they hold less than 3 percent of the nation's total wealth. The median family wealth for white people is $171,000 compared with just $17,600 for black people." Jones, "A Vast Wealth Gap, Driven by Segregation, Redlining, Evictions, and Exclusion, Separates White and Black America," *New York Times Magazine*, August 14, 2019, https://www.nytimes.com/interactive/2019/08/14/magazine/racial-wealth-gap.html. For a comprehensive account of the material economic impact of America's past on contemporary African Americans, see Oliver and Shapiro, *Black Wealth/White Wealth*. We discuss the current economic conditions of African Americans more deeply in chapter 7.

Chapter 4: The Call to Own

1. James Forman, "The Black Manifesto," in *Black Manifesto: Religion, Racism, and Reparations*, ed. Robert S. Lecky and H. Elliot Wright (New York: Sheed and Ward, 1969), 119–20. Forman specified that the Black-led NBEDC would receive the funds, allocating them toward programs designed to promote Black economic development and self-determination. These programs included a southern land bank, Black publishing and printing facilities, Black television networks, a Black university located in the South, a research center focused on "the problems of black people," a technical skills training center, funding for welfare recipients through the National Welfare Rights Organization, protection of Black workers through a National Black Labor Strike and Defense Fund, the generation of capital for cooperative businesses in the US and in Africa through the International Black Appeal, and the establishment of a Black Anti-Defamation League for the protection of the African image.

2. The "Black Manifesto" also acknowledges the responsibility of "private business and the United States government." Forman, "Black Manifesto," 126.

3. Forman, "Black Manifesto," 118, 120, 126. Forman later elaborated as follows: "Who brought us to this country? They were not only white, but they were Christian. Who put us on those farms down South and robbed us of our labor? Not only were they white; they were

Christians. . . . Congregationalists, Presbyterians, Episcopalians, Methodists, and Baptists. So when we go to these churches and say that you owe us reparations, we know we are on sound political grounds whether we get a dime or not." Elaine Allen Lechtreck, "'We Are Demanding $500 Million for Reparations': The Black Manifesto, Mainline Religious Denominations, and Black Economic Development," *Journal of African American History* 97, no. 1–2 (2012): 48.

4. Forman, "Black Manifesto," 123, 126.

5. Thomas A. Johnson, "Blacks Press Reparations Demands," *New York Times,* June 10, 1970, https://www.nytimes.com/1970/06/10/archives/blacks-press-reparations-demands -blacks-press-demands-for.html.

6. Emanuel Perlmutter, "Black Militant Halts Service at Riverside Church," *New York Times*, May 5, 1969.

7. Forman, "Black Manifesto," 122–23.

8. These included the Episcopal Church, Lutheran Church in America, Southern Baptist Convention, United Methodist Church, United Presbyterian Church, United Church of Christ, American Baptist Convention, Christian Science Church, Roman Catholic Archdioceses of New York, Baltimore, Cincinnati, St. Louis, and Chicago, Reformed Church in America, Unitarian Universalist Association, Union Theological Seminary (New York), Christian Church (Disciples of Christ), Presbyterian Church in the United States, Washington Square United Methodist Church, Riverside Church, National Council of Churches, and the World Council of Churches.

9. The editors of the evangelical magazine *Christianity Today*, for example, described Forman as a leader of "the new anti-church revolution," and blamed "this whole ridiculous situation" on "the implicit repudiation of biblical revelation in today's seminaries and ecclesiastical bureaus." Russell Chandler, "Manifest(o) Destiny: IFCO and the Church," *Christianity Today* 13 (June 6, 1969): 42; "Union Seminary: An Ethical Dilemma," *Christianity Today* 13 (June 6, 1969): 27.

10. Lecky and Wright, *Black Manifesto*, 18. The official reply from the office of the Archdiocese of New York is representative of this type of reaction: "The people of the Archdiocese of New York have always had, and will ever continue to have, a deep and practical concern for the needy, the disadvantaged, and all who are unjustly deprived because of racial prejudice." However, the Archdiocese wrote, the Black Manifesto and its demands could not be endorsed insofar as they are "closely joined to political concepts which are completely contrary to our American way of life." "Response of the Archdiocese, May 21, 1969," in Lecky and Wright, *Black Manifesto*, 145, 146.

11. For examples of such programs, see Lecky and Wright, *Black Manifesto*, 21–25. Washington Square United Methodist Church, a predominantly White congregation in New York City, furnished Forman with a check for $15,000 and urged "all members of the religious community to recognize the 'Black Manifesto' as a God-given imperative." The General Assembly of the United Presbyterian Church committed $100,000 for distribution to NBEDC "out of love and obedience to God." The Episcopal Church later provided $200,000, but required the funds to be channeled through an alternative organization, the National Committee of Black Churchmen. See Lechtreck, "'We Are Demanding $500 Million,'" 51–54, 57–59.

12. Lechtreck, "'We Are Demanding $500 Million,'" 62. In the assessment of historian Arnold Schuchter, "To no one's surprise, the churches thanked God for the challenge and then went about business as usual." Schuchter, *Reparations: The Black Manifesto and Its Challenge to White America* (Philadelphia: Lippincott, 1970), 62.

13. See Raymond A. Winbush, ed., *Should America Pay? Slavery and the Raging Debate on Reparations* (New York: Amistad, 2003), xxii; and Alfred L. Brophy, *Reparations: Pro*

and Con (New York: Oxford University Press, 2006), 37–38; cf. Boris Bittker, *The Case for Black Reparations* (New York: Random House, 1973), 3–7.

14. Gayraud S. Wilmore, "A Black Churchman's Response to the Black Manifesto," in James H. Cone and Gayraud S. Wilmore, eds., *Black Theology: A Documentary History, 1966–1979* (Maryknoll, NY: Orbis, 1979), 93.

15. According to recent national surveys, only about one-fourth of Americans support some form of reparations for descendants of African slaves—Marist: 26 percent (2016); Data for Progress: 26 percent (2016); Rasmussen: 21 percent (2019); NPR/PBS NewsHour/ Marist: 27 percent (2019). See http://maristpoll.marist.edu/wp-content/misc/usapolls/us160 502/Point%20Taken/Reparations/Exclusive%20Point%20Taken-Marist%20Poll_Reparati ons%20Banner%201_May%202016.pdf; https://www.dataforprogress.org/polling-the-left -agenda; https://www.rasmussenreports.com/public_content/politics/questions/pt_survey _questions/april_2019/questions_reparations_for_slaves_april_4_and_7_2019; and http:// maristpoll.marist.edu/wp-content/uploads/2019/07/NPR_PBS-NewsHour_Marist-Poll _USA-NOS-and-Tables_1907190926.pdf.

When Barna asked Christians, "How do you think the Church should respond to the African American community now because of this 400-year history?" (with multiple responses allowed), they responded as follows: "There's nothing the Church should do" (28 percent), "Don't know" (26 percent), "Repair the damage" (26 percent), "Repent" (16 percent), "Pursue restitution" (12 percent), "Lament" (8 percent). See Barna Group, *Where Do We Go from Here?* (Ventura, CA: Barna Group, 2019).

16. Brophy, *Reparations*, 40–45.

17. Lesslie Newbigin, *The Gospel in a Pluralist Society* (Grand Rapids: Eerdmans, 1989), 233.

18. Our goal in what follows is not to articulate a formal or comprehensive ecclesiology. For this, see, for example, Edmund P. Clowney, *The Church* (Downers Grove, IL: InterVarsity, 1995); and Herman Bavinck, *Reformed Dogmatics*, trans. John Vriend, ed. John Bolt (Grand Rapids: Baker Academic, 2008), 4:273–588.

19. Lesslie Newbigin, *Truth to Tell: The Gospel as Public Truth* (Grand Rapids: Eerdmans, 1991), 86.

20. Regional and national publications also played a significant role in the public debates over slavery and the Bible and in the Christian resistance to desegregation in the 1950s. See Julia Kirk Blackwelder, "Southern White Fundamentalists and the Civil Rights Movement," *Phylon* 40, no. 4 (1979): 334–35.

21. Abraham Kuyper, "Common Grace," in *Abraham Kuyper: A Centennial Reader*, ed. James Bratt (Carlisle, UK: Paternoster, 1998), 189, 195; see also Miroslav Volf, *After Our Likeness: The Church as the Image of the Trinity* (Grand Rapids: Eerdmans, 1998), 137; Newbigin, *Truth to Tell*, 81–90.

22. On Citizens' Councils, see Waltraut Stein, "The White Citizens' Councils," *Negro History Bulletin* 20, no. 1 (1956): 2–23; Neil R. McMillen, *The Citizens' Council: Organized Resistance to the Second Reconstruction, 1954–64* (Urbana: University of Illinois Press, 1971), 171–79.

23. These movements have been commonly formed by Christian "folk theology"—a syncretistic blend of cultural values with the historic language, Scriptures, symbols, and rituals of the church—more so than by the formal confessions of the church. Carolyn Renée Dupont invokes the concept of "segregationist folk theology," a phrase coined by historian Paul Harvey, to describe the religious case for segregation in the civil rights era. Dupont, *Mississippi Praying: Southern White Evangelicals and the Civil Rights Movement, 1945–1975* (New York: New York University Press, 2013), 80–81. Similarly, in his analysis

of the lost cause, historian Charles Reagan Wilson identifies at the heart of that cultural dream a "Southern civil religion, based on Christianity and regional history," that sought to provide meaning to life amid Confederate defeat. With its mix of symbols, myth, ritual, and theology, this cultural religion functioned as a "well-organized, multidimensional spiritual movement" that stood apart from, yet invariably intersected with, southern Protestantism. Wilson, *Baptized in Blood: The Religion of the Lost Cause, 1865–1920*, 2nd ed. (Athens: University of Georgia Press, 2009), 1, 8, 14. In the view of Dupont and Wilson, Christian civil religion and folk theology were a significant driving force of White supremacy from the end of the Civil War through the civil rights era.

24. Exod. 19:5; Ezek. 16:32; Mark 12:30; John 15:9; Acts 20:28; Eph. 1:6–8; 5:25–30; 1 Peter 2:9.

25. The phrase "impoverished power" is taken from Michael Card's song "The Basin and the Towel."

26. Howard Thurman, *Jesus and the Disinherited* (Boston: Beacon, 1976), 3.

27. Isaiah 61:1–2; Luke 4:18–19; cf. Luke 14:12–24.

28. "In U.S., Decline of Christianity Continues at Rapid Pace," Pew Research Center, October 17, 2019, https://www.pewforum.org/2019/10/17/in-u-s-decline-of-christianity-continues-at-rapid-pace.

29. Albert Barnes, *The Church and Slavery* (Philadelphia: Parry & McMillan, 1857), 20–21.

30. Martin Luther King Jr., "Address Delivered at a Meeting Launching the SCLC Crusade for Citizenship at Greater Bethel AME Church," in *The Papers of Martin Luther King, Jr.*, vol. 4, *Symbol of the Movement, January 1957–December 1958*, cd. Clayborne Carson, Tenisha Armstrong, Susan Carson, Adrienne Clay, and Kieran Taylor (Berkeley: University of California Press, 1992), 370–71.

31. Frederick Douglass, "Love of God, Love of Man, Love of Country: An Address Delivered in Syracuse, New York, on 24 September 1847," in *The Frederick Douglass Papers*, vol. 2, ed. John W. Blassingame (New Haven: Yale University Press, 1982), 99–101.

32. In the excerpt quoted above, Douglass paraphrases or alludes to James 3:17; Luke 10:30–35; Matt. 7:12; Isa. 58:6.

33. Manisha Sinha, *The Slave's Cause: A History of Abolition* (New Haven: Yale University Press, 2016), 12.

34. Benjamin Lay, "All Slave-Keepers . . . Apostates, 1737," in *Am I Not a Man and a Brother: The Anti-Slavery Crusade of Revolutionary America, 1688–1788*, ed. Roger Bruns (New York: Chelsea House, 1977), 49.

35. On the Quaker manumission movement, see, e.g., Michael J. Crawford, "The Pace of Manumission among Quakers in Revolutionary-Era North Carolina," *Quaker History* 102, no. 1 (2013): 1–16.

36. Some influential works include Peter Williams Jr., "An Oration on the Abolition of the Slave Trade" (1808); Theodore D. Weld, *The Bible against Slavery* (1837); Beriah Green, *The Chattel Principle* (1839); George Cheever, *God against Slavery* (1857); George Bourne, *A Condensed Anti-Slavery Bible Argument* (1845); Theodore Sedgwick Wright, "The Progress of the Antislavery Cause" (1837); and Henry Highland Garnet, "An Address to the Slaves of the United States" (1843).

37. David Brion Davis, *The Problem of Slavery in the Age of Emancipation* (New York: Vintage Books, 2014), 260.

38. Theodore Dwight Weld, "Weld to William Lloyd Garrison, Hartford [Conn.], January 2, 1833," *Letters of Theodore Dwight Weld, Angelina Grimké Weld, and Sarah Grimké, 1822–1844*, ed. Gilbert H. Barnes and Dwight L. Dumond, 2 vols. (Gloucester, MA: P. Smith,

1965), quoted in David Brion Davis, *Inhuman Bondage: The Rise and Fall of Slavery in the New World* (New York: Oxford University Press, 2006), 253.

39. For a helpful analysis of the relative weakness of the abolitionists' biblical arguments in the face of the proslavery literalist, plain reading of biblical texts, see Mark A. Noll, *The Civil War as a Theological Crisis* (Chapel Hill: University of North Carolina Press, 2006), 31–50; and Noll, *America's God: From Jonathan Edwards to Abraham Lincoln* (New York: Oxford University Press, 2002), 367–421.

40. Davis, *Inhuman Bondage*, 260.

41. Laura L. Mitchell, "'Matters of Justice between Man and Man': Northern Divines, the Bible, and the Fugitive Slave Act of 1850," in *Religion and the Antebellum Debate over Slavery*, ed. John R. McKivigan and Mitchell Snay (Athens: University of Georgia Press, 1998), 148, quoted in Noll, *Civil War as a Theological Crisis*, 57. Mark Noll observes that an "inability to distinguish the Bible on race from the Bible on slavery meant that when the Civil War was over and slavery was abolished, systemic racism continued unchecked." *Civil War as a Theological Crisis*, 52; see also 73–74.

42. On this, see David W. Blight, *Race and Reunion: The Civil War in American Memory* (Cambridge, MA: Belknap, 2002); Edward J. Blum, *Reforging the White Republic: Race, Religion, and American Nationalism, 1865–1898* (Baton Rouge: Louisiana State University Press, 2005); Mark A. Noll, *God and Race in American Politics: A Short History* (Princeton: Princeton University Press, 2008), 77–78.

43. Eric Foner, *Reconstruction: America's Unfinished Revolution, 1863–1877* (New York: Harper Perennial, 1988), 88.

44. Harvey, *Through the Storm, Through the Night: A History of African American Christianity* (Lanham, MD: Rowman & Littlefield), 69–96; Foner, *Reconstruction*, 405.

45. Henry McNeal Turner, *Respect Black: The Writings and Speeches of Henry McNeal Turner*, ed. Edwin Redkey (New York: Arno Press, 1971), 72, quoted in Harvey, *Through the Storm*, 81.

46. Harvey, *Through the Storm*, 75.

47. Mary Beth Swetnam Mathews, *Doctrine and Race: African American Evangelicals and Fundamentalism between the Wars* (Tuscaloosa: University of Alabama Press, 2017), 131.

48. Jonathan Frank, "The Negro Problem in Theory and Practice," *National Baptist Union-Review*, August 25, 1917, 8, quoted in Mathews, *Doctrine and Race*, 133.

49. A. W. Jackson, "Does Your Present-Day Protestantism Conform to the Program of Jesus Christ?—Christ's Program," *A.M.E. Christian Recorder*, June 16, 1927, 12–13, quoted in Mathews, *Doctrine and Race*, 135.

50. Noll, *God and Race*, 106–7.

51. Charles Marsh, *The Beloved Community: How Faith Shapes Social Justice, From the Civil Rights Movement to Today* (New York: Basic Books, 2005), 2.

52. Noll, *God and Race*, 119.

53. Harvey, *Through the Storm*, 110.

54. David Walker, *Walker's Appeal in Four Articles; Together with a Preamble, to the Coloured Citizens of the World, but in Particular, and Very Expressly, to Those of the United States of America, Written in Boston, State of Massachusetts, September 29, 1829*, 3rd ed. (Boston: David Walker, 1830), 60; Angelina Emily Grimké, *Appeal to Christian Women of the South* (New York: American Anti-Slavery Society, 1836), 15–16; James Gillespie Birney, *The American Churches: The Bulwarks of American Slavery* (Newburyport, MA: Charles Whipple, 1842); Albert Barnes, *An Inquiry into the Scriptural Views of Slavery* (Philadelphia: Perkins & Purves, 1846), 383–84; Frederick Douglass, "What to the Slave Is

the Fourth of July? An Address Delivered in Rochester, New York, on 5 July 1852," in *The Frederick Douglass Papers*, vol. 2, ed. John W. Blassingame (New Haven: Yale University Press, 1982), 377–79; Francis J. Grimké, "Christianity and Race Prejudice" (1910), in *The Works of Francis J. Grimké*, vol. 1, ed. Carter G. Woodson (Washington, DC: Associated Publishers, 1942), 461; James F. Findlay Jr., *Church People in the Struggle: The National Council of Churches and the Black Freedom Movement, 1950–1970* (New York: Oxford University Press, 1997), 207–8.

55. See Jemar Tisby, *The Color of Compromise: The Truth about the American Church's Complicity with Racism* (Grand Rapids: Zondervan, 2019); and Robert P. Jones, *White Too Long: The Legacy of White Supremacy in American Christianity* (New York: Simon & Schuster, 2020).

56. John G. Fee, *Non-Fellowship with Slaveholders the Duty of Christians* (New York: John A. Gray, 1855), 26. Fee provides the following breakdown according to denominations: Methodists (219,563); Presbyterians, Old and New School (77,000); Baptists (125,000); Disciples, or Reformed Baptists (101,000); Episcopalians (83,000); other denominations (50,000).

57. Jennifer Oast, "'The Worst Kind of Slavery': Slave-Owning Presbyterian Churches in Prince Edward County, Virginia," *Journal of Southern History* 76, no. 4 (2010): 867–900. For more on institutional slavery, see Jennifer Oast, *Institutional Slavery: Slaveholding Churches, Schools, Colleges, and Businesses in Virginia, 1680–1860* (New York: Cambridge University Press, 2016).

58. This is one important example of how White Christians were financial beneficiaries of slavery—that is, through the church—even if they and their families were not slaveholders themselves. In being relieved of their responsibility to support the church financially, they profited personally from church-owned slavery.

59. Oast, "'Worst Kind of Slavery,'" 879, 899.

60. Oast, "'Worst Kind of Slavery,'" 867, 879.

61. Museum of the Bible, "Slave Bible Exhibit Examines Use of Religion in Colonial Period," November 26, 2018, https://www.museumofthebible.org/press/press-releases/slave-bible-exhibit-examines-use-of-religion-in-colonial-period. The most prominent example of such a slave Bible is *Parts of the Holy Bible, Selected for the Use of the Negro Slaves, in the British West-India Islands* (London: Law & Gilbert, 1808).

62. J. R. Balme, *American States, Churches, and Slavery*, 3rd ed. (London: Hamilton, Adams & Co., 1864), 39–40.

63. Gayraud S. Wilmore, *Black Religion and Black Radicalism: An Interpretation of the Religious History of African Americans*, 3rd ed. (Maryknoll, NY: Orbis Books, 1998), 47.

64. Robert L. Dabney, *Ecclesiastical Relation of Negroes: Speech of Rev. Robert L. Dabney, in the Synod of Virginia, Nov. 9, 1867; against the Ecclesiastical Equality of Negro Preachers in Our Church and Their Right to Rule Over White Christians* (Richmond: Printed at the Office of the Boys and Girls Monthly, 1868), 5, 6, 11.

65. Dabney, *Ecclesiastical Relation of Negroes*, 11.

66. For more on scientific racism, see Craig Steven Wilder, *Ebony and Ivy: Race, Slavery, and the Troubled History of America's Universities* (New York: Bloomsbury, 2013).

67. Samuel Cartwright, "Diseases and Peculiarities of the Negro Race," *DeBow's Review* 11 (1851), quoted in Henry Louis Gates Jr., *Stony the Road: Reconstruction, White Supremacy, and the Rise of Jim Crow* (New York: Penguin, 2019), 61.

68. Cartwright, "Diseases and Peculiarities of the Negro Race."

69. Charles Carroll, *The Negro, a Beast; or, "In the Image of God"* (St. Louis: American Book and Bible House, 1900), 87.

70. Carroll, *The Negro, a Beast*, 161.

71. Wilder, *Ebony and Ivy*, 11.

72. Given the interwovenness of slavery in the American economy during this period, no one escaped from being a beneficiary of slavery. After all, the bodies of enslaved people had become the nation's largest financial asset, and the cotton they tended to became the nation's most exported commodity; on this see Edward E. Baptist, *The Half Has Never Been Told: Slavery and the Making of American Capitalism* (New York: Basic Books, 2014); Sven Beckert, *Empire of Cotton: A Global History* (New York: Vintage, 2014). Even so, we acknowledge that there is a difference between this broader sense of complicity and the various ways in which churches benefited from slave labor *more directly*.

73. Princeton Theological Seminary, "Princeton Seminary and Slavery: A Report of the Historical Audit Committee," 11, https://slavery.ptsem.edu/wp-content/uploads/2019/10/Princeton-Seminary-and-Slavery-Report-rev10-19.pdf.

74. Southern Baptist Theological Seminary, "Report on Slavery and Racism in the History of the Southern Baptist Theological Seminary," December 12, 2018, 7, 35, 38, https://sbts-wordpress-uploads.s3.amazonaws.com/sbts/uploads/2018/12/Racism-and-the-Legacy-of-Slavery-Report-v4.pdf. Joseph E. Brown, the seminary's most important donor and chairman of its board of trustees from 1880 to 1894, earned much of his fortune from the brutal exploitation of Black men in the convict-lease system. One donation by Brown in particular, a gift of $50,000 in 1880, was "instrumental in saving the seminary from financial collapse." The seminary's report also concedes, "It is impossible to know how many of the seminary's donors and trustees were involved in the convict-lease labor system, but given its extensive implementation throughout the South, it is reasonable to conclude that Joseph E. Brown was not the only one. Donors were donors because they engaged in a range of business operations of such scale that they could not have avoided all involvement in the common business and labor practices of the day." Further, two of the seminary's most important donors, who also played leading roles as trustees, were the Levering brothers from Baltimore. The report concludes, "It is likely that their [coffee] fortune derived in significant measure from slave labor in Brazil and Cuba."

75. "Princeton Seminary and Slavery," 11. On October 18, 2019, the seminary announced that it would set aside $27.6 million from its endowment as reparations for its historical ties to slavery.

76. E.g., Gen. 9:25–27; 17:12; Lev. 25:45–46; Deut. 20:10–11; Eph. 6:5–9; Col. 3:22; 4:1; 1 Tim. 6:1–2; and Philem. 1–26. On biblical texts used by proslavery advocates in the nineteenth century, see Mark A. Noll, *The Civil War as a Theological Crisis* (Chapel Hill: University of North Carolina Press, 2006), 34–35. Regarding Genesis 9 and the so-called curse of Ham, David Brion Davis comments, "This text would become absolutely central in the history of antiblack racism. No other passage in the Bible has had such a disastrous influence through human history as Genesis 9:18–27." Davis, *Inhuman Bondage*, 64. On the biblical debate over slavery more broadly, see David Brion Davis, *The Problem of Slavery in the Age of Revolution, 1770–1823* (New York: Oxford University Press, 1975); Larry E. Tise, *Proslavery: A History of the Defense of Slavery in America, 1701–1840* (Athens: University of Georgia Press, 1987); Mark A. Noll, *America's God: From Jonathan Edwards to Abraham Lincoln* (New York: Oxford University Press, 2002), 367–438.

77. Wilson, *Baptized in Blood*, 101.

78. One minister, Reverend John Paris, preached that these "simple minded people" believed they had been "freed from the restraints that servitude had thrown around them," so they "abandoned themselves to a cause of reckless dissipation." Quoted in Wilson, *Baptized in Blood*, 106.

79. Wilson, *Baptized in Blood*, 111.

80. Southern churches remained remarkably silent on the issue of Klan violence. See Daniel W. Stowell, *Rebuilding Zion: The Religious Reconstruction of the South, 1863–1877* (New York: Oxford University Press, 1998), 159. On the relationship between southern evangelicalism and the Ku Klux Klan, see Wilson, *Baptized in Blood*, 100–101, 110–18.

81. For a summary of biblical arguments and passages used in support of segregation, see David L. Chappell, "Religious Ideas of the Segregationists," *Journal of American Studies* 32, no. 2 (1998): 237–62; and Chappell, *A Stone of Hope: Prophetic Religion and the Death of Jim Crow* (Chapel Hill: University of North Carolina Press, 2004), 105–78.

82. Quoted in Chappell, *Stone of Hope*, 114.

83. "Tuscaloosa Presbytery Protests against Assembly's Advice," *Southern Presbyterian Journal* (August 4, 1954): 17.

84. For a full transcript of the radio address, see Justin Taylor, "Is Segregation Scriptural? A Radio Address from Bob Jones on Easter of 1960," *Gospel Coalition*, July 26, 2016, https://www.thegospelcoalition.org/blogs/evangelical-history/is-segregation-scriptural-a-radio-address-from-bob-jones-on-easter-of-1960.

85. On silence as a form of complicity, see Gregory Mellema, *Complicity and Moral Accountability* (Notre Dame, IN: University of Notre Dame Press, 2016), 19–20, 26, 134–41; see also our discussion on the responsibility of the accomplice in chapter 5.

86. Martin Luther King Jr., "Letter from a Birmingham Jail," in *Where Do We Go from Here: Chaos or Community?* (Boston: Beacon, 2010), 90.

87. Chappell, *Stone of Hope*, 122–23. For a helpful analysis of the Presbyterian doctrine of the "spirituality of the church" as related to the church's complicity with racial injustice during the Civil Rights era, see Sean Michael Lucas, "Owning the Past: The Spirituality of the Church in History, Failure, and Hope," *Reformed Faith & Practice* 1, no. 1 (2016): 25–38; cf. Peter Slade, *Open Friendship in a Closed Society: Mission Mississippi and a Theology of Friendship* (New York: Oxford University Press, 2009), 94–106.

88. Francis Grimké, "Discouragements: Hostility of the Press, Silence and Cowardice of the Pulpit" (1900), in *Works of Francis J. Grimké*, 240–41; cf. Lucas, "Owning the Past," 27; and Slade, *Open Friendship*, 119–20.

89. John G. Fee, *Non-Fellowship with Slaveholders the Duty of Christians* (New York: John A. Gray, 1855), 31, 37.

90. Albert Barnes, *The Church and Slavery* (Philadelphia: Parry & McMillan, 1857), 169–70. Barnes also set forth a similar argument some years earlier in *An Inquiry into the Scriptural Views of Slavery* (Philadelphia: Perkins & Purves, 1846), 383–84: "There is not vital energy enough; there is not power of numbers and influence enough out of the church, to sustain it. . . . There is no power *out* of the church that could sustain slavery an hour if it were not sustained *in* it."

91. Oliver Johnson, *William Lloyd Garrison and His Times; or, Sketches of the Anti-Slavery Movement in America, and of the Man Who Was Its Founder and Moral Leader* (Boston: B. B. Russell, 1880), 245–46.

92. Ida B. Wells, *Southern Horrors: Lynch Law in All Its Phases* (New York: Age Print, 1892), 17, in *On Lynchings* (Mineola, NY: Dover, 2014).

93. Ida B. Wells, *Crusade for Justice: The Autobiography of Ida B. Wells*, ed. Alfreda M. Duster (Chicago: University of Chicago Press, 1970), 154–55. On the silence of southern churches in the face of lynching, see Amy Louise Wood, *Lynching and Spectacle: Witnessing Racial Violence in America, 1890–1940* (Chapel Hill: University of North Carolina Press, 2009), 50–51.

94. Grimké, "Christianity and Race Prejudice," 464. For a more extended critique of the silence of the White Christian pulpit, see also Grimké, "Discouragements," 240–47.

95. Martin Luther King Jr., "Letter from a Birmingham Jail," in *Why We Can't Wait* (New York: Mentor Books, 1963), 86.

96. King, "Letter from a Birmingham Jail," in *Why We Can't Wait*, 90. And again: "Millions of American Negroes, starving for the want of the bread of freedom, have knocked again and again on the door of so-called white churches, but they have usually been greeted by a cold indifference or a blatant hypocrisy." Martin Luther King Jr., *Strength to Love* (Philadelphia: Fortress, 1981), 63.

97. Fannie Lou Hamer, Project South Interviews, Stanford University, Mississippi Freedom Democratic Party, chap. 55, quoted in Chappell, *Stone of Hope*, 72.

98. Tony Evans, "America's Racial Crisis Is a Result of the Failure of the Church to Deal with Racism," *Dallas Morning News*, June 15, 2020, https://www.dallasnews.com/opini on/commentary/2020/06/15/tony-evans-americas-racial-crisis-is-a-result-of-the-failure-of -the-church-to-deal-with-racism.

99. See, e.g., Exod. 16:27–28; Num. 16:24–27; Deut. 13:12–17; 17:7; 19:13; 21:1–9; Josh. 7:1, 24–26; 22:16–18; 1 Sam. 14:37–38; 2 Sam. 21:1–8; 2 Kings 9:26; 2 Chron. 7:19–20; 12:12; 32:25; Ezra 9:6–15; Neh. 1:4–11; 9:6–37; Dan. 9:3–19; Matt. 23:37–38; Rev. 2:14; 2:20; 3:9. See Brian S. Rosner, *Paul, Scripture, and Ethics: A Study of 1 Corinthians 5–7* (New York: Brill, 1994), 66–67, for representative examples of when "the entire nation suffers, or is threatened with, some degree of divine displeasure on account of the presence of a gravely sinning member." For a helpful overview of the ethics of collective responsibility, see Gregory F. Mellema, *Collective Responsibility* (Atlanta: Brill Rodopi, 1997).

100. John Murray, "Corporate Responsibility," in *Collected Writings of John Murray*, vol. 1 (Carlisle, PA: Banner of Truth Trust, 1989), 275.

101. See, e.g., Deut. 24:16; Ezek. 18:20–21 (but cf. Deut. 21:8–9; Ezek. 9:5–6; 20:23–26; 24:21).

102. See Mellema, *Complicity*, 66–75; Mellema, *Collective Responsibility*, 1–82, 95–104; Larry May and Stacey Hoffman, eds., *Collective Responsibility: Five Decades of Debate in Theoretical and Applied Ethics* (Savage, MD: Rowman & Littlefield, 1991).

Chapter 5: Owning the Ethic of Restitution

1. Henry J. Cadbury, *John Hepburn and His Book against Slavery, 1715* (Worcester, MA: American Antiquarian Society, 1949), 89–113.

2. John Hepburn, *The American Defence of the Christian Golden Rule, or an Essay to Prove the Unlawfulness of Making Slaves of Men* (New York, 1715).

3. Hepburn, *American Defence*, 21–22.

4. John Tillotson, *Two Sermons on the Nature and Necessity of Restitution* (London, 1707), 14.

5. For helpful overviews of tax collection and tax collectors in first-century Palestine, see Thomas E. Schmidt, "Taxes," in *Dictionary of Jesus and the Gospels*, ed. Joel B. Green and Scot McKnight (Downers Grove, IL: InterVarsity, 1992), 804–7; Otto Michel, "τελώνης," in *Theological Dictionary of the New Testament*, vol. 8, ed. Gerhard Friedrich, trans. and ed. Geoffrey W. Bromiley (Grand Rapids: Eerdmans, 1972), 88–105; and John J. Rousseau and Rami Arav, *Jesus and His World: An Archaeological and Cultural Dictionary* (Minneapolis: Augsburg Fortress, 1995), 275–79.

6. Michel, "τελώνης," 99–100. Michel observes that although one had legal recourse to file a complaint if defrauded, the sheer complexity of the procedures and rules typically discouraged the average person from doing so.

7. Philo, *On the Special Laws* 2.92–94; 3.158–62, in *The Works of Philo*, trans. C. D. Yonge (Peabody, MA: Hendrickson, 1993).

8. Schmidt, "Taxes," 806. Rabbinical Judaism placed tax collectors in the same moral and legal category as robbers, usurers, gamblers, shepherds, and slaves. See Michel, "τε-λώνης," 102.

9. See, e.g., Luke 5:30; 7:34; 15:1–2; N. T. Wright, *Jesus and the Victory of God*, Christian Origins and the Question of God 2 (Minneapolis: Fortress, 1996), 266.

10. See Craig L. Blomberg, *Jesus and the Gospels: An Introduction and Survey* (Nashville: Broadman & Holman, 1997), 60–61; Douglas E. Oakman, *Jesus and the Peasants* (Eugene, OR: Cascade Books, 2008), 140, 150–51; Rousseau and Arav, *Jesus and His World*, 278. The predatory nature of the Roman Empire's system of taxation is well-documented. Taxes in Judea where Zacchaeus lived and worked were a crippling economic burden for the overwhelming majority of the Judean population, most of whom lived on close to minimum subsistence. The total annual tax liability for small farmers (who had the double burden of Roman and Jewish taxes) has been estimated at half or more of all their wages. When overwhelmed by unpayable taxes and left unable to repay their creditors, these peasants would often lose not only their land but also their freedom; oftentimes they would be cast in debtors' prisons or sold into slavery as a form of debt repayment.

11. See, e.g., Gen. 20:14; Exod. 12:35–36; 22:1; Judg. 17:1–4; 2 Sam. 12:6; 2 Kings 8:1–6; Neh. 5:11; Job 20:10, 18–19; Prov. 6:31; Ezek. 33:15.

12. These three foundational passages differ in form and emphasis, but they are united and complementary in content. Exodus 21:33–22:15 presents various real-life "case studies" of injuries that require recompense. By contrast, Lev. 6:1–7 and Num. 5:5–8, which are closely related linguistically and thematically, outline the basic procedures for making restitution and atonement for stealing. For more on the relationship between these texts, see Timothy R. Ashley, *The Book of Numbers* (Grand Rapids: Eerdmans, 1993), 111; and Gordon Wenham, *Numbers: An Introduction and Commentary* (Downers Grove, IL: InterVarsity, 1981), 78–79.

13. According to Exod. 22:3, those who are unable to make full recompense are expected to sacrifice their own livelihood in order to fulfill their obligation, even to the point of selling themselves into servitude to pay off the debt. The law of restitution is stunningly unyielding.

14. Scholars over the centuries have expressed different opinions about the purpose of these penalties: Do they represent "punitive damages"? Is this compensation for lost economic opportunity, for instance, the value of produce that would have been harvested on the field had it not been stolen, the wool produced by a sheep, or the lost labor of an ox? As we will explain later, Christian interpreters uniformly believe these added penalties have been abrogated in Christ. At the very least, the variations in size and proportions of these penalties reflect a recognition of difference in the severity of sins and degrees of responsibility on the part of the guilty parties.

15. Jay Sklar, *Leviticus: An Introduction and Commentary* (Downers Grove, IL: InterVarsity, 2014), 121–22, 125; Gordon Wenham, *The Book of Leviticus* (Grand Rapids: Eerdmans, 1979), 105, 108–9. Sklar helpfully explains the reparation offering in the context of ancient Near Eastern practice as follows: "In the Ancient Near East, one could atone for a breach of covenant loyalty by acknowledging the wrong and paying an appropriate penalty (cf. 2 Kings 18:7, 13–14). The penalty served as a ransom payment: a mitigated penalty in place of the one deserved. In this case, the reparation offering served as just such a payment" (119).

16. R. K. Harrison, *Leviticus: An Introduction and Commentary*, Tyndale Old Testament Commentaries (Downers Grove, IL: InterVarsity, 1980), 73–74; Ashley, *Numbers*, 115; Sklar's and Wenham's comments are succinct and clarifying. Sklar, *Leviticus*, 125: "Only after this [restitution] is done can they bring a reparation offering to the Lord for atonement

and forgiveness." Wenham, *Leviticus*, 122: "Divine forgiveness was contingent on reparation to the neighbor and sacrifice to God."

17. Sklar, *Leviticus*, 125.

18. For an accessible discussion on whether Old Testament laws are binding on Christians today, see Timothy Keller, *Generous Justice: How God's Grace Makes Us Just* (New York: Dutton, 2010), 19–24.

19. We may cite two influential examples. Thirteenth-century theologian and philosopher Thomas Aquinas devotes an entire section of his classic work *Summa Theologiae* to an examination of the ethics of restitution, drawing extensively from the Mosaic law in defining its practice for his and our time (see Aquinas, *Summa Theologiae* II-II, Q. 42). Similarly, John Calvin—who carefully distinguished timeless moral and natural laws from Israel's temporal, ceremonial, and civil regulations—classified the restitution laws in Num. 5:5–7 as "affixed" to the eighth commandment and part of the "general equity" of the Old Testament's civil laws. He also evaluates portions of Exod. 22:1–15 as having important yet secondary value as a type of law (he classifies them as "political supplements to the eighth commandment") that do not add, detract, or change the substance of the moral law but "aid in the observance of the Moral Law." John Calvin, *Commentaries on the Four Last Books of Moses: Arranged in the Form of a Harmony*, 2 vols., trans. Charles William Bingham (Grand Rapids: Baker, 1989), 2:135–36; 2:140–48; 1:xvi–xvii.

20. Aquinas stipulates that "since the coming of Christ no man is bound to keep the judicial precepts" in Exod. 22:1 that command a specifically "fourfold" and "fivefold" restitution (*Summa Theologiae* II-II, Q. 42, Art. 3). Referring to the added penalty in Num. 5:7, John Tillotson states that the law is no longer binding specifically "as to this measure and proportion." He explains: "Altho' we be free from the *Letter* of the Law, yet we are tyed to the *Equity* of it." Tillotson, *Two Sermons*, 26–27.

21. Wright, *Jesus and the Victory of God*, 257.

22. Wenham, *Leviticus*, 112.

23. Augustine, *Letter* 153.20, in *Augustine: Political Writings*, ed. E. M. Atkins and R. J. Dodaro (Cambridge: Cambridge University Press, 2004), 83–84; Thomas Aquinas, *Summa Theologiae* II-II, Q. 62, vol. 3, trans. Fathers of the English Dominican Province (Westminster, MD: Christian Classics, 1981), 1449–56; John Hooper, *A Declaration of the Ten Holy Commandments of Almighty God* (1548), in *Early Writings of John Hooper*, ed. Samuel Carr (Cambridge: Cambridge University Press, 1843); Henry Bullinger, *The Decades of Henry Bullinger, Minister of the Church of Zurich*, vol. 2, trans. H. I., ed. Thomas Harding (Cambridge: Cambridge University Press, 1850); Calvin, *Four Last Books of Moses*, vol. 2; Robert Some, *A Godly Treatise against the Foul and Gross Sin of Oppression* (1562), in James Scholefield, ed., *The Works of James Pilkington* (Cambridge: Cambridge University Press, 1842), 469–75; John Wemyss, *An Exposition of the Second Table of the Moral Law* (London, 1632); William Fenner, *The Spiritual Man's Directory* (London, 1648); Thomas Watson, *The Doctrine of Repentance* (1668; repr., Carlisle, PA: Banner of Truth Trust, 2016); Watson, *A Body of Practical Divinity, in a Series of Sermons on the Shorter Catechism* (Aberdeen: D. Chalmers, 1838); Richard Baxter, *A Christian Directory, or a Sum of Practical Theology and Cases of Conscience* (1673), in *The Practical Works of Richard Baxter in Four Volumes*, vol. 1 (Ligonier, PA: Soli Deo Gloria, 1990); Ezekiel Hopkins, *An Exposition of the Ten Commandments, 1692* (New York: American Tract Society, 1846); John Tillotson, *Two Sermons on the Nature and Necessity of Restitution* (London, 1707); William Beveridge, *The Nature and Necessity of Restitution. On Luk. XIX.8* (London, 1711); Randolph Ford, *The Great Duty of Restitution* (London, 1711); White Kennett, *Charity and Restitution: A Spital Sermon Preached at the Church of St. Bridget, on Easter-Monday,*

March the 30th, 1719 (London, 1719); Thomas Boston, *An Illustration of the Doctrines of the Christian Religion*, vol. 2 (1773; repr., Aberdeen: George and Robert King, 1848); Thomas Ridgley, *A Body of Divinity: Wherein the Doctrines of the Christian Religion Are Explained and Defended*, vol. 2 (Philadelphia, 1814); James Durham, *The Law Unsealed, or a Practical Exposition of the Ten Commandments* (Glasgow, 1777); and William S. Plumer, *The Law of God as Contained in the Ten Commandments* (Philadelphia: Presbyterian Board of Publication, 1864).

24. Aquinas, *Summa Theologiae* II-II, Q. 62, Art. 2, 4; Bullinger, *Decades of Henry Bullinger*, 2:35–36; Baxter, *Christian Directory*, 513; Hopkins, *Exposition of the Ten Commandments*, 386. Withholding includes *preventing* others from receiving their due (e.g., withholding wages, Deut. 24:14–15) and *keeping* what justly belongs to them, including lost or misplaced items that are found and not returned (Exod. 23:4; Lev. 6:3–4; Deut. 22:2).

25. Two closely related terms commonly used to describe the return of ill-gotten goods are *restitution*, which refers to the return of "the same thing" (i.e., the identical goods that were originally taken), and *satisfaction*, which refers to the payment of "something of equal value or use to the receiver." Restitution is required whenever possible, satisfaction only if restitution is "unavoidably hindered or forbidden by some effectual restraint." These constraints include the loss of the stolen goods or the difficulty of quantifying certain types of stolen goods, including nonmaterial possessions (see Wemyss, *Exposition of the Second Table*, 247, 249; Baxter, *Christian Directory*, 896; Hopkins, *Exposition of the Ten Commandments*, 393; Tillotson, *Two Sermons*, 20, 27; Beveridge, *Nature and Necessity of Restitution*, 21). It should be noted that by these definitions the work of reparations, because of the passage of time and the unquantifiable nature of many losses, will typically entail the making of *satisfaction*, strictly speaking, the endeavor to return the *equivalent value* of what was originally taken. In most cases of reparations, it will in fact be impossible to make a "perfect and plenary" return of what was plundered and to restore the injured persons fully to their "original condition," the wounds and losses being incalculably great. By God's mercy, nevertheless, and for the sake of our neighbors, we must do all that we can.

26. Aquinas, *Summa Theologiae* II-II, Q. 62, Art. 1.

27. Aquinas, *Summa Theologiae* II-II, Q. 62, Art. 2; Wemyss, *Exposition of the Second Table*, 247–48; Hopkins, *Exposition of the Ten Commandments*, 395; Tillotson, *Two Sermons*, 20–22; Ford, *Great Duty of Restitution*, 9–10; Boston, *Illustration of the Doctrines*, 296. Notably, Boston speaks of a particular kind of "indirect stealing" that he calls "heart theft." He includes in this category "heart-adultery," discontentment, envy, and covetousness.

28. Practically speaking, one might wonder how compensation can be made for an intangible sort of theft. The case of slander illustrates this well. Baxter raises the question, "How must satisfaction be made for slanders, lies, and defaming of others?" His response: "By confessing the sin, and unsaying what was said, not only as openly as it was spoken, but as far as it is since carried on by others, and as far as the reparation of your neighbour's good name requireth, if you are able." Baxter, *Christian Directory*, 89; see also Tillotson, *Two Sermons*, 22.

29. Tillotson, *Two Sermons*, 36.

30. Aquinas, *Summa Theologiae* II-II, Q. 62, Art. 5; Some, *Godly Treatise*, 470; Wemyss, *Exposition of the Second Table*, 250; Fenner, *Spiritual Man's Directory*, 37; Watson, *Doctrine of Repentance*, 25; Baxter, *Christian Directory*, 897; Hopkins, *Exposition of the Ten Commandments*, 394; Beveridge, *Nature and Necessity of Restitution*, 22; Ford, *Great Duty of Restitution*, 14; Kennett, *Charity and Restitution*, 17; Boston, *Illustration of the Doctrines*, 290; Ridgley, *Body of Divinity*, 403; Plumer, *Law of God*, 529.

31. Hopkins, *Exposition of the Ten Commandments*, 394; Tillotson, *Two Sermons*, 35. Tillotson also argues that the restored goods must be directed to the person or place "where I most reasonably presume the Party injur'd would have bestow'd his Estate, and this part of it among the rest, had he been Possessor of it."

32. Hooper, *Declaration of the Ten Holy Commandments*, 404; Bullinger, *Decades of Henry Bullinger*, 2:51; Some, *Godly Treatise*, 470; Wemyss, *Exposition of the Second Table*, 251; Fenner, *Spiritual Man's Directory*, 37; Watson, *Doctrine of Repentance*, 25; Baxter, *Christian Directory*, 897; Hopkins, *Exposition of the Ten Commandments*, 394; Tillotson, *Two Sermons*, 29, 36; Beveridge, *Nature and Necessity of Restitution*, 22–24; Ford, *Great Duty of Restitution*, 15; Kennett, *Charity and Restitution*, 17; Boston, *Illustration of the Doctrines*, 290; Ridgley, *Body of Divinity*, 403; Plumer, *Law of God*, 529; cf. John Chrysostom, *Homily 39* on 1 Cor. 15:11, in *A Select Library of the Nicene and Post-Nicene Fathers of the Christian Church*, 1st series, vol. 12, ed. Philip Schaff (New York: Christian Literature Company, 1898).

33. Ridgley, *Body of Divinity*, 403; Beveridge, *Nature and Necessity of Restitution*, 22; Watson, *Doctrine of Repentance*, 25; Baxter, *Christian Directory*, 897; Kennett, *Charity and Restitution*, 17.

34. See Tillotson, *Two Sermons*, 29; Beveridge, *Nature and Necessity of Restitution*, 23–24.

35. Beveridge, *Nature and Necessity of Restitution*, 23–24; Wemyss, *Exposition of the Second Table*, 251; Tillotson, *Two Sermons*, 29; cf. Chrysostom, *Homily 39* on 1 Cor. 15:11.

36. Aquinas, *Summa Theologiae* II-II, Q. 62, Art. 7. For a helpful summary and analysis of Aquinas on complicity, see Gregory Mellema, *Complicity and Moral Accountability* (Notre Dame, IN: University of Notre Dame Press, 2016), 18–30.

37. Aquinas, *Summa Theologiae* II-II, Q. 62, Art. 7 (emphasis added).

38. Aquinas, *Summa Theologiae* II-II, Q. 62, Art. 7. Aquinas also argues that primary actors and complicit actors may both share responsibility for an act of theft, and may also be bound to make restitution in certain cases, yet they may not be *equally* responsible for the theft. Hence: "He is bound chiefly to restitution, who is the principal in the deed; first of all, the *commander*; secondly, the *executor*, and in due sequence, the others." Aquinas recognizes different degrees of responsibility.

39. Baxter, *Christian Directory*, 897; cf. Beveridge, *Nature and Necessity of Restitution*, 21.

40. Boston, *Illustration of the Doctrines*, 290, 303; cf. Beveridge, *Nature and Necessity of Restitution*, 21.

41. Watson, *Doctrine of Repentance*, 25; Aquinas, *Summa Theologiae* II-II, Q. 62, Art. 6; Tillotson, *Two Sermons*, 32, 52; Boston, *Illustration of the Doctrines*, 290; Durham, *Law Unsealed*, 374.

42. Boston, *Illustration of the Doctrines*, 308.

43. It is for this reason that the moral duty to return stolen possessions does not contradict scriptural passages (e.g., Ezek. 18) that affirm personal responsibility for sin.

44. Preaching in the fourth century, John Chrysostom, the archbishop of Constantinople, explains, "He that has succeeded to an inheritance full of injustice, though he have committed no rapine himself, details nevertheless the property of others. . . . For if this or that person had robbed and you received a thing, and then the owner came and demanded it back; would it avail you in defence to say that you had not seized it? By no means. For what would be your plea when accused! Tell me. That it was another who seized it? Well: but you are keeping possession. That it was he who robbed? But you are enjoying it. Why these rules even the laws of the heathen recognise, which acquitting those who have seized

and stolen, bid you demand satisfaction from those persons in whose possession you happen to find your things all laid up." Chrysostom, *Homily 15* on 1 Cor. 5:1, 2 (*NPNF*[1] 12:87).

45. Calvin, *Four Last Books of Moses*, 2:135; Fenner, *Spiritual Man's Directory*, 37; Hopkins, *Exposition of the Ten Commandments*, 393; Tillotson, *Two Sermons*, 52; Beveridge, *Nature and Necessity of Restitution*, 26–27; Ford, *Great Duty of Restitution*, 1, 4–5; Boston, *Illustration of the Doctrines*, 302; Ridgley, *Body of Divinity*, 402.

46. Hopkins, *Exposition of the Ten Commandments*, 393; Beveridge, *Nature and Necessity of Restitution*, 24–25, 27; Tillotson, *Two Sermons*, 51. Tillotson argues his point memorably: "For how art thou sorry for doing of it, if thou continuest to do it, if thou wilt go on to do it and do it again? How dost thou hate thy Sin, if thou enjoy the Benefit and reap the Advantage of it? If thou dost this, it is an Argument thou lovest the Sin still; for thou didst never love it for it self, but for the Profit of it, and so long as thou retainest that, thou canst not be quit of the Sin."

47. Beveridge, *Nature and Necessity of Restitution*, 27.

48. Augustine, *Letter* 153.20.

49. Hopkins, *Exposition of the Ten Commandments*, 381, 393; see also Watson, *Doctrine of Repentance*, 25; Tillotson, *Two Sermons*, 33–34, 59, 64–65; Beveridge, *Nature and Necessity of Restitution*, 28–29; Boston, *Illustration of the Doctrines*, 309.

50. Watson, *Body of Practical Divinity*, 438; cf. Hopkins, *Exposition of the Ten Commandments*, 382.

51. Calvin, *Four Last Books of Moses*, 2:136.

52. Bullinger, *Decades of Henry Bullinger*, 50.

53. Aquinas, *Summa Theologiae* II-II, Q. 62. Art. 8; cf. Tillotson, *Two Sermons*, 38–43. The early commentators believed that the Bible requires an abiding urgency and blood-earnest diligence before the call to make restitution. Citing Prov. 27:13 and Exod. 22:3 (in which the convicted thief parts with his garment and his freedom, respectively, in an effort to restore his neighbor), Boston and Fenner declare that the repentant thief must "go all the length he can," for indeed, "a readiness to restore to the utmost of our power is absolutely necessary." Fenner, *Spiritual Man's Directory*, 37; Boston, *Illustration of the Doctrines*, 290.

54. Brian Cummings, ed., *The Book of Common Prayer: The Texts of 1549, 1559, and 1662* (New York: Oxford University Press, 2011), 396 (emphasis added).

55. One can only imagine the stunning dissonance of the aforementioned liturgy being administered in an assembly of Anglican enslavers and traders—and in the company of enslaved Africans no less—in churches throughout colonial Virginia, for instance, where the Church of England was the established church.

56. This was, in fact, the explicit reasoning of the proslavery Presbyterian minister Robert L. Dabney. See Dabney, *A Defence of Virginia (and Through Her, of the South) in Recent and Pending Contests against the Sectional Party* (New York: E. J. Hale & Son, 1867), 122–24.

57. Ralph Sandiford, *A Brief Examination of the Practice of the Times, by the Foregoing and Present Dispensation* (Philadelphia, 1729); Roger Bruns, ed., *Am I Not a Man and a Brother: The Antislavery Crusade of Revolutionary America 1688–1788* (New York: Chelsea House, 1977), 32.

58. "Arguments against Making Slaves of Men," in Hepburn, *American Defence*, 35.

59. Thomas Paine, "Essay on Slavery," in Bruns, *Am I Not a Man and a Brother*, 379. Paine was a deist who had a distaste for the Old Testament, yet he frequently employed biblical reasoning in his writing. In this essay, he notes the devastating spiritual consequences of slavery ("the past treatment of Africans must naturally fill them with abhorrence of Christians") and calls for the evangelization of Africans "in their own countries." This appears

to be an example of nonmaterial (spiritual) restitution—i.e., the restoration of losses and damages to the soul.

60. Samuel Hopkins, *The Works of Samuel Hopkins*, vol. 1 (Boston: Doctrinal Tract and Book Society, 1852), 131–32.

61. Samuel Hopkins, *A Dialogue concerning the Slavery of the Africans, Showing It to Be the Duty and Interest of the American Colonies to Emancipate All the African Slaves* (Norwich, 1776), in Bruns, *Am I Not a Man and a Brother*, 422. In addition to the Old Testament passages we examined earlier, early abolitionists often appealed to a different but closely related line of reasoning found in Deut. 15:13–15, a passage that commands not only the manumission of slaves after a term but also the generous provision of goods "out of your flock, out of your threshing floor, and out of your winepress" upon their departure. In doing so, they are commending a practice akin to the provision of "freedom dues"—money, clothing, supplies, and sometimes land that was commonly given to indentured servants at the expiration of their term of service. On freedom dues, see Abbot Emerson Smith, *Colonists in Bondage: White Servitude and Convict Labor in America, 1607–1776* (Chapel Hill: University of North Carolina Press, 1947), 238–41.

62. James Swan, *A Disuasion to Great Britain and the Colonies* (Boston, 1772), 30–31.

63. Timothy Dwight IV, "The Charitable Blessed: A Sermon, Preached in the First Church in New-Haven, August 8, 1810" (New Haven: Sidney's Press, 1810), 20. At this point in the sermon, Dwight was encouraging his listeners to provide funding for local schools that had been established for African American children.

64. Dwight, "Charitable Blessed," 22–23.

65. Lynda J. Morgan, *Known for My Work: African American Ethics from Slavery to Freedom* (Gainesville: University Press of Florida, 2016), 24, 45, 114.

66. David Ruggles, *The Abrogation of the Seventh Commandment by the American Churches* (1835), in *Early Negro Writing, 1760–1837*, ed. Dorothy Porter (Boston: Beacon, 1971), 487. Ruggles also argued that Christian slaveholders were "perpetual and impenitent transgressors" who "should be discarded from Christian fellowship peremptorily."

67. Herbert Aptheker, ed., *A Documentary History of the Negro People in the United States*, vol. 1 (New York: Citadel, 1990), 37. For the riveting account of Henrietta Wood, a former slave who in 1878 was awarded the largest financial settlement by an American court in restitution for slavery, see W. Caleb McDaniel, *Sweet Taste of Liberty: A True Story of Slavery and Restitution in America* (New York: Oxford University Press, 2019).

68. See "Peter Bestes and Other Slaves Petition for Freedom (April 20, 1773)," in Aptheker, *Documentary History*, 7–8; Chernoh M. Sesay Jr., "The Revolutionary Black Roots of Slavery's Abolition in Massachusetts," *New England Quarterly* 87, no. 1 (March 2014): 115, 124; "Negro Petitions for Freedom," in *Collections of the Massachusetts Historical Society*, vol. 3, Fifth Series (Boston: Massachusetts Historical Society, 1877), 434–35.

69. Aptheker, *Documentary History*, 14–16.

70. Maria W. Stewart, "An Address Delivered at the African Masonic Hall, Boston, February 27, 1833," in *Meditations from the Pen of Mrs. Maria W. Stewart (Widow of the Late James W. Stewart), Now Matron of the Freedman's Hospital, and Presented in 1832 to the First African Baptist Church and Society of Boston, Mass.* (Washington, DC: Enterprise, 1879), 69.

71. Henry Highland Garnet, *Walker's Appeal, with a Brief Sketch of His Life. And also Garnet's Address to the Slaves of the United States of America* (New York, 1848), 94.

72. *Proceedings of the National Emigration Convention of Colored People Held at Cleveland, Ohio, on Thursday, Friday, and Saturday, the 24th, 25th, and 26th of August, 1854* (Pittsburgh: A. A. Anderson, 1854), 68.

73. Sojourner Truth, *Narrative of Sojourner Truth; a Bondswoman of Olden Time, Emancipated by the New York Legislature in the Early Part of the Present Century; with a History of Her Labors and Correspondence, Drawn from Her "Book of Life,"* ed. Olive Gilbert and Frances W. Titus (Boston, 1875), 197.

74. Quoted in Mary Frances Berry, *My Face Is Black Is True: Callie House and the Struggle for Ex-Slave Reparations* (New York: Vintage, 2005), 50.

75. Morgan, *Known for My Work*, 114.

76. "Go Down, Moses," in *The Norton Anthology of African American Literature*, vol. 1, 3rd ed., ed. Henry Louis Gates Jr. and Valerie Smith (New York: Norton, 2014), 14–15.

77. See Albert J. Raboteau, *Canaan Land: A Religious History of African Americans* (New York: Oxford University Press, 2001), 44:

> From the earliest period of their migration to America, British colonies had spoken of their journey across the Atlantic as the exodus of a New Israel from bondage in Egypt to the Promised Land of milk and honey. For African Americans the opposite was true: whites might claim that America was a new Israel, but blacks knew that it was Egypt because they, like the children of Israel of old, still toiled in bondage. . . . The story of Exodus contradicted the claim made by defenders of slavery that God intended Africans to be slaves. On the contrary, Exodus proved that slavery was against God's will and that slavery would end someday. The where and the how remained hidden in divine providence, but the promise of deliverance was certain.

One early example of this reversal is found in a letter written anonymously in 1723 by Anglican slaves in Virginia to the bishop of London. They described their cruel masters as being as "hard with us as the Egypttions was with the Chilldann of Issarall." See Thomas N. Ingersoll, "'Releese Us out of This Cruell Bondegg': An Appeal from Virginia in 1723," *William and Mary Quarterly* 51, no. 4 (October 1994): 781–87.

78. Hopkins, *Exposition of the Ten Commandments*, 386. Hopkins's reading of Exod. 3:21–22; 11:2–3; 12:35 is consistent with a significant interpretive tradition that has viewed the Israelites' plundering of the Egyptians as a case of corporate restitution. See, e.g., Jubilees 48:18: "They asked the Egyptians for vessels and garments, vessels of silver, and vessels of gold, and vessels of bronze, in order to despoil the Egyptians in return for the bondage in which they had forced them to serve." Philo, *On the Life of Moses* 1.141, in *The Works of Philo Judaeus*, vol. 2, trans. Charles Duke Yonge, ed. Anthony Uyl (Woodstock, Ontario: Devoted, 2017), 179: "They were thus receiving the necessary wages from those whom they had served for so long a time." Tertullian, *Against Marcion* 4.24, in *Writings of Tertullian*, vol. 2, ed. Anthony Uyl (Woodstock, Ontario: Devoted, 2017), 176: "For they who had built for the Egyptians their houses and cities, were surely workmen worthy of their hire, and were not instructed in a fraudulent act, but only set to claim compensation for their hire, which they were unable in any other way to exact from their masters." Calvin, *Four Last Books of Moses*, 1:226: The Egyptians "dress up in spoils those whom they had pillaged before." James K. Bruckner, *Exodus* (Peabody, MA: Hendrickson, 2008), 118, 47: "The children of Israel delivered the Egyptians of their wealth, of their slaves, as well as of their guilt for the years of slavery. The slaves were released with material goods to begin their new lives (Deut. 15:12–15). . . . The Lord had inverted the power structure. . . . Where Pharaoh would not give, the Lord would make sure that the pharaoh's people give generously. This may have been a token of compensation for the years of forced labor" (on Exod. 3:21–22; cf. Gen. 15:14; Deut. 15:13). T. Desmond Alexander, *Exodus* (Grand Rapids: Baker Books, 2016), 23, 59: "The Israelites are now suitably rewarded for their many years of service to the Egyptians. . . . As compensation for the years of hard labor, God will cause the Egyptians to be generous when the Israelite women request items of silver and gold and clothing." Umberto Cassuto,

A Commentary on the Book of Exodus, trans. Israel Abrahams (Jerusalem: Magnes, 1967), 44, 147: "They were entitled to liberation, and upon liberation the bounty was also due to them. This was required by law—that is, absolute justice demanded it—and although no earthly court could compel the king of Egypt and his servants to fulfil their obligation, the Heavenly Court saw to it that the requirements of law and justice were carried out, and directed the course of events to this end."

Chapter 6: Owning the Ethic of Restoration

1. Levi Coffin, *Reminiscences of Levi Coffin, the Reputed President of the Underground Railroad* (London: Sampson Low, Marston, Searle & Rivington, 1879), 12–13.

2. Coffin, *Reminiscences of Levi Coffin*, 12–13; see also Mary Ann Yannessa, *Levi Coffin, Quaker: Breaking the Bonds of Slavery in Ohio and Indiana* (Richmond, IN: Friends United Press, 2001), 3–4.

3. Coffin, *Reminiscences of Levi Coffin*, 268. Coffin enthusiastically affirmed abolitionist Charles Stuart's view of slavery's theft as a "consummate" evil: "Their bodies are stolen, their liberty, their right to their wives and children, their right to cultivate their minds and to worship God as they please, their reputation, hope, all virtuous motives, are taken away by a legalized system of most merciless and consummate iniquity" (268).

4. This view, championed by abolitionists across the country, was articulated clearly and succinctly by the American Anti-Slavery Society in 1833: "Freeing the slaves is not depriving [slave owners] of property, but restoring it to its rightful owners; it is not wronging the master, but righting the slave—restoring him to himself." *Declaration of Sentiments of the American Anti-Slavery Society: Adopted at the Formation of Said Society in Philadelphia on the 4th Day of December, 1833* (New York: William S. Dorr, 1833), 2.

5. Coffin, *Reminiscences of Levi Coffin*, i, 511.

6. Coffin, *Reminiscences of Levi Coffin*, 189.

7. Coffin, *Reminiscences of Levi Coffin*, 109, iii.

8. Coffin, *Reminiscences of Levi Coffin*, 108. Levi and Catherine would also serve as an inspiration for the Quaker characters Simeon and Rachel Halliday in Harriet Beecher Stowe's bestselling antislavery novel *Uncle Tom's Cabin*; see Manisha Sinha, *The Slave's Cause: A History of Abolition* (New Haven: Yale University Press, 2016), 441.

9. Coffin, *Reminiscences of Levi Coffin*, 190.

10. Coffin, *Reminiscences of Levi Coffin*, 109–10, 192.

11. Levi Coffin, *Reminiscences of an Abolitionist, Thrilling Incidents, Heroic Actions, and Wonderful Escapes of Fugitive Slaves, in Connection with the Anti-Slavery Underground Railroad of the United States, Related by Its President, Levi Coffin* (London: Dyer Brothers, 1877), 10.

12. See, e.g., from the mid-nineteenth century alone: Benjamin Drew, *The Refugee: Or the Narrative of Fugitive Slaves in Canada* (Boston: John P. Jewett, 1856), 16, 37; Gamaliel Bradford, quoted in *Massachusetts Anti-Slavery Society, An Account of the Interviews which Took Place on the Fourth and Eighth of March, between a Committee of the Massachusetts Anti-Slavery Society, and the Committee of the Legislature* (Boston: Massachusetts Anti-Slavery Society, 1836), 24–25; John G. Fee, *Non-Fellowship with Slaveholders the Duty of Christians* (New York: John A. Gray, 1855), 60–61; Frederick Douglass, "Love of God, Love of Man, Love of Country: An Address Delivered in Syracuse, New York, on 24 September 1847," in *The Frederick Douglass Papers*, ed. John W. Blassingame (New Haven: Yale University Press, 1982), 2:99–100; Beriah Green, "The Chattel Principle: The Abhorrence of Jesus Christ and the Apostles; or, No Refuge for American Slavery in the New Testament," *Anti-Slavery Examiner*, no. 12 (New York: American Anti-Slavery Society, 1839), 23–24. On

the common appeal to the second great command in abolitionist literature, see Caroline L. Shanks, "The Biblical Anti-Slavery Argument of the Decade 1830–1840," *Journal of Negro History* 16 (1931): 132–57.

13. I. Howard Marshall, *The Gospel of Luke*, New International Greek Testament Commentary (Grand Rapids: Eerdmans, 1978), 447.

14. One notable example of a White theologian's retelling of the parable in light of early twentieth-century White supremacy is that of Princeton's B. B. Warfield, who published a poem in 1907 (originally under the pseudonym Nicholas Worth Jr.) entitled, "Wanted—A Samaritan," in *The Independent* 62 (January 31, 1907): 251. It reads as follows:

> Prone in the road he lay,
> Wounded and sore bested:
> Priests, Levites past that way
> And turned aside the head.
> They were not hardened men
> In human service slack:
> His need was great: but then,
> His face, you see, was black.

15. Martin Luther King Jr., *Strength to Love* (Philadelphia: Fortress, 1981), 32, 37. In a powerful reversal, King and Howard Thurman also used the parable to teach the obligation of African Americans to love the "enemy-neighbor from whom you can expect no good in return, but only hostility and persecution," namely, the White man. See Martin Luther King Jr., "An Experiment in Love," in *A Testament of Hope: The Essential Writings and Speeches of Martin Luther King Jr.*, ed. James Melvin Washington (New York: HarperCollins, 1991), 19; Howard Thurman, *Jesus and the Disinherited* (Boston: Beacon, 1976), 79, 90–92.

16. Toni Morrison, *Beloved* (New York: Vintage Books, 2004), 36–42, 92; Carolyn A. Mitchell, "'I Love to Tell the Story': Biblical Revisions in *Beloved*," in *Understanding Toni Morrison's "Beloved" and "Sula": Selected Essays and Criticisms of the Works by the Nobel Prize–Winning Author*, ed. Solomon O. Iyasere and Marla W. Iyasere (Troy, NY: Whitston, 2000), 173–89.

17. It should be noted, however, that the application of this text to the plunder of a historically oppressed people may be warranted by the text itself. The parable, while fictional, appears to have been based in part on the real-life events recorded in 2 Chron. 28:5–15. Several scholars have noted the numerous linguistic, structural, and thematic parallels between this passage and Luke 10:30–35. See, e.g., F. Scott Spencer, "2 Chronicles 28:5–15 and the Parable of the Good Samaritan," *Westminster Theological Journal* 46, no. 2 (1984): 317–49; and Isaac Kalimi, "Robbers on the Road to Jericho: Luke's Story of the Good Samaritan and Its Origins in Kings/Chronicles," *Ephemerides Theologicae Lovanienses* 85, no. 1 (2009): 47–53. Jesus may have intended the Old Testament text to serve as the moral and narrative framework for his parable—first, by bringing to the fore the tribal hostility shared by a people who, despite actually being of one blood, are socially and politically divided; and second, by situating the climactic act of mercy within a context of corporate injustice and repentance. Indeed, the parable of the good Samaritan teaches more than charity as a response to individual misfortune.

18. Darrell L. Bock, *Luke*, vol. 2, Baker Exegetical Commentary on the New Testament (Grand Rapids: Baker, 1996), 1024.

19. See Matt. 22:37–40; cf. Rom. 13:8–10; Gal. 5:14.

20. James 2:8; 1 John 3:17–18; Matt. 25:31–46.

21. Fee, *Non-Fellowship with Slaveholders*, 60–61.

22. Howard Thurman, "The Good Samaritan (Luke 10:25–37)," in *Sermons on the Parables*, ed. David B. Gowler and Kipton E. Jensen (Maryknoll, NY: Orbis Books, 2018), 105, 108. On the importance of the good samaritan in Howard Thurman's life and thought, see David B. Gowler, "Sit and Listen; Go and Do: The Parables of the Good Samaritan and Prodigal Son in Howard Thurman's Life and Thought," in *Anatomies of the Gospels and Beyond the Gospels*, ed. Mikeal C. Parsons, Elizabeth Struthers Malbon, and Paul N. Anderson (Leiden: Brill, 2018), 434–51.

23. King, *Strength to Love*, 35.

24. King, *Strength to Love*, 36.

25. W. M. Christie, "Inn," *International Standard Bible Encyclopedia*, vol. 3, ed. James Orr, John L. Nuelsen, Edgar Y. Mullins, and Morris O. Evans (Chicago: Howard-Severance, 1915), 1470.

26. Martin Luther King Jr., "I See the Promised Land," in *A Testament of Hope*, 284.

27. King, *Strength to Love*, 34, 35.

28. Thurman, "Who Is My Neighbor?," in *Sermons on the Parables*, 184–85.

29. King, *Strength to Love*, 37–38. On the theme of "unenforceable obligations," see also Martin Luther King Jr., *Where Do We Go From Here: Chaos or Community?* (Boston: Beacon, 2010), 106–7; King, "A Walk through the Holy Land," in *The Papers of Martin Luther King, Jr.*, vol. 5, *Threshold of a New Decade, January 1959–December 1960*, ed. Clayborne Carson, Tenisha Armstrong, Susan Carson, Adrienne Clay, and Kieran Taylor (Berkeley: University of California Press, 2005), 169–70.

30. Joel Green, *The Gospel of Luke* (Grand Rapids: Eerdmans, 1997), 426 (emphasis added).

31. Cf. Matt. 5:43–47. See Heinrich Greeven, "πλησίον," *Theological Dictionary of the New Testament*, vol. 6, ed. Gerhard Kittel and Gerhard Friedrich, trans. Geoffrey W. Bromiley (Grand Rapids: Eerdmans, 1968), 315–16; Marshall, *Gospel of Luke*, 444; Bock, *Luke*, 1035–36. Certainly, Lev. 19:18 applies to members of the covenant community (i.e., "native" Israelites in the land) and not self-evidently to all people. Jesus, however, reads the call to "love your neighbor as yourself" in light of 19:34, which draws the sojourner into the scope of neighbor love: "You shall treat the stranger who sojourns with you as the native among you, and you shall love him as yourself."

32. See Rebecca Anne Goetz, *The Baptism of Early Virginia: How Christianity Created Race* (Baltimore: Johns Hopkins University Press, 2012).

33. J. Duncan M. Derrett, *Law in the New Testament* (London: Darton, Longman & Todd, 1970), 225.

34. Marshall, *Gospel of Luke*, 448.

35. Marshall, *Gospel of Luke*, 448; see also R. T. France, *Luke* (Grand Rapids: Baker Books, 2013), 190. France describes them as the "pious elite" in Jewish society.

36. Green, *Gospel of Luke*, 430–31.

37. Green, *Gospel of Luke*, 430–31.

38. King, *Strength to Love*, 33.

39. Jeremias, "Σαμάρεια," in *Theological Dictionary of the New Testament*, vol. 7, ed. Gerhard Kittel and Gerhard Friedrich, trans. Geoffrey W. Bromiley (Grand Rapids: Eerdmans, 1971), 91–92. The New Testament often alludes to these long-standing cultural hostilities; see, e.g., Matt. 10:5; Luke 9:52–54; 17:16; Acts 8:25. Most Galilean travelers in the first century detoured around Samaritan territory, and those who passed through did so at risk of harassment and physical harm. In 128 BC, John Hyrcanus destroyed the Samaritan temple. As if to return the favor, Samaritans in AD 6–7 desecrated the Jewish temple by scattering human bones during Passover under the cover of night, after which time "the old hatred became more implacable than ever." Jeremias, "Σαμάρεια," 90.

40. Samaritans established their own temple in Gerazim, demurred on the Jewish antici- pation of a Davidic Messiah, and embraced only the Pentateuch—the first five books of the Hebrew Scriptures—as canonical, unapologetically rejecting the rest.

41. H. G. M. Williamson and C. A. Evans, "Samaritans," in *Dictionary of New Testa- ment Background,* ed. Craig A. Evans and Stanley E. Porter (Downers Grove, IL: InterVarsity, 2000), 1060.

42. France, *Luke*, 190. In a 1972 essay entitled "Lost in Non-Translation," renowned author Isaac Asimov suggests that readers think of the story as taking place in Mississippi in the days of Jim Crow, with a minister and deacon passing by a White traveler who has been robbed and left half dead, and the role of the Samaritan played by a Black sharecrop- per. See Isaac Asimov, "Lost in Non-Translation," in *The Tragedy of the Moon* (New York: Dell, 1973), 174–75.

43. Marshall, *Gospel of Luke*, 450.

44. France, *Luke*, 191. See also G. V. Jones, *The Art and Truth of Parables* (London: SPCK, 1964), 115, quoted in J. Massyngbaerde Ford, *My Enemy Is My Guest: Jesus and Violence in Luke* (Maryknoll, NY: Orbis Books, 1984), 93: "The parable is not a pleasant tale about the traveler who did his good deed: it is a damning indictment of social, racial, and religious superiority."

45. Christopher J. H. Wright, *Old Testament Ethics for the People of God* (Downers Grove, IL: InterVarsity, 2004), 52–57.

46. On this contrast between the economics and cultural order of extraction in opposition to restoration, see Walter Brueggemann, *Money and Possessions* (Louisville: Westminster John Knox, 2016), 222; Brueggemann, *Tenacious Solidarity: Biblical Provocations on Race, Religion, Climate, and the Economy*, ed. Davis Hankins (Minneapolis: Fortress, 2018), 33, 38–39; and Brueggemann, *God, Neighbor, Empire: The Excess of Divine Fidelity and the Command of Common Good* (Waco: Baylor University Press, 2016), 8.

47. This comprehensive character of restoration is rooted in the law of neighbor love in Leviticus 19, which the parable of the good Samaritan imaginatively expounds. In the verses that lead up to the climactic command (Lev. 19:9–18), neighbor love is shown to express itself in nearly every sphere of life: in the sharing of one's possessions, the use of one's words, the treatment of employees in the course of one's daily work, the judgments rendered in public life, and even the inner attitudes and dispositions of one's heart (see, e.g., Lev. 19:9–10, 13–14, 15). What is more, it is revealed as a love that expresses itself preeminently in the care of neighbors who are poor, disadvantaged, and oppressed. Neighbor love, therefore, seeks our neighbors' wholeness and lifts up the totality of their humanity—refreshing their bodies and restoring their souls, healing their pasts and investing in their futures. And it does so, most of all, in the lives of the disinherited.

48. Coffin, *Reminiscences of Levi Coffin*, 577–78.

49. Coffin, *Reminiscences of Levi Coffin*, 268.

50. King, *Strength to Love*, 34; King, "I See the Promised Land," in *A Testament of Hope*, 284; and King, "The One-Sided Approach of the Good Samaritan," in *The Papers of Martin Luther King, Jr.*, vol. 6, *Advocate of the Social Gospel, September 1948–March 1963*, ed. Clayborne Carson, Susan Carson, Susan Englander, Troy Jackson, and Gerald L. Smith (Berkeley: University of California Press, 2007), 240. When he wrote and preached on the good Samaritan, King often interjected in this manner, calling his listeners to address the systemic causes of racial prejudice and poverty.

51. Desmond Tutu, *No Future without Forgiveness* (New York: Doubleday, 1999), 31.

52. On this observation, see Mikeal Parsons, *Luke* (Grand Rapids: Baker Academic, 2015), 180; Green, *Gospel of Luke*, 426.

53. See Luke 1:50, 54, 58, 72, 78; 17:13; 18:38–39.

54. See Luke 7:13; 15:20.

55. Kelly M. Kapic, *God So Loved, He Gave: Entering the Movement of Divine Generosity* (Grand Rapids: Zondervan, 2010), 33.

56. Kapic, *God So Loved*, 211–12.

57. Kapic, *God So Loved*, 211–12.

58. King, *Strength to Love*, 38.

59. King, *Strength to Love*, 38.

60. King, "Walk through the Holy Land," 171.

Chapter 7: The Call to Repair

1. Joseph Rosenbloom, *Redemption: Martin Luther King Jr.'s Last 31 Hours* (Boston: Beacon, 2018), 1.

2. Martin Luther King Jr., "I See the Promised Land," in *A Testament of Hope: The Essential Writings and Speeches of Martin Luther King Jr.* (San Francisco: HarperCollins, 1986), 285.

3. For a detailed treatment of King's last two days, see Rosenbloom, *Redemption*.

4. Anasa Troutman, personal interview, June 2020. Unless otherwise indicated, all quotations in this chapter from Anasa Troutman, Taj James, David Bailey, Justin Merrick, and Nwamaka Agbo come from personal interviews conducted by the authors in June 2020.

5. Of course, not all of our interviewees use either our same language or the same language as one another. But each conceives of cultural repair in a way that maps generally onto the framework that we have used in this work. Taj James, for example, describes the work of repair primarily in terms of power, as the restoration of cultural power (the power to define narratives), political power (the power to make rules), and economic power (the power to control wealth). Similarly, Anasa Troutman defines the work of reparations in terms of the cultivation of narrative power (the power to shape stories), political power (the power to act in sovereignty), and economic power (the power to deploy assets). Justin Merrick, however, thinks of the work as building capacity for communities to access and deploy various forms of capital: political, economic, cultural, and so on. While slightly different in language, these categories resonate with the repair of truth, power, and wealth. More on this below.

6. For more information on Taj James's work, see https://fullspectrumcapitalpartners.us.

7. For more information on David Bailey's work, see https://arrabon.com and www.urbandoxology.com. See also the important work of Latasha Morrison at Be the Bridge, https://bethebridge.com.

8. Nwamaka Agbo, "Restorative Economics for a Just Transition," keynote address, COCAP, October 9, 2017, Oakland, California, https://youtu.be/Y855wYAdnnc.

9. For more information on Justin Merrick's work, see www.ctcmidsouth.org.

10. For more information on Nwamaka Agbo's work, see www.nwamakaagbo.com/restorative-economics.

11. This sentiment from Nwamaka Agbo is also echoed by Troutman and James. Troutman's advice is to "center the needs and interests of the most impacted populations and make decisions that provide dignity and good quality of life for that population." James encourages churches to "focus on communities systematically excluded from capital access and community ownership who experience generational income and wealth inequality."

12. For important explorations of this dynamic, see Anand Giridharadas, *Winners Take All: The Elite Charade of Changing the World* (New York: Knopf, 2018); and Edgar Villanueva, *Decolonizing Wealth: Indigenous Wisdom to Heal Divides and Restore Balance* (Oakland: Berrett-Koehler, 2018).

13. See, e.g., the ten-point plan created by the Caribbean Reparations Commission, https://caricomreparations.org; the road map to reparations created by the American Descendants of Slavery, https://ados101.com/roadmap-to-reparations; the proposals drafted by the National Coalition of Blacks for Reparations in America, www.ncobraonline.org/reparatio ns; the specific recommendations contained in the H.R. 40, www.congress.gov/bill/116th-con gress/house-bill/40/text; as well as proposals found in Katherine Franke, *Repair: Redeeming the Promise of Abolition* (Chicago: Haymarket, 2019), chap. 4; and William A. Darity Jr. and A. Kirsten Mullen, *From Here to Equality: Reparations for Black Americans in the Twenty-First Century* (Chapel Hill: University of North Carolina Press, 2020), chap. 13.

14. For a helpful reflection on the role of public memorials, see Gail Dexter Lord and Ngaire Blankenberg, *Cities, Museums, and Soft Power* (Washington, DC: American Alliance of Museums, 2015).

15. This emphasis on bringing one's power directly to bear on the work of repairing White supremacy would be a helpful topic for exploration by the current faith and work movement in the American church. This movement, while often helpful in thinking about the stewardship of power, is less articulate on the meaning of doing so against the backdrop of White supremacy.

16. Troutman refers to this work as "restorative development."

17. As Justin Merrick notes, "A huge part of the work is psychological rehabilitation: providing people with the opportunity to heal from multigenerational trauma. This is important because it creates a form of psychological power. Self perspective is a huge part of the reparative process."

18. E.g., David Bailey urges churches to "develop a pipeline of empowered leaders that serve not only the church but the whole neighborhood."

19. As Justin Merrick notes, "The work is to use place-based organizing to create a form of community empowerment. Only when we do this will people have the capacity to do what we all want to do: make decisions that impact their own lives and communities."

20. For more on the important work of Hernandez and Gripne, see www.devlabs.vc and www.impactfinancecenter.org, respectively.

21. Agbo, "Restorative Economics for a Just Transition."

22. Agbo, "Restorative Economics for a Just Transition."

23. James notes, "One of the greatest needs is the cultivation of leaders who can help to reabsorb the return of resources into the black commons."

24. Justin Merrick helpfully observes, "Communities need the ability to spend time in a more sacred way, to think not just in terms of immediate deliverables, but in terms of how to nurture the beloved community."

25. For an important paradigm for addressing land reform, see the pioneering work of Ed Whitfield at both the Southern Reparations Loan Fund (https://southernreparations.org) and the Fund for Democratic Communities.

Epilogue

1. Curt Dalton, "Jourdon Anderson, Dayton History Books," Dayton History Books Online, accessed September 22, 2012, https://web.archive.org/web/20160303234714/http://www.daytonhistorybooks.com/jourdon_anderson.html.

INDEX

abolition, abolitionists, 63, 64, 65, 111–12, 133–34, 214n6, 228n39
accomplices of theft, and restitution, 146–48
Adams, John, 61
African Americans
  humanity of, 214n9
  as inferior, 121
  invisibility of, 172–73
  limited personal and moral capacity of, 63
  theft of social identity, 123
  work on reparations, 186
  wronged by culture of White Supremacy, 24
African Methodist Episcopal Church, 113–14
agape, 115
Agbo, Nwamaka, 185, 192, 194, 203, 245n11
Alaska Native Claims Settlement Act (1971), 100–101
Alexander, T. Desmond, 239n78
Allen, Richard, 61, 154
amalgamation, 120–21, 220n16
America
  as "cursed" nation, 43
  two Christianities of, 111
American Anti-Slavery Society, 102, 112, 240n4
American church
  as accomplice, 121–25
  as bystander, 125–30
  emerged in context of White supremacy, 16–17
  history of failure, 115–21

  history of faithfulness, 111–15
  as perpetrator, 117–21
American Colonization Society, 64
American Defence of the Christian Golden Rule (Hepburn), 134, 136, 153–54
American Descendants of Slavery (ADOS), 20
American dream, 41, 48
American economic policy, subsidized White Americans, 25
American founders
  brought slavery into the New World, 60
  White Supremacy of, 62–63
American history, romanticization of, 78–81, 95
American independence, as exclusively for White people, 52
American racism, 15, 26, 31–37, 40, 42, 45–47, 55, 59, 81, 214n8, 219n9
American South
  agrarian slave economies, 64
  and Black land ownership, 92
  convictions of ministers after Civil War, 124
  myth of an honorable war, 78–79
  political and economic power of, 64
  preservation of racial hierarchy, 113
Anderson, Jourdon, 11–14, 156, 209
Anderson, Patrick, 11
antineighborly culture, 175–76, 178
anxiety, in restoration, 169–70
Arbery, Ahmaud, 209

247